Pop Music and Hip Ennui

Pop Music and Hip Ennui

A Sonic Fiction of Capitalist Realism

Macon Holt

BLOOMSBURY ACADEMIC
NEW YORK • LONDON • OXFORD • NEW DELHI • SYDNEY

BLOOMSBURY ACADEMIC
Bloomsbury Publishing Inc
1385 Broadway, New York, NY 10018, USA
50 Bedford Square, London, WC1B 3DP, UK
29 Earlsfort Terrace, Dublin 2, Ireland

BLOOMSBURY, BLOOMSBURY ACADEMIC and the Diana logo
are trademarks of Bloomsbury Publishing Plc

First published in the United States of America 2019
Paperback edition first published 2021

Copyright © Macon Holt, 2019

For legal purposes the Acknowledgments on p. xiii constitute
an extension of this copyright page.

Cover design: Louise Dugdale
Cover illustration: Hip Ennui by Joakim Drescher

All rights reserved. No part of this publication may be reproduced or
transmitted in any form or by any means, electronic or mechanical,
including photocopying, recording, or any information storage or retrieval
system, without prior permission in writing from the publishers.

Bloomsbury Publishing Inc does not have any control over, or responsibility for,
any third-party websites referred to or in this book. All internet addresses given
in this book were correct at the time of going to press. The author and publisher
regret any inconvenience caused if addresses have changed or sites have
ceased to exist, but can accept no responsibility for any such changes.

Library of Congress Cataloging-in-Publication Data
Names: Holt, Macon, author.
Title: Pop music and hip ennui: a sonic fiction of capitalist realism / Macon Holt.
Description: New York, NY: Bloomsbury Academic, 2019. |
Includes bibliographical references, discography, filmography, and index.
Identifiers: LCCN 2019026058 (print) | LCCN 2019026059 (ebook) |
ISBN 9781501346668 (hardback) | ISBN 9781501346675 (epub) |
ISBN 9781501346682 (pdf)
Subjects: LCSH: Popular music–Economic aspects. | Popular music–Social
aspects. | Capitalist realism (Economic theory)
Classification: LCC ML3918.P67.H658 2019 (print) |
LCC ML3918.P67 (ebook) | DDC 306.4/8424–dc23
LC record available at https://lccn.loc.gov/2019026058
LC ebook record available at https://lccn.loc.gov/2019026059

ISBN: HB: 978-1-5013-4666-8
PB: 978-1-5013-8321-2
ePDF: 978-1-5013-4668-2
eBook: 978-1-5013-4667-5

Typeset by Integra Software Services Pvt. Ltd.

To find out more about our authors and books visit
www.bloomsbury.com and sign up for our newsletters.

For Mark Fisher

Contents

Preface	viii
Acknowledgments	xiii
Part 1 Pop Music and Hip Ennui	1
1 Kodwo Eshun: Sonic Fiction at Century's End	3
2 Mark Fisher: Capitalist Realism after the Crash	21
3 Sounds Like the Future Will Never Arrive	35
Part 2 A Sonic Fiction of Capitalist Realism	43
Vignette: Jessie J at the Closing Ceremony of the 2012 London Olympics	45
1 Attention	51
Vignette: Busking on the London Underground	77
2 Complicity	81
Vignette: On "Bored in the USA" on Letterman on YouTube (Now Removed)	100
3 Catharsis	105
Vignette: The Stones	128
4 Home	133
Vignette: One of Two: Carly Simon's New Boyfriend	156
5 Conjunction	159
Vignette: Two of Two: On Xiu Xiu and Mixing	183
Notes	187
References	190
Index	200

Preface

This is a book about the difficulties of living in a world in which the soundscape of popular music infuses so many moments of our lives with an intensive sense of possibility, only for it to be immediately disavowed. This is a world in the permanent aftermath of the financial crash and on the perpetual brink of ecological collapse, wherein the only potential for change seems to be the ever increasing sophistication of our streaming services and wireless ear buds. Yet we live in an atmosphere that reverberates with a potential that is so often drained from many of the activities necessary for the reproduction of life. A potential that is desired to such an extent that many structure their lives around its pursuit. This book is about how it can feel to be inescapably entangled in such an atmosphere, the circumstances upon which this atmosphere is predicated, and the implications that these circumstances present. This book is about the experience of the possibilities and desires popular music can provide while, at the same time, recognizing the involvement of this music in oppressive modes of cultural production and social organization.

The terms "popular" and "pop music" are used interchangeably in this book and taken to mean the broadest definition of contemporary vernacular musics; this intentionally verges on conceptual disintegration. Despite this, I cling on to the term because, as Deleuze and Guattari put it, "it's nice to talk like everybody else" (2013, 1). Indeed more than nice, this usage allows for an interrogation of the differences that inhere in the same term as each iteration causes it to drift into different inflections. To that end, this is a book less about popular music and its interpretation, than it is about an attempt to come to some kind of understanding of what it is to live with popular music as it exists within the contingencies that brought it forth and the relations that these entail. Although this book is far from comprehensive, it attempts to draw lines between concentrations of power and potential, between sound and sensation, and between liberatory expression and disciplinary suppression, which I and others can perhaps use as a frame for further investigation into the affects of living in the soundscape of contemporary pop. Above all, however, this book should be considered as an experiment that attempts to address a slippery object of research without reducing it to something more tangible or declaring it as ineffably unknowable.

To attempt to grasp this slippery object—found in the space between the popular music of the culture industry, the production of subjectivity in (post) modern society, the aesthetics of pop and their ethical potentials, and the material conditions under which this takes place—this book is divided into two uneven sections. The first section provides a background to the conceptual and theoretical tools that will later be engaged with and developed in the second section. In that section an attempt is made to more precisely diagnose the maladies of popular music and the experience of it under capitalist realism before pointing to some tentative ways through the impasses with which we are faced.

The first section, "Pop Music and Hip Ennui," serves as an introduction in which I explore, in detail, two works by two thinkers over two chapters: *More Brilliant than the Sun* (1999) by Kodwo Eshun and *Capitalist Realism* (2009) by Mark Fisher. These provide an examination of the main conceptual tools that are applied in this book, the methodology of Sonic Fiction, and the analytical perspective of capitalist realism. In the third chapter of this section, I attempt to situate these works in relation to myself as a reader of them and in regards to the problems contained in the experience of contemporary pop music. To do so, I bring in a third and very different resource in the form of David Foster Wallace's novel *Infinite Jest* (2007) to provide a frame or disposition of "hip ennui." This disposition is characterized by a combination of a paranoid drive to normatively correct behavior in the pursuit of cultural capital and a disappointed resignation to the immovability of the status quo. This is the backdrop upon which the tools of Fisher and Eshun can be engaged.

It should be made clear, however, that these engagements are not intended as critiques of these thinkers but rather an excavation of the conceptual tools that may be useful to the project at hand. Critiques of these works and thinkers are, of course, welcome and necessary. Especially in the years to come as the corpus of Fisher's work becomes canonized and as *More Brilliant* is to be republished and thus soon to be rediscovered. Wallace too is increasingly deified online. It is not that my readings of these thinkers are uncritical, but that mine is not a thoroughgoing critical project. What is offered up here are instead readings as a means of expanding the ideas expressed by each of these thinkers, particularly Eshun and Fisher, into new contexts, periods, and in relation to different theoretical considerations. The question asked here is, what can be done with the ideas of these two thinkers in combination? The question of their limitations is to be asked by others at other times. If there is something that Part 1 of the book can contribute to later critical work, it will be to provide a reading that may complexify our understanding of the work of these thinkers.

In the second section, "A Sonic Fiction of Capitalist Realism," I work through the previously identified space between popular music and contemporary culture as subjectively experienced. This section should itself be regarded as an attempt to produce academic writing as a kind of Sonic Fiction by making use of Holger Schulze's (2020) clarifying expansion of Eshun's concept. Traces of this shift begin to surface in the last chapter of the first section, which attempts to contextualize my readings of Fisher and Eshun, and my experience of music. Drawing inspiration from Jacques Attali's *Noise: The Political Economy of Music* (2011), Part 2, "A Sonic Fiction of Capitalist Realism" is divided into five conceptual chapters that attempt to perform a diagnosis of what is at stake in the experience of contemporary popular music and to propose ways of addressing these problematics. These conceptual chapters chart a theoretical journey starting with the tension that exists between the critical perspective of the Frankfurt School and the anti-elitist stance of what could be called the Birmingham school of cultural studies. As this is worked through, a new position is developed that highlights the ambivalence of popular music in the contemporary world. And from this position new possibilities become apparent. This starts with a chapter on the contentious field of "Attention," which was considered by the Frankfurt school to be the battleground of the culture industry, a concern that needed to be problematized but which also must remain a concern. From here, I move on to what was really at stake in controlling our attention: our "Complicity." This chapter provides a critique of the notion that some kinds of music are essentially more complicit in the reproduction of capital than others, but also of the impulse to flatten such concerns into the field of cultural capital. After this, the underlying cause of this problematic field is exposed: our desire for "Catharsis." In this chapter, the critique of cathartic desire is taken seriously, though ultimately found to be wanting. What it apparently wants is a different conception of the state to which catharsis returns us, a "Home" state if you will. With much of the difficult work of establishing this position of ambivalence done, this chapter starts to refocus the critique to more constructive ends. These ends are found in the final conceptual chapter "Conjunction," which through a deep analysis of Beyoncé's *Lemonade* lays out the implications for considering the experience of popular music under capitalist realism. All the while, it is pop music that gives this investigation its capacity for discovery. These chapters are framed by six vignettes of particular musical experiences that intensify, confound, confirm, and interrupt the project.

The conceptual chapters themselves also contain interruptions, as attempts to produce a piece of cultural theory of contemporary popular music are made all the more difficult by the unwieldy nature of the practice, of its experience, and the changing circumstances of the world/culture. Indeed, the writing and the arguments of the chapters themselves are constantly destabilized by the slippery nature of the object under consideration, and exposing some of the inadequacies of theory in addressing it also reveals possibilities in this tension. At other points, the tendencies of a theorist push the object out of earshot and become enraptured with the apparent clarity of semantic propositions. But echoes of the object haunt even these moments, destabilizing them and causing it to return even louder and more intrusively upon the cozy abstractions of such reductive thought than it was before.

The perspective presented in this book, by me, is, of course, particular. This writing comes from a tradition that claims both that cultural production is of import to the constitution of politics (and vice versa), and that the current hegemonic arrangement of neoliberal capitalism is insufficient to the realization of human emancipation. This perspective connects to another concern about what this book attempts to address. As a British-(anglophone) Canadian residing in Denmark in recent years, I have been living between languages, which has meant I have constantly been faced with the question of what is meant by terms such as "science" and "knowledge." Within a Danish linguistic context, a book, such as this one, would be thought to contain "scientific" work, though not in the strict sense meant by the English use of the term. Nonetheless, it does seem to imply that such work must necessarily add to the sum of human knowledge in the world. Knowledge here is considered the output of *a* scientific method (rather than *the* scientific method) and is thus a cumulative phenomenon with an implicit teleology toward a completion that is perhaps only ever notional. But between this difficult-to-grasp object of analysis and the moves made in attempting to cope with its slippery qualities, this book would seem to be a bad fit with such an understanding of knowledge.

To flesh out what I mean by this, I began the project upon which this book is based as something of an Adornian, without fully grasping the implications of what holding that position would mean. I started from the assumption, like Adorno, that there was something inherently (within a particular historical position) different about the kind of music I believed to be infantilizing and that which I considered to be emancipatory. However, I quickly realized that this position was untenable. It didn't with fit the music. It didn't fit with how it was produced. It didn't fit with how it was consumed. Most importantly, it didn't fit with the notion that cultural production could produce political change. If the revolution was to be predicated on everyone enjoying Schoenberg or Radiohead in the right ways and for the right reason, then the project seems a little silly. The poststructuralist approach of thinkers like Deleuze and Guattari seems to offer a better picture of how to understand this space I was actually interested in and which this book examines as an intersection of intensive flows of capital, desire, power, and sound. But such a perspective makes a clear articulation of a necessary political project more difficult. There's no simple way to reconcile these tensions. Yet because we can find moments when both of these perspectives, as well as many others, are audible through pop music, it might be possible to expose certain resonant potentialities of different configurations of the flows that brought it in to being. Potentialities that we may already on some level know to exist but that don't fit into existing categories.

All this is to say that when I approach popular music in the conditions of contemporary capitalist realism, I do not consider my contribution to this field as one that takes it in the direction of some kind of completion. Rather, through the practice and perspective of Sonic Fiction opened up by Eshun, this project is one of intensification. Intensification of problematics, intensification of sonic experience and, after Fisher, intensification of the desire for the world to be other than it is. The intention of this book is not to finally reveal the truth about pop music, but rather to make clear the impossibility of such a project from where we currently stand. The world in which we live cannot realize or fully contain the potential that inheres in pop, nor what it expresses and affects. The project of this book is to amplify the resonances of this potential to the extent that the sonic reflections of a world that could come to be are made audible.

Acknowledgments

Monographs such as this have the name of one person on the cover and they feature prominently on a single CV but, in truth, the creation of things like this are never the result of only one individual's efforts. So, first I would like to thank those who have helped this book come into the world in this form and helped to make it make sense to the extent that it does. I would like to thank my editor at Bloomsbury, Leah Babb-Rosenfeld and her assistant Amy Martin for guiding me through this process of transforming my manuscript into a book. And I would like to thank Joakim Drescher for creating the cover artwork, which has made this look exactly like the book I always wanted to write. I would also like to thank Holger Schulze, whose help and encouragement throughout this process may be the main reason why this artifact is before you now, rather than languishing within an unedited manuscript on my hard drive. I would also like to thank the reviewers of my proposal and manuscript, whoever they are, for their vital critical input.

This book was developed from my graduate school research at the Centre for Cultural Studies at Goldsmiths, University of London. The center no longer exists for reasons that are too convoluted to get into here, but it must be said that it was truly a privilege and an inspiration to study there. The intellectual rigor and the originality of the work produced by the scholars and students at the center has left an indelible mark on me and has expanded my idea of what is possible through academic work in ways that continue to thrill me. It has set a bar that I am constantly reaching for in my work, which seems perpetually to be outside of my grasp. In particular, I would like to thank the convener of the PhD program, Luciana Parisi, whose class, "Critical Theory of Interactive Media," changed the way I think about pretty much everything. To this day I'm not sure I have caught up to where her class has sent my thinking.

I also need to thank my graduate school advisors, Anamik Saha and the late Mark Fisher, without whom there would have been nothing to develop into a book. Their guidance and expertise was invaluable to both the refinement of this project and actually getting it done. Anamik kept me disciplined and constantly reminded me that what I was working on needed to be ostensibly "PhD shaped," though he was immensely supportive of my vision for the project and encouraging of my drive to try out odd things with it. To the extent that I am any sort of scholar today, it is Anamik's doing. Mark's theoretical work was such an inspiration to me that the title of his first book is in the subtitle of this one. In the months between the initial hand-in of my research and my viva, Mark took his own life. This tragedy was a great shock to me and literally thousands of others, one we are all still coming to terms with. The influence of Mark on my research had become somewhat invisible to me at the point of its handing in, though it was clear to my examiners, Mark's colleague, S. Ayesha Hameed and Holger Schulze. With their and Anamik's guidance, I was able to further develop this influence and thus produce the work before you today. I hope that this book can both honor Mark's legacy and contribute something to the projects he started.

A book like this can only come into being if one is surrounded by other forms of support in their daily life. So I would like to thank Ark Books of Copenhagen for giving me a welcoming place of camaraderie when writing alone in my own cave became an insurmountable task. In particular, I would like to thank Franek Korbanski for showing me exactly what dedication to something looks like, whenever I have needed a reminder, and Giovanna Alesandro for getting me into the store in the first place and bringing a drive and intensity into every project that we work on together. I also need to thank the reading group of which I have been a part for this last year of transforming my old ideas into a new book. Sheri Hellberg, Alexander Buk-Swienty, Niklas Birksted, and Neus Casanova Vico have all injected new energy into my thinking. They continue to make me to explain myself more clearly and to listen more carefully and have helped me to find the joy in what can be an exhausting way of working. I would like to thank my parents, Duncan Holt and Fiona Bannon, for their unceasing support and showing me, by example, that this kind of undertaking is something possible. They taught me how to think and showed me just how much there was out there to think about. A note of gratitude also needs to be extended to my brother Lewys, whose patience with me as I pontificated over the years is to be commended. And as both my audience and critic, he helped me grow my confidence to where I felt able to wax on for this many pages. That said, he is also quite the performative pontificator in his own right. Finally, I would like to thank Katrine Pram Nielsen, who has been there at almost every stage of this project since nearly the very beginning. It would not exist were it not for her immeasurable support and inspiration. Even though it is nowhere near enough, Tusind tak my dearest friend.

Part 1

Pop Music and Hip Ennui

1

Kodwo Eshun: Sonic Fiction at Century's End

Sonic Fiction Is a Theory-Fiction

We could start with the book. In the opening pages of *More Brilliant than the Sun: Adventures in Sonic Fiction* (1998), Kodwo Eshun asserts that music is a means of thinking in itself and not merely something to be thought about. This doesn't mean it is something just to be "felt," as if it were in some kind of transcendental black box, alien to conceptualization and the world of signs, but something more connective and powerful than mere signification.

Respect due. Good music speaks for itself. No sleevenotes required. Just enjoy it. Cut the crap. Back to basics. What else is there to add?

All these troglodytic homilies are Great British cretinism masquerading as vectors into the Trad Sublime. Since the 80s, the mainstream British music press has turned to Black Music only as a rest and a refuge from the rigorous complexities of white guitar rock. Since in this laughable reversal a lyric always means more than a sound, while only guitars can embody the zeitgeist, the Rhythmachine is locked in a retarded innocence. You can theorize words or style, but analyzing the groove is believed to kill its bodily pleasure, to drain its essence.

[...]

In CultStud, TechnoTheory and CyberCulture, those painfully archaic regimes, theory always comes to Music's rescue. The organization of sound is interpreted historically, politically, socially. Like a headmaster, theory teaches today's music a thing or 2 about life. It subdues music's ambition, reins it in, restores it to its proper place, reconciles it to its naturally belated fate.

Much of the text in the chapter has been taken from a chapter I contributed to the *Bloomsbury Handbook to Sound Art*. It appears here in an edited and expanded form.

> In *More Brilliant than the Sun* the opposite happens, for once: music is encouraged in its despotic drive to crumple chronology like an empty bag of crisps, to eclipse reality in its wilful exorbitance, to put out the sun. Here music's mystifying illogicality is not chastised but systematized and intensified – into MythSciences that burst the edge of improbability, incites a proliferating series of mixillogical mathemagics at once maddening and perplexing, alarming, alluring. (Eshun 1999, -007--004)

In his book, Eshun dives into this sonic thinking and the corporeality that extends the body into the vibrant electronic networks of (post-)modernity as a space of invention and "desiring-production" (Deleuze and Guattari 2013a, 11), racing toward intensive intersections of posthuman potentiality and into Afrofutures through "futurhythmachines" (Eshun 1999, -005). These were concepts that other media had, up until then, seemed able only to glance at. Eshun claimed that these ideas could be better actualized through understanding music as the production of Sonic Fictions. By engaging with music and the experience of it as a means of producing new fictive worlds that he would then document through writing, Eshun could connect this sonic thinking to other kinds of thinking. Eshun's Sonic Fictions allowed us to explore the logics, systems, and narratives from which particular musics emerge and through which they flow without reducing them to the virtue morality of the sublime, the strictures of western harmony, or the narratives of black redemption under white hegemony.

We could also start with the concept, but it might be a little premature. Sonic Fiction may have been something that was implicit in all music making; indeed, as Holger Schulze notes, perhaps all experience of sound:

> Sonic fiction is everywhere. Where one can find sounds one will also detect bits of fiction. As a consequence sonic fiction might then *mainly* be found in the tiny and ephemeral, often rapidly vanishing intersections and interferences *between* texts and lifestyles, between a given recording medium, its material properties, its design and processes of storing, retrieving and reproducing sound – as well as all its listeners appropriating all these qualities of the recording medium to play an intrinsic and radiating part in their lives. (Schulze 2020, 1)

Sonic Fiction as a concept has, for Schulze, proven to be a vital conceptual frame for understanding the entwining of sonic experience with more readily communicable forms of knowledge and subject construction. This extends far beyond the experience of music and beyond the particularities of the theoretical concerns of Eshun's work. And while this makes sense, in order to give this expansion of the concept the necessary moorings we need to reconstruct the kernel from which it started, because it was not until Eshun's book that Sonic Fiction, the concept, was given form. The book has become a point from which lines can be drawn backward into Sonic Fiction's emerging origin myths that connect the theory-fictions of anglophone Deleuzians in the 1990s (Schulze 2020, 11) and through them to the already fictionalized milieu of Parisian intellectual life in the 1970s, which in turn clearly connects to the counterculture and the techno-utopianism of a Silicon Valley built from the jetsam, flotsam, and lagan of military contracts following World War Two. This produced a world of consumer electronics in the 1980s, which points to the turntables, turned to as the expense of traditional musical means became too great in the deindustrializing urban centers of the USA later that decade; this in a country whose existence is predicated on the middle passage—the disavowed source of human energy, hundreds of years before—that allowed it to become a global hegemon.

But Eshun's book also produced lines that emanate forward, pulling the reader into the future. A future in which so much of this history could be left behind as we build anew upon its wreckage. Sonic Fiction is Eshun's means of thinking all this through music.

But perhaps we are already ahead of ourselves. In Eshun's Sonic Fiction, there are so many concepts to excavate and deconstruct. It needs to be recognized, as Eshun does, that the world in which we now live—a world of cloud-dwelling archivists, isolated by the "ecstasy of communication" (Baudrillard 2012)—has been fermenting since before the fall of the wall. Before the turntable transformed reproduction into production. Before the televisual spectacle of moptops from Liverpool on the Ed Sullivan show. Before record labels made profits by making paupers out of bluesmen. Before humanity cast upon itself the mushroom cloud shadow of its own potential end. And before the horrors of rationalized death and before the mechanized war. The infrastructure of this world, for Eshun, starts with the production of a fiction. The fiction of modernity, which leads the creature from another, slightly earlier, fiction, that of the cogito, to work from the delusory assumption that it can separate itself from both its flesh and the world (Eshun 1999, 38), and thus affectlessly appraise the both of them. For Eshun, we had already produced a reality built upon the innumerate fictions that stem from this. And the way in which we treat the sounds we are surrounded by is utterly entangled in these fictions also. Thus, we sought to be able to store and organize them rationally. This should not be considered as a simple opposition to Sonic Fictional experience, even though it can at times obscure our recognition of it, because it was through this organizing, fictionalizing logic—which for music meant the development of recordability—that the tools needed to make Sonic Fictions recognizable were produced (160). It is through recording and repetition and recontextualization that Sonic Fictions can be understood and are shared. The novel required the printing press: Sonic Fiction required the wax cylinder. But the question remained of how to actualize this virtual capacity.

In the years leading up to the publication of *More Brilliant than the Sun*, Eshun's investigations into musical Afrofuturism were to collide with the invention, or perhaps rather articulation, of theory-fiction by the Cybernetic Cultures Research Unit (CCRU) based then, unofficially, at the University of Warwick (Hameed 2017, 257). While Eshun had been mining the intersections of black music technology for hints at the science fictions yet to come, CCRU had been incessantly reading Baudrillard and Ballard until the distinction between these texts seemed to evaporate. For CCRU, this was a moment in which the continued discursive impositions of categorical limitations upon the world/culture were becoming ever more exposed as fictions as they were rapidly deterritorialized by the flows of techno-capital. Nation states were dissolving into globalized trade networks facilitated by the accelerating entanglement of communications networks. In turn, this also allowed for the possibility that identity as we knew it could be shed or reinvented in new online environments (CCRU 2014, 317). All the while, political ideologies that had structured the struggles of the previous 150 years were disappearing and being replaced by technocracies whose power was tied to the free flow of capital. All of this meant that the notion of the subject was effectively crumbling, even if, discursively, it remained in play. The theory-fictions of the CCRU were part of an attempt to map the world from a perspective inside the disintegration of these certainties. As above with Sonic Fiction, theory-fiction engaged with the affects of a world in technological flux at the end of human history and the affects of the very theories that had tried to explain them. They saw this as a kind of knowledge that exceeds the limited notion of rationality upon which liberal democracy was founded (CCRU 2017).

The point of convergence between theory- and Sonic Fiction is science fiction. A genre that, while rife with its own blind spots, could at least articulate some of the problematics listed above that were often so happily ignored by the more "refined" forms of literary fiction as defined by the status quo. Chief among these problematics was the paranoiac attachment to the status quo. Against this frame, science fiction offered resources that revealed that the claims that music needed either the limitation of some explanatory theory coherent only in terms of a historically limited notion of rationality or the *cretinous* (Eshun 1999: -007) assertion that it was beyond theoretical engagement, could clearly be seen as a nonsense. If we take Jungle, a favorite musical subgenre of CCRU (CCRU 2014, 329) and Eshun (1999, 076) that captured the energy and aesthetics found in cyberpunk—a form of music with a rigidity so rapid that it takes on the auditory appearance of flows darkly libidinal in character—the conventional tools for the theoretical judgment of music, which fixate on semantic decoding toward a final analysis, reveal nothing of this sound world *qua* the experience of it in context. Jungle is fast, Jungle is repetitive, Jungle is dissonant. But these are crass observations. Jungle envelops the listener/dancer to such an extent that the fiction of *an analysis from nowhere* is even more laughable than usual. At the same time, to seal this material of such clear cultural relevance, which is to say on the material condition in which it emerged, in a black box of the ineffable subjective experience simply reproduces the banality of ideology. These modes of dismissal and mystification are the inevitable outcome of the normalization of the impulse, championed by capitalism, to leave enjoyment unexamined in service of the perpetuation of the reduction of humans to rational economic actors (Gilbert and Pearson 1999, 42). But the way in which Jungle exceeds this is also complex, as even as a Sonic Fiction, it rejects the reduction to symbolic narratives while building fictive worlds as networks of sonic and sensual complexity, all while remaining aesthetically entangled with digital technology. "The Jungle Is a Futurhythmachine," asserted Eshun (1999, 076). Eshun gave form to this intuition of critical insufficiency and tied Jungle to other musics of the computer/human conjuncture. But more importantly, as he did this, he built a new operating system to explore the theory-fiction of music.

But we are already ahead of ourselves. To even ask: What is Sonic Fiction? We must first, of course, ask: What is theory-fiction? But also, simultaneously, what is Afrofuturism? And, to some extent, what is science fiction?

Afrofuturist Science Sonic Theory-Fiction

We should start with science fiction; the genre that catalyzed this fictive approach to inquiry. It is from science fiction that Eshun and others found the imaginative resources to uncover and invent whole fictive words from sound, owing to this genre's particular relationship to reality. In his 1971 essay "Fictions of All Kinds," the science fiction author J.G. Ballard argued the case for this speculative mode of writing, which has so often been dismissed as merely pulpy entertainment. He claimed that the focus of mainstream cultural discourse on so-called "serious fiction" is leading to a failure of imagination. A failure that, with the increasing rate of technological development, we can no longer afford to indulge. Ballard claimed that we were (and perhaps we still are) in desperate need of a science fiction that rides these currents of development if we are to even begin to understand what is happening to us and the world under the condition of ever accelerating modernity. He writes:

> In essence, science fiction is a response to science and technology as perceived by the inhabitants of the consumer goods society, and recognizes that the role of the writer today has totally changed. [...] To survive, he must become far more analytic, approaching his subject matter like a scientist or engineer. If he is to produce fiction at all, he must out-imagine everyone else [...] (Ballard 2014, 238)

Ballard claims that we no longer have the option of considering technology and human life as barely overlapping magisteria; as if we are the ones who simply "use" the tools. Instead we have to realize, as numerous philosophers have, that these tools are our world and thus also they are parts of us. The writers of science fiction need to be able to practice some kind of scientific distancing to rid us of the notion that the human condition is something timeless and of universal importance. Instead, these writers need to consider our existential condition under the contingencies of our changing situation. Though an imperfect way of addressing this situation, it is through this that we can perhaps place our pervasive humanism into the context of a variable. By doing so we may be able to imagine what is to come for the world that we have built while we have been so enraptured and distracted by more immediate goals.

We find hints of Eshun taking up this cause on his bio page in *More Brilliant than the Sun*: "He is not a cultural critic or cultural commentator so much as a concept engineer, an imagineer at the millennium's end writing on electronic music, science fiction, technoculture, gameculture, drug culture, post war movies and post war art" (1999, -017). When Eshun writes about music he does so outside of the accepted frames of music criticism. He doesn't contribute to a corpus of cultural production but engineers the production of a new culture. But, more to the point, Eshun accelerates the central claim of Ballard's essay. If

Ballard wanted us to ask, in morally disinterested terms, what was becoming of humanity? then Eshun asked, who's asking? *More Brilliant than the Sun* is, more than anything, an attempt to wrest so-called black music from the essentialists and romantics, and to bring it into a world that so often relegates such music and its meanings to the position of a "minority" interest in every sense of the term. The intention of Eshun was to use this music to help forge the future beyond this patrician restriction just as Ballard envisaged for science fiction. Because—more than the present, which is arguably always so very impoverished by the weight of history—for Eshun, the future is the actual territory that is at stake in Sonic Fiction. It is the space that most easily occupies the border between possibility and actuality.

This was also the paradigm under which science-fiction writers such as Philip K. Dick, Octavia Butler, and William Gibson operated, and from which Eshun and CCRU drew inspiration. In addition to the well-established capacity of this art form to offer a critique of its contemporary moment, the preemptive, or hyperstitional,[1] capacities of certain pieces of science fiction were such that a direct real-world application of what had been described in a piece of writing could appear not so long after its original publication. However, due to the powerful yet banal circumstance of late capitalism becoming neoliberalism, these real-world realizations often appear like deformed reflections in a bad mirror. For example, the hackers of the matrix, addicted to the thrill of cyberspace in Gibson's *Neuromancer* ([1984] 2017), find their real-world corollary in dopamine junkies staring at the infinite scroll of social media. However, there is much more to this formal capacity than a simple predictive parlor trick.

Such is the hyperstitional capacity of science fiction that it allows for the actionable recognition of the "immanent continuity between epistemology and ontology" (Parisi 2017, 223). To flesh this idea out, the (science) fictional convention of building of a world plausibly connected to our own, but in some important way other-than-it-is, is a practice that exposes the manner by which the conditions we find ourselves "being" establish what we can consider ourselves "knowing." And on top of this, it is through this conditioned "knowing" that we are aware of our "being" and the conditions of it.

We find an example of this at work in the characters that populate Dick's *The Man in the High Castle* (2016)—a novel about the geopolitics following an Axis victory in World War Two. The conceptual novelty of such a conceit, were these characters to read a book with the same premise, would be utterly lost on these people. They would know it as simply contemporary realist fiction perhaps of the thriller genre. In the novel, on the east coast of the USA, Nazi "race science" would be considered as an undeniable fact that defines the being of particular humans. This kind of knowledge would go beyond political designation and become a part of the human condition and the fabric of reality. Here, to know someone's race is to know the conditions of their existence. For the characters in the novel, as it is for us reading it, the epistemic revelation, or the expansion of what is knowable and thinkable, is tied to a situational reversal. Thus the characters are fascinated and perplexed by *The Grasshopper Lies Heavy*, a novel within the novel that presents an alternate history that, from their perspective, reverses the winners and losers of World War Two. We as readers are then made aware that what we presume to be the conditions under which we exist, and how we come to know and understand them, can be thought of as part of a story. And the effectiveness of this story, the means by which we know what we are, is tied to the extent that it is recognized and sanctioned by structures of power. Our being is understood by our knowledge of it and our knowledge of it established through the conditions of our being. This is, of course, the kind of insight we find in the post-structuralist work of thinkers like Foucault (1998). However, this recognition taken in conscious combination with the capacities of science fiction by the sonic/theory-fictionalists actually enhanced the power of sci-fi beyond the understanding for which Ballard had hoped. This capacity of the genre to force the recognition of the kind of contingencies revealed by post-structuralism is taken by some to reveal the possibility of making interventions in the hegemonic power structures that rest on the illusory distinction between knowledge and being through culture. It allows for the exposure of contingency in certain systems of thought that had had the ability to appear natural (Cuboniks 2017, 242–243).

It is with science fiction as this kind of paradigm-rupturing device in mind that we should consider the practice of Afrofuturism. And through this, we can see how Afrofuturism was a necessary component in the conceptual development of Sonic Fiction as such. There are a great many takes on Afrofuturism that range from the radical and revolutionary to reassuring liberal banality. But, in Eshun's use of the term, we find an intrinsically speculative form of Afrocentric conceptual engineering. Of course, it is entangled with the historical legacy of both racism and colonialism but, nonetheless, this concept is orientated firmly toward the future. A future in which there is the possibility that this history of violence and oppression that runs through post-colonial blackness, that reduced so many of those with black bodies to objects and commodities, may no longer be definitional. Indeed, perhaps a future in which the horrors of plunder may barely be remembered at all. This opens up the question of what it will be possible to know, with a radically different conception of the subject that does the knowing. That being said, these fictions are, however, always read by those of us existing in a present that is inseparable from the traumas upon which our world is built, meaning that the reality of this past is folded into the possibility of the future. As Eshun writes in the essay "Further Considerations on Afrofuturism," when imagining the conclusions arrived at as a team of archaeologists from the United States of Africa (USAF) start to examine artifacts from the early 21st century:

> In our time, the USAF archaeologists surmise, imperial racism has denied black subjects the right to belong to the enlightenment project, thus creating an urgent need to demonstrate a substantive historical presence. This desire has overdetermined Black Atlantic intellectual culture for several centuries. To establish the historical character of black culture, to bring Africa and its subjects into history denied by Hegel et al., it has been necessary to assemble countermemories that contest the colonial archive, thereby situating the collective trauma of slavery as the founding moment of modernity. (Eshun 2003, 287–288)

For Afrofuturism, the project is nothing less than an attempt to assert the existence and validity of, for want of a better term, black subjectivities that had been disavowed by so much of western philosophical, cultural, and political history. This is not something that can simply be argued to be an oversight, a mere mistake of (white wealthy western) reason. Rather, in Eshun's sci-fi, the materials of cultural production understood to be Afrofuturist highlight the blind spots endemic to the hegemonic "image of thought" (Deleuze 2011, 164) and the thinking subject envisioned as the white bourgeois European man of property. This is nowhere more evident than in music.

Traditional Western musicology, with its privileging of harmony as some kind of mechanistic riddle to resolve the conundrum produced by the conceptual collision of truth and beauty, is and has been poorly equipped to deal with other musical priorities and socialites (Small 2011). One need only look to one of the more radical practitioners of this mode of musical analysis, Theodor Adorno, to find a truly unforgivable lack of comprehension of music that deviates from the imperatives of the Western harmonic tradition. Despite the inherently counter-hegemonic tendencies in jazz aligning with his own desire to see capitalism come to an end in a way that would eschew authoritarianism, Adorno's commitment to the Western musical tradition leads him to denounce it as "cynical barbarism" (Adorno 1991, 34). Even as recently as the mid-2000s, the "avant-garde" composer, Karlheinz Stockhausen, struggled to find anything more incisive about the use of repetitive syncopated rhythmic devices used in contemporary electronica other than to request they stop with all "these post-African repetitions" (Stockhausen et al. 2008, 382). And in the nominally empirical/scientific field of audio signal analysis, a 2012 research paper, "Measuring the Evolution of Contemporary Western Popular Music," by Serra et al., attempted to draw conclusions about the relative state of contemporary Western popular music with no consideration for rhythm, and not even a mention of its omission.

The work of Gilbert and Pearson in *Discographies* (1999) has helped to shape the critique of connection between this outmoded form of musicology and its relation to the conceptualization of the bourgeois individual under liberal capitalism. But for the Afrofuturist, against the stupidity that Gilbert and Person so aptly identify, there is no argument to be made on the terms as they stand, and thus none is directly attempted. Instead, Afrofuturism illustrates the insufficiency of the status quo through the presentation of a richness derived from what is understood as an otherness incomprehensible to the dominant discourse. We can hear this in the way melody, harmony, timbre, and rhythm are organized as a continuum in so-called black music; it as much the drag of the stick against the snare as the syncopation of beat; as much the duration of the horn note as the production of the artificial harmonics; as much the quality of the sawtooth synth as it is the tune you hum for days afterward; as much Flying Lotus's infusion of the dragged "soulful" rhythms of jazz samples, as it is the "postsoul" (Eshun 1999, -006) of laptop drum machines.

Indeed, it is with a complex conceptualization of rhythm that Eshun rewrites that science fiction of future music and in doing so decolonizes the field of aesthetics through the technological potential of the rhythmachine, and thus is simultaneously able to challenge those who would essentialize blackness:

> Traditionally, the music of the future is always beatless. To be futuristic is to jettison rhythm. The beat is the ballast which prevents escape velocity, which stops music breaking beyond the event horizon. The music of the future is weightless, transcendent, neatly converging with online disembodiment. Holst's Planet Suite as used in Kubrick's 2001, Eno's Apollo soundtrack, Vangelis' Blade

Runner soundtrack: all these are good records – but sonically speaking, they're as futuristic as the Titanic, nothing but updated examples of an 18th C sublime.
[...]
Hyperrhythm's digital supersession of the human immediately alters your perception of the percussive act. As an actional event in times pace, drumming loses its solidity. Breakbeat science scrambles the logic of causation, opens up a new illogic of hypercussion and supercussion. (Eshun, 1999, 068)

Eshun's Sonic Fiction charts its route through the baggage of history, musicology, capitalism, technology, and rationality at the level of the concept. It is not enough to expand musicology to include appropriate consideration for rhythm or to simply understand the music of the Black Atlantic (Gilroy 2007) as being tied to a history of capitalism and colonial exploitation, which has played a part in producing those technologies now considered integral to contemporary musical expression. All these things are insufficient appendages to established ways of containing music as either the "trad sublime" or just theoretically significant diversions. Eshun wants to use Sonic Fiction to explore the logic of sensation that runs through musical experience as an experience of technology, history, and possibility. The concept engineer working in the bowels of these ossified ideas, to redirect from certain structures and overpower other capacities to find new openings and new means of conjunction and disjunction.

We see this in Eshun's narration of Sun Ra. A musician who, according to Eshun, knew more than any other at that time how to exploit the collapse of science and technology into magic and mythology that one finds in recorded and electronic music. While there may be the temptation to dismiss it as hyperbole, Eshun's fictioning of Ra provides an incisive analysis of what is at play in the composer's practice, and is able to avoid the pitfalls of reductionism.

From Marconi to Tesla to Moog to Ra, electrification opens up a discontinuum between technology and magic. Why a discontinuum instead of a continuum? Because alternating current transmits across gaps and intervals, and not by lineage or inheritance. From now on, Electronic Music becomes a technology-myth discontinuum. Traditional Culture works hard to polarize this discontinuum. Music wilfully collapses it, flagrantly confusing machines with mysticism, systematizing this critical delirium into information mysteries.
[...]
Music is the science of playing human nervous systems, orchestrating sensory mixes of electric emotions: the music of yourself in dissonance. Ra hears humans as instruments, sound generators played by the music they listen

to. The tone scientist's role is to engineer new humans through electronics. (Eshun 1999, 161)

There is a dry academic way to put this notion of Sun Ra's MythScience. One could, in line with Deleuze and Guattari's notion of stratification (2013b, 46–85), say that what Ra does is move freely between different strata of material organization. He is able to manipulate tools derived from the insights of physics and use the biological reaction to these manipulations to produce new systems of signification, while translating fragments of this new system into more conventional language, which allows people to be let into this musical experience. But such an analysis subsumes Ra into the concepts of French intellectuals via the conventions of the white academy. Eshun's Sonic Fiction of Ra allows the musician and his work to exceed such analytic categories. It allows something of Ra's work and practices to be glimpsed, heard and understood more thoroughly while never confusing these articulations for a final analysis.

The standard take on this jazz composer is that his experimental style was supplemented with an eccentric performative engagement with ancient Egyptian iconography and science fiction references. For Eshun, this misses most of what is actually taking place in Ra's work. Eshun hears and sees the production of a space of possibility encompassing Ra's music, performance, writing, and filmmaking in the production of a new MythScience fiction. Ra's music resonified and thus reconceptualized space as something other than the void of the trad sublime, and entangled in this reconceptualization are implications for our world. Ra puts forth an idea of black emancipation that is uncomfortably Nietzschean in its willingness to cast aside the apparent naturalism of the world as it is, and in doing so opens the possibility of becoming despotic.

> Soul affirms the Human. Ra is disgusted with the Human. He desires to be alien, by emphasizing Egypt over Israel, the alien over human, the future over the past. In his MythScience systems, Ancient Africans are alien Gods from a despotic future. Sun Ra is the End of Soul, the replacement of God by a Pharaonic Pantheon. (Eshun 1999, 155)

And here we have the problematic potential of Sonic Fiction. The capacity "fictive ideality" (Parisi 2017, 226) that it shares with its precedent, theory-fiction is without a necessary politics. Ra's desire to anoint himself the despot of an empire of ancient African aliens is, at once, able to appear terrifying and reasonable. He wants to occupy the position of the powerful rather than that of the oppressed whose redemption is eternally deferred. "Rather than identifying with the replicants [...] Ra is more likely to dispatch blade runners after the Israelites. He's the Tyrell Corporation's unseen director" (Eshun 1999, 155).

However, it would be incorrect to call Sonic Fictional practices relativist because, as Schulze notes in his examination of Sonic Fiction (2013), these practices are based in empiricism, which is to say that they start from experiences that precede them. There is first something concrete, absolute in ontological terms but particular in experiential terms, from which they stem. An *a priori* condition from which the production of Ra's Sonic Fictions unfurl. A being that precedes his capacity for knowing but that can only be understood through this capacity. We could say that, in the first instance, there is the sound. There is the music of Sun Ra with its particular qualities, which moves to the edges of a particular mode of signification (Jazz with experimental ideation), which is then combined with Ra's utterances and descriptions (the despotic space pharaoh, the galactic empire of black people). But we're getting ahead of ourselves again. Even prior to this there are the histories both of Western and African musical practices and their intersection in colonialism. On the one hand, this means that despite his desire to break "violently with Christian redemption, with soul's aspirational deliverance, in favor of posthuman godhead" (Eshun 1999, 156), the circumstance from which Ra attempts to escape haunts his desire to do so. On the other hand, the actualization of this desire in his music and other artistic practices does move into a space that is beyond, or other than, the telos of the hegemonic ideologies that are inherent to these conditions.

All this is to say that it is incorrect to consider Sonic Fiction to be relativistic because it is grounded in existing systems of what can empirically be said to be. Speculations from here may follow but they are routed in the given. This speaks to the intentions of sonic fiction as a practice. The goal is not to produce new absolutes on a universal scale, but nor is the practice of writing Sonic Fiction one that can be reduced to a particular partial slice of given conditions. The goal is to occupy that space *between* that fiction so often does. In the terms of Alexander Weheliye, this is a space of singularity, where particulars and universals are not held above one another but held in parallel tension (Weheliye 2005: 206–207).

Regardless of what one may think of Ra's expressed desire for a kind of musical despotism—which is nothing new in the white musical avant-garde (see for example Luigi Russolo or Karlheinz Stockhausen)—it is the mode of expression itself that carries the potential of Sonic Fiction. Sonic Fiction offers the tools to engage empirically and explore the skepticism found in the postmodern tradition of "incredulity towards the grand narratives" (Lyotard 2006, xxiv); a notion that is so often misread. Incredulity does not mean dismissal or abandonment. Instead, it means only that one is unwilling to believe in these narratives of history or progress *prima facie*. Rejection or criticism of these narratives may follow from this initial skeptical move, but this is more likely to point to a problem with the narrative in question than the stance of incredulity. But Sonic Fiction is more than just a skeptical, critical project: it is a creative practice. A way of producing new narrative worlds and systems of signification that, while they may start from the conditions that can be said "to be," do not remain constrained by the hegemonic insistence that these conditions "must be."

Eshun's Sonic Fiction, despite being the instantiation of the concept as such, must too be considered as singular. It is soaked with the orientation toward the future that is both derived from its connection to the accelerationist theory-fiction of the CCRU and the science fiction of Afrofuturism. Certain imperatives, problematic and less so, are thus baked into it. However, just as each singular instantiation of Sonic Fiction that can be said to exist in music exceeds that music, the practice itself exceeds the circumstance from which it emerged. And while Sonic Fiction emerged through the concepts churned up by the musics produced in the latter half of the first full century of recorded sound, Sonic Fiction exceeds this first instantiation.

The Postsoul

At the Century's End, the Futurhythmachine has 2 opposing tendencies, 2 synthetic drives: the Soulful and the Postsoul. But then all music is made of both tendencies running simultaneously at all levels, so you can't merely oppose a humanist r&b with a posthuman Techno.

[…]

From the outset, this Postsoul Era has been characterized by an extreme indifference towards the human. The human is a pointless and treacherous category. And in synch with this posthuman perspective comes Black Atlantic Futurism. Whether it's the Afro Futurist concrete of George Russell and Roland Kirk, the Jazz Fission of Teo Macero and Miles Davis, the World 4 Electronics of Sun Ra and Herbie Hancock, the Astro Jazz of Alice Coltrane and Pharoah Sanders, the cosmophonic HipHop of Dr Octagon and Ultramagnetic MCs, the post-HipHop of The Jungle Brothers and Tricky, the Spectral Dub of Scientist and Lee Perry, the offworld Electro of Haashim and Ryuichi Sakamoto, the despotic

Acid of Bam Bam and Phuture, the sinister phonoseduction of Parliament's Star Child, the hyperrhythmic psychedelia of Rob Playford and Goldie, 4 Hero and A Guy Called Gerald, Sonic Futurism always adopts a cruel, despotic, amoral attitude towards the human species. (Eshun 1999, -005)

A final point needs to emphasized in the conceptualization of Sonic Fiction and its connection to "black music"; a term that Eshun believes, "so often sounds stupid, so dated and pointless" (37). This is the notion of postsoul. The problem with the concept of "black music" is its deployment as a counter to the supposed techno-rationality of so-called white music. While this may point to certain limitations in the dogmatic application of harmonic telos as aesthetic justification, and help us to identify the joyless pretensions of certain progressive rock practices, it does so by dehistoricizing and essentializing blackness. The assertion that what is called black music is somehow soulful commits the naturalistic fallacy, deconstructed above, by making the musical practices that emerged from the culturation of those with particular bodies into some kind of mystic, essential racial expression. Not only does this ignore the history of technological entanglement and innovation found in predominantly black cultural practices, but it is also dehumanizing as it applies a condescending notion of purity (read uncomplicated) to particular musical practices as the basis for aesthetic judgment.

Like in the above discussion of Western philosophy's reluctance to grant black people the status of a subject, as this concept has elided with the vague secular humanism of liberal capitalist democracies, so too has followed this concept's connection to hegemonic power. And so we read in Eshun's work from this time—when he was still proximate to the philosopher Nick Land in his desire to rid the world of the "human-security system" (2018, 54) and usher in some nominally liberated posthuman future—the desire to be rid of this corrupt institution of bestowing value through humanity, because this has always been a fragile whimsical criteria. The music he cites can be heard as attempts at this. Alice Coltrane's casting off of geo-cultural determinism, Tricky's technological reappropriations of white appropriations of blackness (whose soul is it anyway?), and the rhythmmachines of Haashim are all challenges to the post-colonial notion of inducing redemption through the assertion of human nature being more proximate to the victims of its plunder. With such an offer on the table, refusal in favor of cosmic despotism seems a reasonable counter.

But the soul haunts Eshun even as he wishes to diminish its essential power. Otherwise, why not simply oppose it in the paragraph above? The answer is at the strategic level. For Eshun this project was about the reorganization of what had come before so as to be able to move beyond the impasses of our contemporary cultural/political/onto-epistemic conditions. This is why he regards the claims of Sun Ra to have been born on Saturn with such credulity:

> I try to exaggerate that impossibility, until it's irritating, until it's annoying, and this annoyance is merely a threshold being crossed in the readers' heads, and once they unseize, unclench their sensorium, they'll have passed through a new threshold and they'll be in my world. I'll have got them. The key thing to do is to register this annoyance, because a lot of the moves I've described will provoke real annoyance, the lack of the literary, the lack of the modernist, the lack of the postmodern. All of these things should provoke a real irritation, and simultaneously a real relief, a relief that somebody has left all stuff behind, and started from the pleasure principle, started from the materials, started from what really gives people pleasure. (Eshun 1999, 193)

The practice of Sonic Fiction, or perhaps the practices of hearing Sonic Fictions and transcribing them, is a provocation. Considering the entrenchment with which so many ideas about music, and ideas about the humanity of those who make it, are held, the first move of Sonic Fiction is to dislocate the parameters of truth and the powers of skepticism that these ideas rest upon. Its second move is to bring people into contact with that which persists through the dislocation of truth and skepticism; "to start from the pleasure principle." There is something hedonistic about Sonic Fiction that both pious Marxists and the practitioners of respectability politics may wish to disavow. But the strength of this approach is in the recognition of the capacities of music and the experience of it greatly exceeds those of a delibidinized theory of history or the supposed universal rationality that undergird the status quo. It may be more dispersed, but the capacities for action in music reorient the lives of millions, changing the future in ways that politics can only ever try to manage and contain.

This is not to say that this conception of the Sonic Fiction project is not without limitations. The anchoring in the pleasure principle makes a great deal of sense and points to many of the blind spots in the traditional understanding of the relationship between music and its constitution of reality. But it does so by borrowing, albeit knowingly, from the same resource from which capital derives its power. At century's end, a time at which resistance to capitalism seemed impossible, and when the untapped cyborg futures of the internet still gleamed with posthuman possibility, these moves of Eshun's may have seemed like the only ones left to play. Or, indeed, the only ones desirable to play. But the 1990s were an oddly specific time; a window on to an end history that had been made available to those in Western liberal democracies. A window that had opened with the end of the cold war and started to close on September 11, 2001 and which had closed entirely by the time of the 2008 financial crisis. Thus, indebted to Eshun as we are for unlocking this way of knowing and being with music, the Sonic Fictions of the present remain to be written. New strategies need to be developed for a world in which certain fields have been foreclosed and others have opened. When Eshun was writing, it was under the conditions of an ideology for material and affective control that would not receive its name until after its near collapse had exposed its cracks. This was capitalist realism, which must be understood as the setting of the Sonic Fictions of today.

2

Mark Fisher: Capitalist Realism after the Crash

The Birth of Capitalist Realism

When Francis Fukuyama declared that the fall of the Soviet Union marked the end of history (1989), despite the career-making hubris of the claim, he was correct in that a new constellation of power relations needed to be recognized. At the time, from the political scientist's vantage point, then at the US State Department (formerly at the RAND Corporation), this appeared to be the inevitable establishment of liberal market democracies as global hegemony. Which is to say, the establishment of some kind of American empire. But from the classrooms of a further education college in Kent in the mid-2000s, looking back on that same moment and its articulation as the end of history, it could clearly be seen as a part of something very different: the construction of capitalist realism.

> The power of capitalist realism derives in part from the way that capitalism subsumes and consumes all of previous history: one effect of its 'system of equivalence' which can assign all cultural objects, whether they are religious iconography, pornography, or Das Kapital, a monetary value. Walk around the British Museum, where you see objects torn from their lifeworlds and assembled as if on the deck of some Predator spacecraft, and you have a powerful image of this process at work. In the conversion of practices and rituals into merely aesthetic objects, the beliefs of previous cultures are objectively ironized, transformed into artifacts. Capitalist realism is therefore not a particular type of realism; it is more like realism in itself. (Fisher 2009, 4)

This was how it appeared to Mark Fisher as a teacher of young people about to enter adulthood, which was then, as it is now, entirely synonymous with the labor market. Though, for Fisher, Fukuyama's declaration was not the instigating gesture that allowed capitalist realism to emerge. Rather, the key moment for him was the declaration of Prime Minister Margaret Thatcher in the 1980s that "There is no alternative" (Fisher 2009, 8) to (neo)liberal capitalism. The melancholy hubris of Fukuyama's assertion pales in comparison with the near reality-defining certainty of Thatcher's remark. While Fukuyama's comment was perhaps recklessly diagnostic, Thatcher's declaration was a world-defining performative.

If one had to summarize what is meant by the term "capitalist realism," it would be as the making indelible of Thatcher's claim to such an extent that it infuses and taints all lived experience. It is not enough that capitalism has saturated almost every area of contemporary life; more than this, for nearly the last four decades, work has been carried out at the ideological and affective level to foreclose even the possibility that there may be a different way for politics/society/culture/economics to be organized. For Fisher, there were few places in the world where this particular condition of capitalist realism were more apparent than the UK. The hyper-competitive capitalism of the United States manages to keep the depressive revelation of capitalist realism somewhat at bay by submerging its subjects in the libidinizing spectacle of consumption; meanwhile in Scandinavia and much of continental Europe, the influence of post-war social democracy has, to an ever-decreasing extent, slowed the advance of capitalist realism or at least obscured it. The UK is the worst of all worlds in these regards, combining the asset stripping of free markets minus the possibility of excess with the feeling of containment that social democracy can engender but with ever-worsening public services. This was not always the case, however: the UK could have become a more protective social democracy. That was until the late 1970s when economic instability brought about the erosion of the post-war consensus that had, broadly speaking, held to the notion that certain industries and cultural values should be protected by the government from the whims of the market and the logic of capital accumulation. This was, of course, a precarious bargain because, as the contradictions inherent in this arrangement caused it to crumble, it left space for a new individualistic political-economy to take the stage. This was one that would be built upon the Hobbsean assertion of a war against all (Gilbert 2014, 35) but where sovereignty would, at least rhetorically, always be referred to the market.

That said, while capitalist realism does describe a set of material and economic circumstances, it goes beyond this to describe the production of a cultural atmosphere that, for Fisher, foreclosed the future and delibidinized everything as a mere medium of exchange (though paradoxically it often managed to achieve this by crassly libidinizing everything). A country as nostalgic, as stratified by class, and as emotionally repressed as the UK was just the place where the contours of capitalist realism can be most clearly observed. When watching the opening ceremony of the London 2012 Olympics, with its focus on a kind of sanitized version of British history, in which it seemed that colonialism existed just to allow for future diversity, one was struck by the pervasive ideas that *The future cannot be better than the past*, and, more subtly, that *Your social position is the result of some cosmic justice and your complaints about this are hysterical and evidence of your weakness*. This is what Fisher attempts to disentangle in *Capitalist Realism*.

It should be said, however, this is not simply one man's diagnosis of the discomfort of the present. Fisher was a philosopher by training, whose analysis of the world was based in Marxian theories and French post-structuralist thought, which was beginning to permeate the anglophone academy in the 1990s. The simulacra of Baudrillard (Fisher 2009, 18), the power emanating from below of Foucault (22) and the conceptualization of capital as the "'unnamable Thing', the abomination, which primitive and feudal societies 'warded off in advance'" (5) of Deleuze and Guattari were all tools he had at his disposal. But it was not merely the love of francophone obscurantism that had drawn him to these questions of social and cultural organization. As a contemporary of Eshun's in CCRU at Warwick—indeed he was amongst its founders—Fisher too was not content to divorce his intellectual analysis from the culture as practice that surrounded him. Fisher, like Eshun, had come to theory as a means of intensifying the music, films, books, and politics that he saw as already expressive of cultural analysis (Fisher 2018, 31). Thus, when it came time to publish a book of his own after years of blogging under the moniker K-Punk, the intention was that it should amplify what was already there. To do this, he co-founded Zer0 Books with a number of other thinkers and writers with this specific mission in mind. "Zer0 books is committed to the idea of publishing as a making public of the intellectual" (103), reads one line in the publisher's mission statement. And this mission was arguably actualized in the publication of *Capitalist Realism* in 2009, just as the dust of the financial crash was beginning to settle and the state and ongoing nature of the damage was starting to become apparent. This short book cost less than most paperback novels and much less than most academic books, which got it into the hands of people who had previously felt excluded from the dominant methods of understanding the present through radical critique. The book seemed to say something that had long been known about the world in which we have found ourselves, but that had previously defied clear definition. It didn't rest on theory for this explanation; instead it used theory as an amplifier to draw out the resonant frequencies of what was present in both the culture and cultural productions of a world saturated in, what could now be called with confidence, capitalist realism.

But as a part of the theory-fictionalists of CCRU, it is safe to claim that Fisher did not regard his book as the final analysis of the status quo, or as the comprehensive guide to changing it. Rather it was the introduction of an idea as affects to instigate more ideas of what to do. It provided certain analytical frames that allow us to derive new and different kinds of knowledge about the world as it is, and why it seems it has become so difficult to change it, while also providing hope to many that all this is contingent and can well be changed.

The Affects and Materials of Capitalist Realism

You are made aware of the boring dystopia[1] of capitalist realism, as the sensation of hopelessness that washes over you as you stand, sleep deprived and nervous, sardine-like on the early morning commuter train. Wherein, the only safe place upon which to affix your gaze is a post-ironic commercial for a prohibitively expensive personal driver service. The other option is staring at the news updates on what used to be a phone and is now more of an intensive content delivery system. Here you find that a musical icon has lost their battle with cancer above an impotent lamentation on drowning refugees and, as you scroll one story down, the missives of opportunistic politicians warning of a "flood" of migrants descending on *our* neighborhoods and calling for an end to "unchecked immigration." A young pop star has filed for divorce. The train leaves behind the sprawl of less unaffordable housing—you wouldn't be here on this train if you didn't have so much rent to pay—and winds its way through the skyscrapers that house the very financial institutions that both caused and profited from the financial crash of 2008 and absorbed the quantitative easing of the subsequent slow and questionable recovery. It becomes clear to you now that everyone on this train, at least everyone in a well-fitting suit, is on their way to work for one of these institutions. Or, if their suit fits less well or they are perhaps in a uniform, the armor of a private security firm or the t-shirt of a sandwich shop, their labor will be indirectly supporting them. At least you can listen to that new Xiu Xiu album, aptly titled *Forget* (2017), which takes you out of this reality as the sound of Jamie Stewart's quivering vocals provides a sense of possibility that affirms, even through this musical desolation, that there is hope that this will not be forever. This escape is facilitated by a device made of conflict minerals assembled in a sweatshop with suicide prevention nets. A device, the planned obsolescence of which causes it to crash with ever greater frequency as its software is updated. But the prohibitive price tag on the new version of this device means that you cannot even affirm your membership to this exploitative system. Of course, the wireless earbuds lodged in the heads on the train serve as a reminder that there are many around you for whom this expense is but a trifle. But if you can put this out of your mind and attend to the song, and if the phone doesn't crash, then this feeling of possibility found in the music has, of course, come at the price of isolation. But the prospect of talking to anyone here is terrifying.

As you make your way out of the station, you pass a busker playing in one of the pitches licensed by the city. He is a young man with one arm. Yet, he has managed to develop a technique to play melody lines that sound like thrash metal. Today, he is playing interpretations of Coldplay hits over a backing track. A wealthy man in a suit stops him between songs and chats with him about guitar tech, eating into the musician's limited time-slot. A mist of perpetual drizzle hits you as you're exiting the station. Across the road, there is a line of closed and run-down shops that stretch to the final destination of the office building.

This is today, this tomorrow, the day after that, the week after that, the month, the year the decade. There is a possibility open to you that might allow for the mitigation of some of the discomforts. Promotions are possible, which might allow you to one day to improve your commute. But this comes with an increase in responsibility for something about which you truly do not care. The clash between acting in bad faith and the need to do so in the name of survival results in a deep anxiety. You are an imposter and they all know it. Not that the work is hard, because it isn't, but it is draining because it requires all your attention and it is unending and unchanging. This monotony would be dispiriting enough as you are truly not living up to your potential, but this isn't *Fight Club* (2004). You aren't living in a world as a victim of your and its own success. Effort is being deployed to keep this thing afloat. It is not that the work is hard; more than anything it's that you're expected to care about it. The anxiety of maintaining this pretense is overbearing in your current position. So, to increase this obligation through working to promotion for the possibility of, one day, perhaps having a less dispiriting commute, is insufficient motivation to spend more energy investing yourself in this place. But if you don't submit to this, you guarantee that every day will be exactly the same.

Later, at the pub, you sit around with friends—or are they just colleagues?—and find a little relief in the way the second pint has removed some of what you have spent the day worrying about—not so much the work as its inescapability. The pub is closer to the station than it is to the office, one of the few places still open in this street. As you let some of the tension go and even laugh a little, you overhear a group of students at the table next to yours talking about something. The only sentence you hear clearly is when the one holding court says, "Nothing ever happens, things just get worse. That's neoliberalism." And you think to yourself, if only they knew.

***

It is necessary to put some daylight between some related terms here, lest capitalist realism be treated as a synonym for neoliberalism. When at a cultural studies conference or scrolling through left-wing Twitter, one can become numb to the invocation of neoliberalism. And yet, until fairly recently, it seemed that one could have a long career in politics itself and not hear the term mentioned at all. There is an imprecision to the term as it is often used to mean simply "things that are bad." That said, it is a term with a rich history documented by the likes of Philip Mirowski (2013), who also takes it to have a precise historical meaning. In short, neoliberalism is a largely unexplicitated political philosophy that holds that the market, if freed from as much regulation as possible while being protected in its activities by a strong state with a (near) monopoly on the deployment of violence, will efficiently deliver the greatest amount of human well-being possible. But this should not be confused even with utilitarianism. The production of human well-being in this philosophy is a desirable epiphenomenon, not the organizing principle. The organizing principle is to minimize interference in the structural functioning of the market, which is the ultimate arbiter of how much human well-being is possible. Any attempt to interfere in this by a government, for example, will simply lead to a destabilization of market forces, which will ultimately be deleterious to the efficient delivery of the maximum possible amount of human well-being as defined by market conditions. This doesn't lead to all humans having their well-being increased. It is merely that, according to this school of thought, if the system is allowed to work as it is supposed to, then a number of people will experience greater well-being. And this increase in well-being and the number of people who experience it is determined by the market too. Indeed, the inequality inherent to this arrangement is a necessary component of the market mechanism. The practical upshot of this is the privatization of public services and public space, the minimization of progressive taxation, the deregulation of industrial and commercial practices, and the globalization (by force or arrangement) of trade and production. The fact that these actions may lead to things like climate change and wars are externalities that it would be unreasonable to require a market to account for in advance, and are only amenable to calculation once the constituent elements can be said to have a market value. Neoliberalism is a dry notion of political economy built on a bad-faith assertion that humans are rational actors with access to perfect information. When it comes to marketing and selling of commodities, rationality is assumed not to overdetermine society or its members, but when it comes to assigning responsibility for financial disasters, rationality is posited as the rationale for asserting individualized personal responsibility leading to misbehavior in the otherwise functional market. As such, neoliberalism does little to account for the desires of individuals beyond satiating the urge for consumption as it alienates them. And it does little to consider the ethico-aesthetic comportment of the world as its distribution of resources shapes it.

The problem with the use of the term "neoliberalism" isn't that it is actually meaningless, only that it can become meaningless when it is too broadly applied; in other words, when it is used to cover both the cause of our present circumstances and its symptoms. Therefore, to give it some conceptual clarity, we could perhaps say that it is the disavowed ethico-aesthetic comportment of the world inherent to the economics of neoliberalism that produces the conditions in which capitalist realism emerges. The political economy of neoliberalism is the cause of the symptoms of capitalist realism. While conventional wisdom has it that one should try to look past the symptom of a condition in order to treat the underlying causes, it doesn't quite hold true when one is talking about something as globally entrenched and defuse in its power structure as neoliberalism and people's understanding of the condition of possibility as delineated by capitalist realism. Indeed, to ignore how the conditions of capitalist realism serve as an affective filter on the possibility of addressing the underlying causes would only exacerbate them.

This is why Fisher looks to films and music in the books, as much as political theory and experiences from his own life, to diagram out this concept. It allows him to formulate and objectify the disavowal of neoliberalism's ethico-aesthetic comportment of the world with greater clarity than previously seemed possible. An example of this is mapping the aesthetic expressions of post-war Fordist capitalist societies onto the films *The Godfather* (2001 [1972]) and *Goodfellas* (2010 [1990]), while in the film *Heat* (2017 [1995]) we are given a clear depiction of how the post-Fordist labor of neoliberalism manifests in culture.

> In *Heat*, the scores are undertaken not by Families with links to the Old Country, but by rootless crews, in an LA of polished chrome and interchangeable designer kitchens, of featureless freeways and late-night diners. All the local color, the cuisine aromas, the cultural idiolects which the likes of *The Godfather* and *Goodfellas* depended upon have been painted over and re-fitted. *Heat*'s Los Angeles is a world without landmarks, a branded Sprawl, where markable territory has been replaced by endlessly repeating vistas of replicating franchises. (Fisher, 2009, 31)

What this illustration expresses is a compressed and comprehensible take on Luc Boltanski and Eve Chiapello's rigorous analysis of 1990s management literature in *The New Spirit of Capitalism* (2005). Their work argues that motivating principles of capitalism changed following the countercultural movements of the late 60s and early 70s, which railed against both the lack of autonomy and the mundanity of work under capitalism, as well as the poor conditions and pay for this work (28–30). What Boltanski and Chiapello argue is that the management literature of the 1990s shows the desire of businesses to appear as if they have addressed the concerns of autonomy and mundanity and to then oppose these to the concerns around pay and conditions (xxix). Thus, the emphasis was placed on flexibility and self-management. The insecurity of this new arrangement was downplayed as each employee was made to feel as if they were responsible for their own success. They were autonomous. In the terms of the movies above, as restrictive as the family in the *The Godfather* could be, there was something beyond the jobs at hand to which one could feel they belonged. In *Heat* the criminals are freed from all old grudges and loyalties, but all that is left is the work and the building of a personal brand.

Capitalist realism as a concept and as a book helped to crystallize in the minds of many the peculiarity and the recentness of this way of organizing what is possible in the world in line with market demand, to which we are told there is no alternative. It allows us to see—in what is passed off as innocuous, like the proliferation of bureaucracy paperwork (Fisher 2009, 41), or inevitable, like the rising cost of education, or natural, like the depoliticized medicalization of mental health—expressions of the same symptom caused by the mismatch between the political economy of neoliberalism and the desires of those living under it. It was a bridge between that which appeared to be the way of the world and the millions of tiny actions that are required to reproduce it. And this way of understanding appeared at a moment when all that had made capitalist realism appear monolithic seemed like it might just crumble.

But this was a decade ago …

The End of the World and the Specter of Acid Communism

The oft-trotted-out trope that it is easier to imagine the end of the world than the end of capitalism usually offers little more than a knowing description of the depth of contemporary hopelessness. But it also gestures toward a profound lack of imagination. In *Capitalist Realism*, Fisher deploys this cliché of the left with more subtlety and, some might read, even excitement. Imagining the end of the world being easier than ending capitalism doesn't mean that it's easier to imagine a planet-destroying meteor shower than imagining the disentanglement of global techno-capital. That is really easy. There is nothing remarkable about that situation. The key term here though is "world," not "planet." The world is an affective and semiotic concept that we co-produce in an unbalanced relationship with our material conditions (Berardi 2015, 331). It is the systems that give things significance; the structure of meaning by which we are surrounded and penetrated and formed.

This is why Fisher points to the film *Children of Men* (2007) as an example of this easier-to-imagine end of the world. To a tech billionaire, the fact of global infertility would appear as a technical problem that just requires outside-the-box thinking. But as this situation has dragged on, in the film, and the problems seem ever more unlikely to be solvable, the hierarchical social order of capitalism persists and is exacerbated even as the meaning of our systems of signification is being evacuated. Even as the end of the world is all that is on the horizon. The scene in which the film's protagonist visits his friend, who, in the refurbished Battersea power station, has surrounded himself with canonical pieces of art (Michelangelo's *David*, Picasso's *Guernica*, etc.) is a perfect illustration of the difficult work involved in imagining the end of the world. It is not just the sadness of not having children that is at stake here. It is not just about the erasure of the future, but with that also comes the erasure of the past. The expertly sculpted statue will go on existing long after the last human closes their eyes for the final time, but with that closure, everything this formed marble meant will disappear and it will become no more than stuff. Capitalism, however, will persist up until this point and depending on the methods and power sources for an automated transaction, perhaps beyond it.

When Fisher writes that rather than being a particular type of realism, capitalist realism purports to be "realism in itself" (Fisher 2009, 4), he is arguing that the notion of one imagining the end of the world and the end of capitalism as if these were separate categories is actually an effect of capitalist realism itself. In the absence of some kind of AI that can utilize the capital—produced as the automated process of capital accumulation persists after the last human in *Children of Men* has closed their eyes—as capital,[2] the same world-ending death of meaning that afflicts *David* will transform the exercise of capitalism into mere symbols without meaning, flickering on a screen unable to become signs.

Capitalist realism is a bulwark to prevent the realization that capitalism is actually a part of the world and, as such, it is contingent upon the construction of meaning. Even the material factors of capitalist production are only effective in as much as can be coded and decoded semiotically, which is to say, be comprehensible as part of the world. Though, owing to the nature of capitalism's entanglement with both the material world and the world of meaning-making—indeed its capacity to appear as reality in itself—we may not be able to simply extract it from the world. Thus, we should perhaps see the end of the world as part of the plan to end capitalism. As Fisher writes:

> … emancipatory politics must always destroy the appearance of a "natural order", must reveal what is presented as necessary and inevitable to be a mere contingency, just as it must make what was previously deemed to be impossible seem attainable. (Fisher 2009, 17)

This amounts to a major rearrangement of the systems through which we produce meaning. The shift of something from an impossibility to not merely a possibility but something attainable implies a radical change in the common understanding of that idea. A shift that might preclude the continuation of our present world of meaning-making. But as we well know, one cannot simply change what things mean. Fisher's work is less a complete analysis than an invitation to "invent the future" (Fisher 2018, 21) with him and everyone else who wants the world to be otherwise.

There are echoes here of Eshun's approach to Sonic Fiction as a means to liberate blackness from the reductive narratives of humanist soulful authenticity. Indeed, this resonance was something Eshun highlighted himself during his reflections on Fisher's work at the first annual memorial lecture in January of 2018:

> Those of us who are unable to reconcile ourselves to our existence. Those of us whose dissatisfaction and disaffection, whose discontent and whose anger and whose despair overwhelms them and exceeds them. And who finds themselves seeking means and methods for nominating themselves, for electing themselves, to become parts of movements and scenes that exist somewhere between seminars and subcultures, study groups and HangOuts. Reading groups drawn together by the impulse to fashion a vocabulary. (Eshun 2018)

He then went on to list all of the groups that have drawn from Fisher's formulation of capitalist realism to set about the end of this world and the beginning of something new. To mention a few, we can hear the concerns of capitalist realism echoed in Nick Srnicek and Alexander Williams' *#Accelerate: Manifesto for An Accelerationist Politics* (2014, 347), which refuses to cede the notion of progress to the amalgamation of techno-capital and seeks to do so by out-innovating capital toward collective ends. In the manifesto *Xenofeminism: A Politics for Alienation*, the collective Laboria Cuboniks (2017, 321) desire to denaturalize that which appears as unchangeable by identifying specific targets and potential strategies that can start to take hold. And we can hear echoes, too, in the work of the contentiously dubbed "speculative realists," who, like Fisher, have taken up the mission of trying to examine reality beyond the appearances of this world (Eshun 2018).

Not every activity that Fisher influenced could be called progressive. There are scenes in Eshun's list that seek to return some kind of prelapsarian state and others that have nothing but disdain for anything that could be called emancipation. Indeed, at earlier points in his life, Fisher's politics had been quite different; oriented toward the nihilism of a cyberpunk future that seemed just around the corner in the mid-1990s (Fisher 2018, 27). But his politics in the last two decades of his life were firmly on the left. That said, they were always inventive and always attempted to find ways to excite involvement in this project of bringing about the new world.

Before Fisher took his own life in January of 2017, he was working a new book that will tragically remain unfinished. The book was *Acid Communism*, which was to be a reappraisal of the 70s counterculture as something other than a social movement always already co-opted by the forces and interests of capital.

This, he argued, was symptomatic of a mistake those on the left have made about the struggle before them. Fisher writes:

> We on the left have had it wrong for a while: it is not that we are anti-capitalist, it is capitalism, with all its visored cops, its teargas, and all the theological niceties its economics, is set up to block the emergence of Red Plenty. The overcoming of capital has to be fundamentally based on the simple insight that, far from being about wealth creation, capital necessarily and always blocks the production of common wealth. (Fisher 2018, 753–754)

Acid Communism would have sought to recontextualize and revitalize the idea that leftist revolutionary politics are an attempt to bring forth "a world which could be free" (ibid) rather than merely a movement to resist the encroachment of capital. If capitalist realism was a diagnostic work, *Acid Communism* was to have been constructive. It was to be a historical reappraisal in search of clues to answer the question of how to liberate desire from capitalism. Or, more properly, it would articulate the difference between what passes for desire under capitalism and what it actually is and could be (Fisher 2018, 587). It was to reorient the notion of the left as a bulwark against the deterritorializing force of capital and instead cast it in the opposite direction with capital as the great inhibitor to be dismantled. It was to be the kind of book that once seemed more possible to write, before capitalist realism required everything to be put forth as either a comprehensive brand strategy or something as vague as a TED talk. It would have been fantastic to have it to work with.

Over the decade mentioned above, like Sonic Fiction, capitalist realism has ricocheted around culture and resonated in the minds of thousands. The point of this short book was never for Mark Fisher to lead the way into the world to come. As much as many found his work and writing to be an inspiration, his project, as Eshun mentions, was always about creating collectives, spaces, and ideas in and with which we could to think and act together. One could even interpret the brevity of *Capitalist Realism* as a way to make sure that the excitement to hold on to and share what you had just read would still be there after you'd finished it. This has been happening with that book for ten years now, and there are now so many people for whom the mention of it can be the start of something new. *Capitalist Realism* is an opening that might allow us to connect with one another; to share our insights, experience, expertise, and excitement about what can be done. But also our pain, our desolation, and our longing for escape.

We don't have *Acid Communism*, and attempts to produce it in Mark's absence seem to me to be misguided at best. The singularity with which Mark would have formulated this concept will always escape the grasp of even the most affectionate and careful imitation. But what we do have is a community built around a shared critique and a low barrier to entry for the expansion of this community. *Capitalist Realism* is an invitation to make something new happen in the space now open before us, which was always the intention. As we read at the close of *Capitalist Realism*:

> The long, dark night of the end of history has to be grasped as an enormous opportunity. The very oppressive pervasiveness of capitalist realism means that even glimmers of political and economic possibilities can have a disproportionately great effect. The tiniest event can tear a hole in the grey curtain of reaction which has marked the horizons of possibility under capitalist realism. From a situation in which nothing can happen, suddenly anything is possible again. (80-81)

In this book, I want to see what I can do to explore that space of possibility pushed open by the conceptualization of capitalist realism, by producing a Sonic Fiction of our present. I am in search of resources that can help to tear down that grey curtain.

3

Sounds Like the Future Will Never Arrive

There is a string of beaches along the eastern coast of the Danish island of Langeland where the water is entirely still. The distance between the shoreline and the island of Lolland is too small to generate much in the way of waves. During storms, the water, of course, becomes more lively, but this takes a lot of outside force. These beaches are beautiful but small and, owing to the popularity of cheap flights to warmer climes and the island's tiny population, they are often almost deserted. The stillness means that the water is incredibly clear and clean but also a little boring. It can feel somewhat domesticated, floating impassively as the current barely moves you. That is until a little after five in the afternoon when, every day, ferries and container ships pass through the channel, sending waves out in both directions and crashing into the shore of Langeland with just enough force to liven it up a little for adults and to thrill small children. Many who grew up on the island have memories in the summer of racing to the shore by five, to throw themselves into the waves dependably produced by the happenstance of the shipping schedule.

  Container ships have a particular significance to Denmark as the country is the home of the A. P. Møller—Mærsk Group, a logistics and shipping company that declares itself to be the largest in the world (A. P. Møller—Mærsk 2018). Once you become aware of this company, it is impossible to not see at least one of their containers in the shipping and cargo yards in the outskirts of every city and town you pass through both in Denmark and abroad. More likely, you'll see hundreds of them. Mærsk, which stands alone on the branding material, is not just proof of globalization but thrives because of it, allowing billions of tonnes of commodities and dead labor to make their way around the world. This is exactly the kind of business a small nation like Denmark needs to keep its social democratic system afloat under global capitalism. Denmark exports luxury furniture and sound systems and millions upon millions of pig carcasses but, on a global stage, this is next to nothing compared to the business of the world's largest international shipping company. The company gets a taste of millions of transactions each year and, while Mærsk accepts the tax burden, Denmark gets a taste of this business too.

Moving to Denmark directly from London, it took me a while to notice the different way in which capitalist realism manifests itself here. There is something about the way in which things seem so constantly dire in England—"its anonymous pubs" (Lyotard 2015, 124), the sour yellowing interiors of its institutional buildings, the rental property windows that function just as well as insulation open as they do closed, and its political deference of status quo inequalities and cloying nostalgia, all of which are to be greeted with a cheery disposition and without effective complaint—that simply being away from it can convince you that the woes, wherever else you are, are just not comparable. This is especially true if one lands in the bastion of ongoing Scandinavian social democracy that is Denmark. The design, the willingness to speak out to change even some minor inconvenience into a more pleasant experience, the fact that unemployment can be a point in your life when you buy a new laptop, students so insulated from going into debt that the very prospect of racking up a tenth of what the average student accrues as a matter of course in the UK—and a hundredth of what's common in the US—terrifies them, and windows that actually insulate their buildings, all make it difficult to see that Denmark is still inside capitalist realism as well. That said, the capitalism part is clear enough. If you spend two winters here, you will see a completely new set of winter jackets on the street. After visiting a few homes, you can sense the importance that many give to keeping up with their friends in acquiring elegantly understated, immaculately designed pieces of furniture. But this is, of course, a Copenhagen-centric assessment. Indeed, this may speak more to the surveillance inherent to—what can appear at times to outsiders as—a close-knit culture. No different really than the village life in Yorkshire or, more properly, the affluent commuter towns in the home counties or a set of the urban well-to-do in London.

I had written a piece for a small Danish cultural magazine critiquing the racism on display in the marketing of a theater piece by a renowned Danish artist and the seeming inability of many in the cultural establishment to understand it as such (Holt 2018). A week or so later I received an email. After a little research to check to whom I would be addressing with my reply, I came to the conclusion that the author was a low-level member of a far-right party in Denmark, *Den Nye Borgerlige* (The New Right/Citizens), though he sent the email from the account of his confectionary business. While the email was polite enough, the questions he asked seethed with frustration that my account, of how racism functioned in the case of the marketing of the theater piece, had neglected to address an anxiety that clearly occupies him every day. *What if the culture of Denmark changes as a result of immigration?* I tried to reply fairly and in search of understanding with an argument against this being an anxiety on which it is worth expending energy, as change is not only inevitable but desirable. I cited the hugely popular Copenhagen Jazz Festival as an example of how the rest of the world has already changed Denmark. I don't how this was received, nor even exactly what I think of the efficacy of this argument anymore. I don't know if I was really responding to him or if, in my mind, I was writing to every leave voter in the UK's EU membership referendum, whom I had conjured in my imagination as my feelings of alienation from the country in which I grew up increased.

A couple of weeks later, I was at a concert that was part of that festival. It was staged in one of the concert venues of the national broadcaster, DR. The band was a jazz quartet from London, two drummers, sax, and a tuba, called Sons of Kemet. They played with all the chops of formal training but seemed utterly unconcerned with reproducing a carbon copy of jazz greats past. They wanted to make us dance in the way that we actually dance today. They refused the opposition between body and intellect that has infected so much contemporary music and institutionalized jazz. Listening to the band play, I could hear the push and pull of Eshun's postsoul even on these analogue instruments. The refusal to completely shear itself away from tradition but also not to be limited by it. This was especially evident from the tuba. As it turns out, the tuba is the great undiscovered analogue dub bass synth; its throb, its ability to become nothing but space-resonating-bass, or drop its low-pass filter and become something aggressive and jagged. The tuba, atop the looping polyrhythmic beat on tracks like "In the Castle of My Skin," was less a backdrop for the sax and more a way to incessantly produce difference. Like electronic dance music, Sons of Kemet were making the thing we call "reality" softer and less defined by changing it from second to second through repetition. Like jazz, though, their improvisation kept you on your toes. There was an urgency to this music. Despite its lack of concrete declarations, the force it exerted on the room was one that demanded instability. It inserted fragility and precarity with expertise, and in doing so eroded a surface of fixed certainty. Looking around the crowd, I noticed it was taking effect. There were, of course, some who would not be moved but, among this normally impassive crowd, many more than normal were starting to get lost in the sound.

They were starting to become aware that their existence and self-hood could not entirely be bound by physicality or its representation.

This was when the particularity of how capitalist realism functions in Denmark became clear to me. I realized how long it had been since I heard anything like Sons of Kemet out in the world. For various reasons, I hadn't left the country for more than half a year at that point, and so most of my less commercial cultural consumption had taken place in Copenhagen. It became clearer to me how so many of the cultural engagements I had been to in Denmark seemed content to tread water with what was already established, what was already well regarded and guaranteed to perform some kind of tacitly agreed upon function of cultural production. Even the racism in the marketing of the piece I had critiqued in the press had seemed, in some sense, contrived. It was like a situationist prank. Its controversy had played out in camps and through lines of discourse that seemed almost staged. Where capital in the anglophone world has often been rapacious in its willingness to feed of its own people, in Denmark capital has been directed to the formation of a more protectionist reality in which things are able to stay the same. In this way, Denmark is succeeding more than most nations at maintaining the appearance of history's end.

The Danish cultural critic Mikkel Frantzen points out that despite being often lauded as one of the happiest nations in the world, Danes are among the highest users of antidepressants (2019, 4). While one can perhaps point to the incongruity between these the measures, as Frantzen does—the first essentially being a propaganda program for liberal democracy and the second being a coalescence of pharmaceutical companies pushing pills in concert with the pathologization of mental health—something in the irony of this arrangement points to the operation of capitalist realism. Like Fisher, Frantzen places this in temporal terms "as a problem of futurity" (2019, 6), but the problem of futurity manifests itself differently in different localities with their own particular historically formed tributaries through which capitalist realism can flow. In the UK, this manifests itself as a kind of stifling nostalgia, similar to Freud's notion of melancholia. In Denmark, it can, at times, look like this as well, but the more prevalent feeling seems to be an attempt to extend the present forever, hysterically asserting the correctness of the current arrangement of things.

In recent years, the Danish literary scene has been overcome by a fascination with science fiction. The scene is small, so these trends are palpable. A review in the right paper will lead to the author dominating the landscape of cultural consumption for months before they fall out of favor. And while we find interesting work dealing with things like personhood in an alienated world (Ørntoft 2018) and body horror steeped in new materialism (Ravn 2018), there is not much that deals with the more banal, but oddly perhaps more troubling, elements of this speculative turn. There are few that seem to want to acknowledge that the existence of the cultural scene of which they are a part is not the result of the whims of the marketplace of cultural consumer consumption, nor the pure product of critical discourse, nor the provision of culture as public good as democratically decided, but something much trickier to think through. That being that, Denmark is fast becoming a vassal state owned by a shipping company and a handful of other corporations that are currently willing to pay enough in tax to maintain the status quo: to extend the present. Denmark's cultural output exists as it does because of the largesse of these companies in subsidizing it. There is some truth that this arrangement exists everywhere that corporate taxation is spent on cultural production, but in Denmark it is in sharp relief. If capitalist realism in the UK can sometimes feel oppressive in the vein of Orwell's *1984* (2013), then its operation in Denmark might just be the technocratic maintenance of stability found in Huxley's *Brave New World* (2014).

Ten years after the financial crisis, the maintenance of capitalist realism has had to reassert itself in the face of opportunistic right-wing populism. The actions being taken to deal with this distort the appearance of capitalist realism. Actions such as Brexit seem to erect barriers to capital accumulation but, I believe, on a larger scale, this will be recontextualized as a kind of creative destruction. A new settlement to continue this exploitative arrangement will be reached, however unpleasant that may be. Despite Denmark facing its own resurgent populism, I still believe it offers us a more accurate picture of how capitalist realism operates today. While it is profitable, companies will pay to incessantly re-instantiate the present. What we already know to be good can be reproduced in shinier packaging, embracing subtly different trends creating the illusion of development and change, while anything that sounds like the future will be relegated to a distant echo. But Mark Fisher had already noticed this in 2014 (28).

***

Before I read Fisher and Eshun, or was even made aware that such approaches to music and thinking existed, I thought there was little for me to latch on to in academia. I was pursuing a Master's in Sonic Arts, really out of a sense of not being sure what I should do. Following the election of the coalition government in 2010, I was rapidly losing faith in the idea that I should chase audio obscurity as I began to feel that everything I thought had been relatively stable in the UK began to come apart. I was becoming more interested in the way that politics fed into the production of aesthetics and how certain aesthetics seemed to work in tandem with particular organizations of politics. I was starting to be drawn to what is called "cultural theory" as something that could at once grapple with the politics of how aesthetic experiences permeated everyday life, without being seduced by the notion that either could exist independently of the other. That said, I found the language frustrating and arcane and I wondered whether, when academics cited these thinkers and then went on to claim things about art that didn't make sense, this waffle might be meaningless. My supervisor for my research project had noticed the earliest sparks of interest in post-structuralist philosophy, particularly that of Gilles Deleuze, which he tried to curtail by citing David Foster Wallace's novel *Infinite Jest* as an example of an artwork that skewered the vacuous excesses of that school of thought. My interest piqued, I picked up the book but I found nothing of the sort. Instead, it read to me like a book written by someone who had plowed through similar frustration to mine and found vital conceptual frames with which to organize the multifarious and seemingly incoherent sensations and symbols of life in a world that looked so very similar to the one that was emerging around me. There is, of course, a satire of academese that runs through the book, and the over-reliance of some philosophers on grammatical technicalities to produce (meaningful?) critiques. But at the same time, it uses obscure language to incredible effect and illustrates the power of grammatical technicality to produce something subtly meaningful on every page. Where my supervisor had read only the satire and criticism, I saw frustration with the fact that the complex questions that stem from living in the world in which we do, yielded only more complex and incomplete answers. The suggestion to read *Infinite Jest* was the last suggestion I took fully on board from my Master's supervisor before he jumped ship for some start-up he'd founded. Which is why, to this day, I still cannot program in JavaScript or Python.

Eshun and Fisher were friends. They had been "schooled" in the same place, in the same networks. While the specific interests of their projects can perhaps be said to diverge by a matter of degrees, the way they see/saw their role in it was essentially the same; they are/were intensifiers of what was already there (Fisher 2018, 31). Their work brings out the critique and possibilities that inhere in the practices and artifacts of the culture that envelops and constitutes us.

It intensifies the signal in particular ways and makes it not just audible but sonorous. This is not to say they were neutral in this. Leaving to one side the methodological impossibility of this, they are/were amplifiers, the mechanisms of which entail distortion. But something of the signal is always retained; the distortion just lets you know where the resonant frequencies are and gives you a tool to drown out some of the background sound while also producing something new and exciting.

The question for me is, thus, less how to bring these thinkers into the same project, but how to tune their respective conceptual amplifiers so as to accentuate the overlap. How do we deploy a project like Sonic Fiction, which articulated the non-essentialist drive of Afrofuturism in music, in combination with a quasi-samizdat of cultural critique like *Capitalist Realism*? I root this through the strongest commonality they have: a fascination with science fiction. The CCRU, where Eshun and Fisher first met in the 1990s, were fascinated by the cyberpunk of the previous decades because it seemed to point out something about the latent potential of that period of time. And in this regard, the more than ten years between the publication of *More Brilliant than the Sun* and *Capitalist Realism* is quite apparent. At century's end, Eshun was still comfortable with leaning into the discourse of posthumanism as the most plausible escape route available to us by following the pleasure principle. After the crash, Fisher found himself staring down the reality principle as expressed in the film *Children of Men*.

What's needed to bring these tools together today is a science fiction that speaks to the conformity of neoliberalism. A science fiction that depicts neither a glorious unfathomable utopia nor the terrifying/thrilling dystopia of capital's dissolution of the subject, but rather a science fiction of disappointment. A science fiction set in a world long after Baudrillard's semiotic apocalypse (Fisher 2000) in which signs are the only thing that can hold value any longer. To use another term of Fisher's, we need a science fiction for our "boring dystopia" of capitalist realism. And this is how I read Wallace's *Infinite Jest*, a novel about the desperate search for meaning in a world where even time as such has become a commodity. But more than being a depiction of our present moment from the past, it is also self-consciously aware of its positionality. Namely, with regard to the potentials and limitations of theoretical cultural critique, which it holds simultaneously to be enthralling and lacking. If we can hold to this apparent but not actual conflict, which is derived from the condition of capitalist realism's boring dystopia, as we approach the Sonic Fiction of contemporary pop music, we may be able to move past the drive to neoliberal conformity that prevents the politics in this music from being heard. And, instead, we may derive from it the complex conjunctions of mediations, subjects, *and* systems that can produce a difference that is uncontainable. The novel, a tale of depression, addiction, and the absurdity of human connection in the context of ever-expanding techno-capital, is a distillation of the end of the historical epoch that began in the late 1980s, has limped on since 2008, and that may now be coming to its own frightening end. It attempts to put the scale and scars of history and its systems of knowledge and power into dialogue with the affective experiences inside those who live under them and are constituted, in part, by them. Wallace's coinage, "hip ennui" (2007, 694), encapsulates this perfectly by combining the existential vulnerability we all have (ennui) and the fight for survival this implies with the desire for cultural capital that this fight currently entails (hipness). This is the place in which I can grapple with the projects of Eshun's Sonic Fiction and Fisher's capitalist realism; within the ethico-aesthetical frame of *Infinite Jest*.

In the chapters that follow, I will attempt to provide a framework for listening to and looking at what is so often so difficult to discern: the affective soundscape of our world of capitalist realism and its connection to the systems of power we inhabit and manifest. I will narrate a Sonic Fiction that tries to straddle the onto-epistemic boundaries between observation and speculation, empiricism and fantasy, the subjective and the systemic, and the irreducible and the necessary reduction of comprehension. The goal here is not finally saying what the truth of our situation is, but to amplify something of our world. The work of this book is to share some of what I have found out about pop music by reading the works others, from studying the industry and its machinations, and by listening to this music as it exists in the world.

Part 2

A Sonic Fiction of Capitalist Realism

Vignette: Jessie J at the Closing Ceremony of the 2012 London Olympics

This is a moment that exists only for television. The people here are here for the benefit of television. They may have their own reasons for attending woven into the course of their lives, some profound, some banal. Just to call it patriotism is not enough to describe their desire for being here. It's not entirely wrong, but it leaves out too much. However, if it were not for television, they would not be here at all. Their investment in this spectacle, and the dreams it ties into, are contingent upon the mechanisms of this show's production within a technological milieu. Within this milieu, this production is intended to shore up a larger project. The reapplication of the salve of *Cool Britannia*—that seemed to work so well during the ballooning debt of the late 1990s—to plaster over the cracks of post-crash austerity. This is the end of the 2012 London Olympics. One year after the riots.

Music can only be made audible in this stadium if it is amplified to the point of distortion; if it is pushed beyond the limits of its own reproduction. This happens in absolute terms eventually but first in relation to human hearing. If music is to be heard over the noise of so many ecstatic people, whose cheers alone have raised the volume in the stadium beyond the level of pain to that of destruction of the ear, it must be played at a level louder than that which allows for a faithful reproduction of the audio files and signal. The sound system can actually push the signal beyond any level that would be recognizable as music as it vibrates the air and overstimulates the hair cells that start to decode this force issued forth in service of this event. This can lead to the death of many of these cells and degradation of a person's hearing, literally scarring the audience with the force of this spectacle. But we shouldn't be simplistically moralistic here. To point to this excessive force as some inherent wrong is not the point, and not to mention boring. For capital, this is creative destruction, and what is being created will emerge on television and seep into the national imagination. On television, this volume can be dipped sufficiently, perhaps manually or maybe side-chained to a compressor, so a polite voice of newscasted, establishment familiarity can narrate the proceedings. These remarks are made from notes, but it still requires some of the skills of an improviser. Skills that guide those uninitiated into the (pop) cultural relevance of the images before them, and, for those already *au fait*, provide a seal of approval from the patriotic imaginary. After all, this is live and this is already history.

A little more than four years earlier, the world was cast into financial crisis stemming from deregulation in the United States housing market and the proliferation of toxic debt. This crisis was so severe, so empirically obvious in its causes, that it led many to speculate that this could have been the end of capitalism. But this is not what happened, though neither was it properly strengthened. Instead, capitalism became even more vampiric. In its neoliberal form, capitalism's criterion of success is not the generation of widespread wealth, in the style of Keynesian social democracy, but instead it simply has to appear to function better than anything else. This is an easy goal to attain, when the reproduction of life is dependent on the creation of capital so abstract it seems only to exist on balance sheets. Without the actions of the financial sector, we are told, we would be without food. This bind allows for excesses, some of which can be used for yachts—but for it to have this capacity, most of it has to stay on the databases. The markets may fall but capital, or at least the particular capital most readily able to perform its definitive function, will float. Whether or not this survival mechanism of vampirism and yet more abstraction is sustainable is a question that is only of relevance to beings comprised of meat. Or rather, beings willing to concede that they are comprised of meat. To the asignifying semiotic chains in the market, sustainability, survival, and their antonyms are literally without meaning.

Even though this ceremony is not really for them, the audience present in the stadium needs to be supported in their enthusiasm. This enthusiasm is what will give the televisual artifact its force, and thus the resources to produce value. This is accomplished through the strategic deployment of frequency. Their voices and cheers dominate the mid-range of the vibratory spectrum, so, to be heard, the music must occupy the upper and lower extremes. In doing so it surrounds the audience's revelry and provides a context, the context of a party, that is more difficult for an observer, uneasy with anything resembling a rally, to assail. And while this is achievable to an extent, there is a problem here. The kinds of music with a frequency profile designed for this purpose are niche. Far too niche for this undertaking. What is called for is pop. A form that, despite its contemporary proximity to dance music, is lyric driven and relies on the mid-range. But under these conditions, the lyrics can only be understood by those who already know them. And those who already know them know them from a context of libidinal ecstasy, wherein the semantic meaning can simultaneously be enhanced and/or become irrelevant.

In September 2008, a relatively young American author hanged himself while his wife was out of the house. She is the artist Karen Green, and it was she who discovered the body of the author, who had been David Foster Wallace. This is an unconscionably violent thing to do to a loved one, which only serves to compound the tragedy. Wallace had battled depression for many years, and while he had continued to publish stories and essays, he had not published a novel since the mid-1990s. That work, *Infinite Jest*, was an attempt to chart addiction as it relates to entertainment as medicine in a late-capitalist dystopia. At the time of his death, he had been working on the follow-up. That novel, *The Pale King*, which would be published unfinished in 2011, was set in the mid-1980s in an IRS tax office in Peoria, Illinois, at the moment that Reaganomics catalyzed the neoliberal revolution in Western Europe and the United States. A revolution of deregulation that led to the normalization of privatization and eventually led to a financial crisis in the year of Wallace's death.

This ceremony is not the opening ceremony. The eyes of the world have largely lost interest. So, the goals here can be more specific, or targeted, or more insular in who they address. So, they can just broadcast a party and that will work perfectly well. Some may get the sense this evening that these revelries are quintessentially British, which would be both correct and not. It would be more accurate to say that a face is being put forward, as they so often are in countries defined by nostalgia, to hide the decay. But those who wanted to could choose to see only a smile, albeit one through gritted teeth; desperate that everyone know that they are fine, but waiting eagerly for everyone to leave.

A year earlier, in a job center in the north of England, in a town whose glory days as a luxury holiday destination had long since passed and where nothing had ever come to replace them, a middle-aged man sits for what must have been the umpteenth time before a much younger man, no older than twenty-two, his advisor. The man, recently laid off, had been a lawyer, though it was unclear exactly in what capacity. Perhaps he had been in the employ of a law firm or the legal department of some other company that needed to downsize or had simply collapsed. The advisor told him that they didn't really have anything for him here that he could apply for, so to keep doing what he was doing. Rising from his seat, the middle-aged man thanks his advisor for his time and walks out of the open-plan office space.

In the midst of her medley set, Jessie J sings out from the back of a Rolls Royce, part of a motorcade of Rolls Royces, the chorus to her song "Price Tag":

It's not about the *money money money*, we don't need your *money money money*,
We just want to make the world dance forget about the price tag
[my emphasis] (Jessie J & B.o.B. 2015).

This moment could have lent itself to a slew of Žižekian readings, as these lyrics seemed to enunciate the values of the big Other of twenty-first-century Britain. It reminds the people, who are suffering the effects of post-crisis austerity piled upon thirty years of dismantled welfare, that this expensive spectacle has been more than worth it. The games had been severely over budget and one would expect that the insistence, during the closing ceremony, that this money, this spending of the collective/common wealth, was not of any significance when compared to the feeling of celebration it facilitated, would have rung hollow if anyone were to have noticed it. But it's far too loud in there, and on TV there are people to tell you what this all means. A little over a year earlier, news anchors and pundits had expressed worry that the riots in London that summer would sour the world's expectations of the games to come.

Two years before his death, Wallace gave a commencement address at Kenyon College (2009). An address that was no doubt experienced as a pinnacle of profundity by many in the room and indeed by many who heard the widely circulated audio recording from that day for the first time. But through repetition and the marketing push that follows the death of an author, it has been rendered trite. A triteness that even the evidence of the author failing, despite extreme efforts, to heed his own advice, cannot fully set aside. The subject of the speech was the difficulty of overcoming the default mechanisms by which we produce meaning from experience. The difficulty for fish of noticing they are surrounded by water. But in this speech there is a clear, desperate insistence not to pretend this problem of the passive acceptance of normality is only a problem for others. The main subject of Wallace's critique was the reflexive cynicism to which he himself often defaulted; cynicism that, while it may be technically correct, limits the cynic's potential to examine what is really at stake in the subtleties of countless everyday phenomena. This recognition, Wallace thought, needs to be the foremost concern of those engaged in criticism with an interest in navigating a route through the various impasses of culture, society, and the world.

While the moment may have seemed ripe for parody, one reason that there were no critiques of Jessie J's incongruous lyrics at the time was that these words were not just inaudible but irrelevant. To be smarter than the text of a pop song in a bizarre context is a skill of no use to anyone. Such an exercise is an attempt to talk about something whilst refusing to recognize what it actually is. A song is not reducible to an instantiation of ideology. It is of course an instantiation of ideology, but the time in which it made sense to attempt such an analytical coup has long since passed. To the extent that ideology plays a role, it is that of providing the infrastructure through which the energy emanating from the song can be made to course. And that infrastructure itself is built upon something deeper than can be shaken by a pithy examination of ideological irony. That would be the default. It is too easy.

Still, something eerie persists from that night. The question is, to what and how should we pay attention to find it?

O

1

Attention

You're Not Paying Attention

Pop is all around us.[1] Without this, the expansion from which pop is the abbreviation would be nonsensical. There has to be something of it everywhere for it to make sense as being popular. Even unpopular popular music—music that is for the most part forgotten, unplayed and unheard—needs a culture of "listened to" popular music to justify even the tiny space it occupies in an indistinct corner of a digital archive. This is, of course, obvious. But actually thinking about this reveals something undeniably gaudy about the music of this modern age that might actually implicate music going all the way back to its first enunciation in social organization. Music is meant to make you feel something. It is thick with affective potential, which is just what is needed, even desired, to cut through the sludge of enlightenment rationalism as ideology; to be made aware of our bodied existence, our spacial placedness and potential displacement, our temporal displacement-ability from the position of an ever disappearing present. But more often than not, the production of this invisible and irreducibly rich sonic space emanates from intention. Intention that may be semantically inexpressible but that nonetheless gives form to the affective refraction patterns that structure this sonic version of a VanderMeerian shimmer as brought to us by Netflix (VanderMeer, 2015; Garland 2018); the stuff about sound that cannot be entirely expressed/understood as symbols, even when they are chained together at the length of a book. But more than sound, this is music. This sound that surrounds is already overladen with symbols of popular musical meaning, pumped out into and engulfing our lives, which are already entangled in complex relationships with symbols. Lives that are, in part, formed by these relationships with symbols, found by passing through the ubiquitous media of these sonic shimmers.

Unlike the VanderMeerian shimmer, however, one does not choose to enter the "atmosphere" (Stewart 2011) of pop music. The only thing that can prevent you from being engulfed by it is your proximity to a speaker and, so very often these days, we find these next to our eardrums. But even when we are sharing an atmosphere, a heavy intentionality has placed these sonic affects in such close proximity to the symbols—which stand in for the sludge of our world and give it meaning—that they are implicated in one another. These sonic affects become patterns of refraction ossified by symbolic impediments. The capacities of the affects, coursing through our bodies, become entangled in our interpretation of the intentions of others. And here we have an urgent problem taking place at the pace of a dirge: this is hard to describe as anything but normal, which makes it very tricky to understand it as the problematic that it is. To complicate this still further, we can't even point to songs and say they're just shitty, because this too is an acquiescence to systems of thought that would stand in for the sludge and that drags complexity toward ideological reduction. Our object of critique is more difficult to point to; more between than inside. To pay attention to paying attention to popular music is to examine the intensity of being occupied by what often goes unnoticed.

There is, of course, political economy here. But as the price of unsynchronized recorded popular music races ever closer to zero,[2] the notion that we consume music becomes ever more outmoded. We may purchase recordings but these hardly form the bulk of our listening. Ours is an age of *Ubiquitous Listening* as Anahid Kassabian (2013) has so helpfully pointed out. Pop music is streamed but not owned, collectively experienced at festivals or on TV, synchronized with products and stories and symbols, in shopping malls, restaurants, and books shops, in clubs, and far too loud in bars without dance floors, and in adverts that run before music videos on YouTube. All the while, we are made an audience, but an audience that is not cognizant of itself as such. And, all the while, we grant access to our attention to others. But this isn't new. John Oswald knew back in the 80s, as the audio tech market boomed, that the notion of consumer choice—hearing what you want to hear when you want and only what you want—was bogus when it came to music. And he understood that the music pouring out of all these personal hi-fis was not simply a pleasant diversion but also a violent bombardment of affects and intentions, foisted upon us unidirectionally so as to inculcate passivity.[3] This is what is so pernicious about this ubiquitous media form that realizes its potential through the capacities of, first, cheap consumer tech and, then, through ubiquitous computing. The more immediate and convenient the gadgets of conveyance have become, and the more people's lives they and the sounds they emanate seep into, the more closed off their design has become and thus the more closed off the possibilities of creative misuse. This loop of convenient exposure and passivity has made the presence of this music the norm and the absence of this music the exception. To be without pop music is to be in a conspicuous void.

For a while, it seemed like Oswald had it right. The technology of musical consumption placed limitations on how one could interact meaningfully with this, now definitively, recorded and produced medium. Getting a hold of the gear you'd need would be expensive and take up a massive amount of space in a life. But as music has moved into the domain of ubiquitous computing, the possibility of manipulating this particular form of music has moved into the phones in the pockets of particularly those in the global north. The gatekeepers seemed to have been overcome. Even a basic laptop with an internet connection is only a torrent away from becoming a studio. So, have we not realized the dream of the musical futurists (Russolo 2008) and musical modernists (Cage 2008) as any sound can now, seemingly, be produced or captured at will and infinitely manipulated, layered, and arranged (Harper 2011, 118)? No, because this is only a technological possibility; something that is virtually true. A capacity that is always present but only as mediation. As desires coded into the interface but seldom ever expressed. Even the visions that have directed this kind of music making were so very particular and based on traditions that are saturated with elitism. A tradition that seemed to disregard the atmospheric pressure of normative music making. A tradition that seems, even now, to revel in its attentional irrelevance in a world in which the majority have their attention harvested every day, and where drawing attention to yourself can be a necessity for survival.

But isn't this all normal? Is this anxiety about the harvesting of attention through technology geared toward normative music production and consumption just another example of critics trying to ruin a good time? Is attention worthy of our attention, when people everywhere are just trying to get by? Well, it is to those interested in capital accumulation. This is to say, that while we might want to place attention to popular music in a box under the heading "people like what they like," those that make money from this kind of content, both directly and indirectly, are paying a great deal of attention to attention. Attention is what keeps the wolf from their doors. The mistake we've made is to allow ourselves to think of what we live in as some sort of natural outcome of human development, when it is, in fact, emergent from the atmospheric pressure of history, economics, power, and desire. Not things that can easily be swayed, but neither is their particular arrangement anything that could be called natural. When we pay attention, however passively, to the vernacular musics that surround us at nearly all times, we are paying attention to glimmers of this atmospheric pressure, embedded in the intentions of not just the musicians, but also of every entity involved in every step that makes this content consumable. And attention is their point of entry into us.

Traditional critical theory (TCT) has been on to this for a long time: the critique of the power of popular culture and its hold over attention. Though we should be careful not to overstate it, lest it sound like a conspiracy theory. Let's be clear: attention is something quotidian for both humans and non-humans alike. It is a response of something that can sense to sensible phenomena; phenomena originating from both internal and external stimuli, and the points of intersection where this distinction is meaningless. But even with this simple definition, it is really easy to see why this field would be of interest to those in the business of capital accumulation, which adds to the complexity of this. The world around us has a seemingly infinite capacity for producing demands on attention—even before we add to it the cultural productions of capital—and any of these things can be experienced at a variety of depths of cognition and sensation. All the while, however, the finite nature of any human body, of any "humanoid alien" (Schulze 2018, 6), means that the amount of attention available from economic actors is always finite. And with finitude come the market behaviors of scarcity.

Despite its insights, TCT has always lagged behind the marketplace when it comes to working with both the material and libidinal economies. True, the goals of TCT and the market could not be more incompatible; the former was trying to work out how to overcome capitalism and prevent another holocaust, while the later ambivalently shepherded in the production of desire for ever more consumption and simultaneously facilitated the production of its "substitute satisfaction" (Adorno 2012, 324). The shimmer of popular music has been invaluable to the marketplace throughout the twentieth and, so far, twenty-first centuries, as it has, along with film and advertising, made an atmosphere to saturate us with insatiable desire. For the goals of TCT on the other hand, pop music, as it is, hasn't ever made a whole lot of sense, even though the field in which it exercises its power is of vital importance to their realization. There have been attempts by those coming from the practice of TCT to consider attention economics of cultural production under market capitalism, but they often rely on filtering everything through the notion of the spectacle (Crary 2000). This is a notion that unhelpfully elides the desire of people for relief from the suffering of their material conditions with some kind of mass hypnosis. As if it were a trick that prevents the realization of an otherwise evident truth. Which, as a mode of analysis, seems to be an effort to distract from the problem of the persistent absence of a viable political alternative to the material conditions that cause their suffering and deception. What is more, even these interventions have mostly focused on film, which is of course of great onto-epistemological and subjective significance (Deleuze 2018), but music operates in different ways. A film on in the background is a film on in the background. It may well imply a position within a particular socio-historical milieu but, unless it periodically draws your full attention, it does not do much more. Whereas, a song on in the background can become the soundtrack to your life without fully capturing you for even a moment. An unseeable, barely hearable, and perhaps unnoticed lattice, replete with affects, intentions, ideas, and sensations upon which everyday life can be structured and then lodged in your mind and you need never even know its name. So when it comes to producing a critique of this field of experience, we are talking about a critique of moment-to-moment minutiae that scale up to the level of the global economy. To get past the first step of this can be like explaining water to fish.[4]

Attention Economics: I Have to Feeling [Sic]

The attention economy is often discussed in relation to social media: those platforms that tend to have the most readily visualizable metrics. But to stick to this level is a shallow way to think about the attention economy because the imperative to orient one's attention in the "correct" direction has long been a subject of contention predicated on its scarcity as a resource. We saw the economic dimension added to the question of attention direction in the twentieth century as the mediatized commodities of attention capture emerged from the culture industry. The desire here, on the part of the industry, was to get consumers to pay to be able to attend to their productions as fixed media. At the end of the second decade of the twenty-first century, this has shifted once again. This is where we find social media and its stunningly documented attentional data. But what is at stake now is more than just drawing eyeballs, because what is really happening is making us vibrate. Behind the politics of social media as the new news source, in another unseen window, the streaming of playlists assembled by tech-company curators, flesh or algorithmic, monetizes the moment-to-moment sensations of musical experience, be it through subscription fees or ad revenues or even just letting them own the knowledge of what you like.

When this problem gets picked up by the spectacle media theorists of TCT it runs through some well-rehearsed analytical algorithms, which basically amount to the idea that we are being duped, and duped so thoroughly that we can't even tell we are being duped. In Adorno and Horkheimer's chapter "The Culture Industry: Enlightenment as Mass Deception," we find the neat idea that because the specific arrangement of social relations are embedded in the commodities produced under those social relations, cultural production under capitalism cannot help but communicate something of the "might of industrial society" (Adorno & Horkheimer 1997, 127), which then becomes an image lodged in the mind of the population. The unassailable power of capitalism becomes the ideological subtext of enjoyment experienced in attending to the products of the culture industry. There is truth to this, but also something troubling in the tightness of its formulation. It makes it seem like the exit sign is only luminescent to those who can recall their knowledge of Hegel to dissipate the phantasmagoria. We see this move of proclaiming ourselves truly trapped in ways only visible to a select few repeated in the more recent work by Jonathan Crary, who argues that attention is a "specifically modern problem" because it is under the conditions of modernity that the "possibility of presence in perception" has been obliterated as attention becomes a "simulation of presence" and, in a very Adornian turn of phrase, "a makeshift, pragmatic substitute in the fact of its impossibility" (Crary 2000, 4). Basically, these positions spell out a few problems for modern attention that can be summarized thusly: *Following the technological advances of industrial capitalism, mediation has now become an efficient way in which to valorize capital thus reifying the content of this mediation of expression, alienating both the labor of its production and the presence of the audience who consume it from their own lived experience.* Some of this is useful. This formulation helps us to understand that there is an observable trajectory from the pennies charged for admission to a double feature in mid-twentieth century cinemas (which we could think of as commodities directing attention) and the present moment of subscription streaming (where, for the sake of efficiency, we can see attention is no longer the means by which the commodity is consumed but has become the commodity itself).

However, there is another thing about this that is all too neat. Despite protestations to the contrary, spectacle theory and TCT are predicated on the idea that this is all so stunning that we have been stupefied by the shiny shimmering productions of the culture industry. Even when they posit the banality to all this, it is still a "spectacle of banality" (Baudrillard 2001). All this seems too ocular. This is the kind of theory that, once it hears the song start to play, turns its head to be overcome by the *image* of Justin Bieber. Or more properly, this is the theorist observing such things happen to others before slinking off to the bar to grumble. It is a way of doing theory that wants to "[teach] today's music a thing or 2 about life" (Eshun 1999, -004). And while this might work well enough for some forms—for those who might have decided that, because they don't watch crummy TV, they're off the hook—the non-spectacular banality of pop music in the attention economy won't let you off that easily. The situation is at once bleaker but, importantly, so much messier too.

The field of spectacle theory tries to stretch it to include the non-spectacular, the banal, the boring. But doing this hollows out the concept, not to mention the etymology. Yes, we are talking about "a social relationship between people that is mediated by images" (Debord, 1977), which could even be stretched to contain sonic images, but for this to have a political force there has to be something about it that impresses upon a population the might of industrial society. Even if the spectacular may not be found in the content itself but in the delivery of that content, that sounds like an exhausting thought process to go through to simply keep the object of analysis conventionally coherent. It sounds like a cynical point of view, casting a critical eye over other people's enjoyment (Bown 2015, 1) and positioning itself above them in order to appraise it.

The contemporary attention economy that flows through the earbuds and screens of our devices constitutes an atmosphere, not a spectacle. This is not something that is simply being placed before us and that we are taught to desire, but something that emerges from a form of life that we have co-produced. There is nothing artificial in our desire for it. Our desires, entangled with the happenstance of history and power, have made it, and our desires are now of it. Which is not to say that there is not coercion, but that a good deal of the time, we welcome it as a familiar part of our world.

Of course, the spectacle did play a role in all of this and, in particular, in the formation of the popular music phenomenon. Without this, popular music would be lacking the cultural congealment necessary to give it commodity status in the attention economy. But as this commodity mutated from concert attendance to record collection, the forces of value production caused the spectacle to dissipate. Instead, according to Jacques Attali, "in order to accumulate profit, it became necessary to sell stockpiles of sign production, not simply its spectacle.

This mutation would profoundly transform every individual's relation to music" (Attali 2011, 88). For Attali, the notion of the spectacle was bound up in the relationship between power and representation. This is how the might of industrial production could become "lodged in men's minds" (Adorno & Horkheimer 1997, 127). It is not the material forces of production you hear at the club, it is their representation. But the effectiveness of this representation of power, this spectacle of power, is historically specific to a time when power could "make people believe" (Attali 2011, 46) in the consensual and just nature of the form of social organization in which they reside. Prior to representation, for Attali, there had been an order of spectacular violence, which was sublimated during the representational period as the "absence of violence" came to illustrate "a harmony in order" (ibid). This period's time was already running out when the first records were being pressed. The proliferation of representation as facilitated by recordings, and its associated devaluation, stripped the spectacle of its power, of its capacity to convince as it was dislodged from the contexts that gave it meaning. Incidentally, this play of floating signifiers is exactly what Oswald was after. But even with the mechanism for its dissemination destabilized, power was still imprinting itself on musical production. It was no longer a matter of representations, as such, but rather the capacity to stockpile them and, through the capacity of repetition, remove music from phenomenal temporality and locality. And so we witness a shift in the operation of power from the embodied and identifiable to the diffuse and unlocatable (Attali, 2011, 90). As Attali tells it, the question is less about use-value and exchange-value and, instead, about use- and exchange-time. In the period of representation, the meaning of these temporal terms would have been much more clear. The song for the wedding is played at the wedding; the song for the party is played at night in the bar. But now, in the period of repetition—faced with stockpiles of dislocated representations that are both out of context and always available, accessible at your convenience and too much to ever listen to, wedding or no—we are faced with a conundrum for the attention economy of popular music: what is it that this attention pays for?

The answer to this is drenched in capitalist realism. That unspoken system of symbolic structuring that cordons off the perimeter of possibility, that places you in an eternal present of anxiety and offers only momentary distractions to keep it at bay. But it is always there, humming like ground noise, in something as innocuous as an email that needs to be urgently addressed on a Sunday afternoon so you can continue to buy food and shelter. When Mark Fisher describes a former student of his, sitting in class either wearing headphones without music playing or with the music playing while the headphones dangle from his neck, he's pointing out an example of the attention economy at work in capitalist realism. The student can't hear the music. He can't listen to it like Adorno would want him to. But he's never far away from the *"sensation-stimulus matrix"* (Fisher 2009, 24), a place that provides immediate but temporary relief from the boredom of enforced attention to post-industrial education. This isn't an automated chasing of pleasure, though, this is a rationally self-interested defensive maneuver. A move to use sounds to keep pain at bay. An instrumental use of music's capacity to fulfill a need.

This works even as we examine music as an art form rather than a commodity. But it is a weird one. Unlike writing or narrative arts, it does not require semantic language to be produced or expressed. Unlike live performance arts like dance or theatre, it no longer requires liveness. And unlike any ocular art, it doesn't even require your head to be turned in a specific direction. Pop music is a little different because, more often than not, it will include narrative, performance, and visuals, but it can still work pretty well even if these elements go unnoticed. All this makes it pretty slippery when we try to map this onto our day-to-day life; a life that is so often made to focus on that which can be understood by sight and semantics and an agreement on time as something fixed in its progression.

This is something that Adorno actually gets about music and art in general. He sees something in this particular intentional arrangement of material that he thinks reveals that the world can be changed:

> As a musical composition compresses time, and as a painting folds spaces into one another, so the possibility is concretized that the world could be other than it is. Space, time, and causality are maintained, their power is not denied, but they are divested of their compulsiveness. (Adorno 2012, 190)

This is the whole thing. The "why" of "why bother with art?" The possibility that the world could be otherwise is manifest in the artwork and this is a pretty powerful thing to have access to on the wall of a gallery or in impenetrable prose, let alone shimmering through your earbuds.

What Adorno doesn't seem to get, however, is that this is something super ambivalent. Thus he spends page-long paragraph after page-long paragraph, trying to outline why it is that only artworks that he considers to have truth content—which is to say that gesture in some way toward the possibility of emancipatory communism—concretize the possibility that the world can be other than it is. And the thing is, he's not wrong about some of this. If you read Kafka, you can't help but be overcome by the alienation emanating from the page. Embedded in the structure of each exchange the narrator (Gregor, K., Joseph K., and so on) engages in is the totalizing logic of capital; represented in such a way that it denatures this reality by, at the level of content, exceeding the confines of its form of expression (Adorno 2012, 267). The horrifying nature of such a depiction of the world does create a tension, the resolution of which would be to move beyond the material conditions and social relations that produced such horror. And, in the case of Kafka, I would guess that would be something like communism. But the other side of this, that artworks that don't point to the possibility of communism do not concretize the possibility that the world could be "other than it is," doesn't follow. There is a lot more to "other" than just communism.

To make concrete the possibility that the world could be other-than-it-is could be far duller than Adorno might have thought. If we take other-than-it-is to mean exactly that, "other," there exists a vast range of possibilities that we could describe in such a way, from fully-automated-intersectional-space-communism to any one of us just being a little bit richer. This would seem to be abundantly clear when we listen to a song like "I Gotta Feeling" (Will.i.am et al. 2009); a song that kept The Black Eyed Peas in the top five of international pop charts throughout 2009. If we just glance at the surface level of this song, its lyrics, its reified content, we can read it almost as a manifesto outlining the problems and proposing solutions:

> I feel stressed out, I wanna let it go, let's go way out, spaced out, and losin' all control
> [...]
> Let's paint the town, we'll shut it down, let's burn the roof, and then we'll do it again. (Ibid)

This is a pretty straightforward: the 9 to 5 grind sucks and is a source of tension and suffering that needs to be released through hedonism. That this suggests some kind of balanced equation between tension and release is perhaps a vision of the world as other-than-it-is. The useful illusion that is used to sell the products of leisure time. But at a more substantive, formal level, by using the refrain to repeat the assertion that "I gotta feeling, that tonight's gonna be a good night," through the insistent pulse, and the drops that can be looped forever, this song concretizes this vision of the world as other-than-it-is. The air is charged, it shimmers with the possibilities of capital, "I got my money, Let's spend it up."

It is an invocation to use the remuneration accrued from the labor of producing capital to recover from that labor by valorizing capital. Capital has no problem providing this kind of relief, so long as it can further valorize capital. Or, put another way, if completely burning out workers and then simply hiring new ones were the most efficient way to valorize capital, then there would be even more forces of political economy pushing for such an arrangement. But, as long as it's not more efficient, certain concessions have to be made to the needs of the flesh component of the machine (Marx 2014, 54).

Marx recognized that capital was capable of commodifying not only the more immediate biological needs like food and shelter but also the needs of the imagination (Marx 1990, 126); needs that we have, for some reason, been so reluctant to accept as valid that scholars have been forced to spend time on documenting them as such (DeNora 2000; Frith 1981; Hesmondhalgh 2013). So, the curious thing is, why has TCT, and Adorno in particular, felt the need to draw this line around the way in which this need is met, while addressing other needs via the only means available under capitalism is hardly commented upon? A sandwich produced under capitalism can meet your hunger like any other even while being marked with the problematic residue of the social relations that brought it into being. Why, then, must a cultural production of capitalism necessarily not be able to allow us to meet the need of perceiving the possibility that the world could be other-than-it-is? The fact that junk food might be bad for you doesn't make it less filling. And the fact that the "other" provided by a great deal of contemporary pop is simply the promise that you can be less stressed and more hedonistic doesn't mean it doesn't provide relief. Nor that the desire for relief is reducible to the fact that its provision has been reified. When faced with a choice of a piece of music that makes clear the reality of suffering—as expressed through a particular set of formal convolutions through which one can imagine the possibility of a world transformed by communism—and a song that makes the enjoyment of time off more easily accessible and even a well-regarded aspiration, it's easy to see what is going to sell. Especially as all of this can, at a moment's notice, pour out through your earbuds and into the process of becoming that you mistake for your self.

All this is to say that if we want to worry about the effects of cultural production in the attention economy, we can say that what our attention allows us to purchase—after we have bought the requisite gizmos and paid the necessary subscriptions fees—is access to materials that concretize the possibility that the world could be other-than-it-is. The trouble isn't that these materials don't let us dream big enough. It is that the dreams they provide are all we feel we need.

Interlude: On Gambino and Goodman

The images of a shirtless, handsome black man dancing joyfully in one moment, before starting to grimace, to twitch, before striking the pose of Jim Crow and drawing a hand gun and shooting a man on a chair, his head covered by a sack, before declaring, "This is America" (Glover & Göransson 2018) and placing the pistol in a silk handkerchief in the hands of an attendant, addressing the audience through the camera, before dancing again, before grimacing again, before being surrounded by black school children dancing, before a jump cut to a gospel choir singing "black man get your money" (Ibid), before the shirtless handsome black man, entering through a door and dancing with them for a moment before he is handed a Kalashnikov and guns them down, before repeating that "This is America," before dancing again as the chaos and violence in the background intensifies, before grimacing again and being surrounded by dancing black school children again, before gesturing the drawing of a gun with his bare hands and everyone runs away, before lighting a joint and climbing atop of a car, a 90s junker in a sea of 90s junkers, and dancing once again, before descending into the "sunken place" (Peele 2017) where the shirtless handsome black man is chased by a faceless white mob, can be semiotically confusing.

There are critics writing commentaries on Childish Gambino's "This is America" music video (Glover 2018; Muri 2018) who do not once mention the music but for the invocation of the title in the lyrics (Collins 2018). Such critiques easily point out the ambivalence at the core of what is expressed in Gambino's work. There is joy, there is suffering, there is violence, and there is dancing. But without the music, this is incredibly confusing. The mix of signs could be confused for just another piece of edgy media playing with the floating of signifiers. But with the music, this question of comprehensibility is itself brought to the center. Where in the song is the joy and where is the suffering? We find the fragile joy in the section with more conventional tonality, in which the lyrics form melodies in the mid-range of frequencies. But this is constantly destabilized by those looks coming across Gambino's face. Something is rotten in the states of America. As the gunshot falls on the downbeat and rings out over the bar that follows, the structure of meaning that has so far been established, the song's genre, mood, subject matter, relationship to tonality, and even time are all shattered. What we are left with is a deep foreboding menace that defies the easy or even conventionally coherent explanation.

Goodman has this down already. He pointed out that the ears of white Western analysis engage in the "fetishization of midrange frequencies" (Goodman 2009, 28), prizing the space of semantic, albeit au/oral, discourse above registers that sit more properly in the realm of affect. In "This is America," Gambino plays between these worlds. The track may not be dub but its throbbing trap bass and beat are indebted to those "sounds systems cultures," which deploy "a bass materialism" "achieving [a] rearrangement of the sense" (ibid). For Goodman and Gambino, what this communicates cannot simply be heard or seen, but must be felt. The white American mainstream has had the dissonance inherent to black American life explained to them in book after book, in protest after protest, and even by a president. What Gambino tries to do is to reproduce the sensation. Slave/wealthy entertainer, the bedrock of American popular culture/ the trope of black violence. Gambino pretends to gun down a choir but it was Dylan Roof who actually murdered a church congregation in Charleston. What will be on prestige TV?

The shock of the bass is the shock of the discursively disavowed chaos of American life. Its dissonance is as violent as it is hypnotic as it is libidinal. In interviews, Gambino plays it cute. He plays it Donald Glover. When asked about what he wanted to say with this song and video, he says that he just wanted to make a good song and it is really for the audience to decide. While it is always nice to see an artist defer to the wisdom of Barthes, there is something else going on. Just as the music is incomprehensible to much of the chattering classes, a black artist who semantically signifies his activism is easy to ignore. But the bass is seeping in, it is already everywhere. In the final chorus, it sits under all the other elements of the music that came before it. If you're confused by the arrangement of signs up until now, the system is laid out as clearly as it can be here.

Don't get distracted, but don't stop dancing either. Some actually can't stop. They'll be killed.

Paying with Attention: What If You Held a TED Talk and Everyone Came?

There is a paradox at the heart of our free market, in that its dynamism is induced by market forces that are the aggregate of individual behavior. Behaviors that are themselves induced and directed in line with those activities that are the most likely to produce surplus value. This necessitates the sale of labor. Even if one is to labor in a welfare capacity, it is welfare as the facilitation of the production of surplus values. This is to say that selling your labor is a choice in the same way that it is a choice to take action so as not to starve. The wisdom of economists has been to rebrand these as incentives. But, in the "war against all" that undergirds capitalist realism, to "incentivize" can only be read as a synonym for "coercion." These forces mean that the commodities produced by the culture industry, including the music technologies of quasi-infinite capacity for sonic invention, are contained. Instead of exploring the limits of their potential, these tools are focused on producing material geared toward the capture of consumer attention. Put another way, they attempt to fulfill a specific limited need. A need to access an otherwise denied feeling of possibility. A space that is otherwise closed off from daily reality. TV and movies do this too, and we do begin to think and dream with the images of these commercial shows. But when it's pop music, it charges the very air with a current of possibility.

There is still something useful here to hear from the TCT of Adorno and Horkheimer, who argue that the productions of the culture industry stultify the imagination (1997, 126–127). This is true but not in the way they think. The problem here is not that the content is too simple or the forms too familiar or even that the art object, on the whole, has to be somehow corrupted as it passes into the commodity form. The problem isn't that the imagination has been stultified absolutely, only that it can't get outside of capitalism. The imagination is still here, it has just been set a specific task; imagining individual flourishing as an engine for economic activity. And this is what we hear in the sonic shimmer of present-day pop. Our image of music (Harper 2011, 130) is stuck just as is our image of thought (Deleuze 2011, 164). In both cases, the tools to imagine remain; we just seem incapable of arranging them to imagine in ways other than we do. The actual faculty of the imagination, it seems, isn't up to much without the resources of the world to point where it might head to. And, as Attali puts it, the music we pump out into the world, that becomes its sonic shimmer, is inscribed with the power relations of that world's political economy (Attali 2011, 3–4). In the case of our world, that means the drive to valorize capital is embedded in the tracks.

As we saw above, the notion of the attention economy is trotted out evermore frequently as our present shifting paradigm. But even as we are paying for Facebook by gawping at clickbait posted by bot farms and subscribing to cloud services that provide us the perfect playlists with which to start the week, it is worth remembering that this term of attention economics has second-order effects that go beyond even the abstract commodity exchange that has so far been discussed. Back in 2006, the film theorist Jonathan Beller wrote:

> Today, consumption is productive [...] because it is labor-power itself that appropriates and valorizes commodities to particular ends, which are themselves productive of images. In giving his or her attention to an object, the spectator modifies both him or herself and it, thereby producing and reproducing the ever-developing infrastructure of the status quo (2006, 117).

And while this is an all-too-cynical way to consider cinema in general, not to mention a little patronizing, this is what the attention economy in aggregate actually runs on: the production of a normality that accepts clickbait rather than the clicks or the bait themselves. Put another way, this formulation makes a great deal more sense if used to describe some cultural productions like pop, which are not attentively attended to, than (capital "C") Cinema as it can function in a disavowed background. The "fridge hum" (Radiohead 2016) of contemporary pop is incessant and often unnoticed. The analysis of attention economics can be too crass in its materialism; buy a movie ticket and reproduce the system, steal a film online and contribute to monetized web traffic, all in the service of producing an ideological imaginary. Beller's point is a little more subtle and a lot more abstract. It's not just ideology or the material conditions that these products (re)produce but, instead, they teach you how to desire and how to dream in capitalism. These are useful group survival skills, and to acquire them, seemingly, very little is required of you, other than your passive presence and *a priori* submission to engage in actions conducive to the reproduction of your life. Which, hey, you'd be doing anyway, right? With pop, instead of cinema, even less is needed from you. Through no action of your own, you are now in a position, right here in this mall, in this bar, on your laptop, of absorbing material specifically tailored to produce desire conducive to the accumulation of capital. This always sounds so conspiratorial but it isn't; it's simply what makes sense when looking from the inside. And concrete examples of this can be found in the empirical social research of shopping mall marketing conducted by Tia DeNora and others (2000, 131).

But we should be careful throwing this word "passive" around, otherwise, this could all end up sounding like good ol' TCT. It is no longer a good look for cultural theory just to spout that people don't know why they like what they like or listen to. Not just this, but claiming "they know not what they do" is a short-cut that bypasses the actual thinking that this predicament requires. That said, the contemporary bombardment of pop music content far exceeds a level that could be engaged with actively. Trying to do so could actually be damaging. Economically speaking, it would not be an efficient use of time. Like Oswald argued, the passivity of the consumer is more like a marketing strategy than an indictment of the audience's capacities and agency. Still, to behave otherwise, to actively not join in with all this, would be a dangerous deviation.

Even as a marketing strategy, passivity, or, more properly, the space that cultural content that is passively imbibed occupies, has a bunch of added benefits. Chief among them is its appearance of normality. As we said before, displays of power in the form of spectacles can still be effective producers of capitalist desire but, because we live in a time in which "[t]he attitude of ironic distance proper to postmodern capitalism" (Fisher 2009, 5) has produced an audience too jaded to regard such displays seriously, it can be a risky investment. Also, if Deleuze and Guattari's analysis of capitalism as an engine for the deterritorialization of other sociocultural forms is an accurate way understanding how our neoliberal political economy functions, then deference to the spectacles of power can be an obstacle to efficient consumption (Deleuze & Guattari 2013a, 257). Thus, the mechanisms of productive attention, for the most part, need to remain passive and, as such, subterranean.

So, here we have a sonic shimmer of contemporary pop refracting ideologically infused intention as a desire for passive consumption. But with this relentless atmosphere filling the preconscious awareness of ourselves in the world, we begin to witness a "deadening of affect" (Goodman 2009,192). The mall "muzak," which is actually a popular song meant to inspire the rapturous ecstasy of a party, bleeds into the metro station, your shared apartment, and the trailer before a YouTube music video, and all the while you had your own earbuds in. All this implicitly instructs you to feel something important but in ways that should not interfere with your productive activities. Musical material that may have, at one time, been transformative is now little more than fridge hum. Goodman's "military entertainment complex"(31) in action. We are enthralled to it and its subterranean provision of life (Foucault 2003, 241). Feeling is being put in its place, beneath productivity. And, so it seems, we can no longer point to any oppressor outside of ourselves and we may not even want to do that as it is easy enough today to be convinced the best thing to do is to reject the entire concept. No one wants to think of themselves as a victim. The images provided by the sonic shimmer of contemporary pop cannot disrupt this status quo alone.

Anything that overtly strays from this becomes instantly largely unacceptable or at least cannot gain traction. Images of radical otherness are filtered out by shock or horror or even simply the rolling of eyes. There is a passive pressure at play that maintains our norms, adjusting itself only ever so slightly to the discourses of most profitability. This is the value of attention to the valorization of capital: *through its proper direction, attention helps ensure the valorization of all capital by maintaining the imaginary of capitalist realism.*

Art-Objects-Oriented Subjectivity

Before we can get any further into what this means for the future of popular music in relation to the glorious arrival of post-capitalism, there are some persistent ghosts of TCT that need to be dealt with. The first is the pseudo-Adornian reification of "content" found in the work of Bernard Stiegler. The second is the situation of this within anthropocentric phenomenology. And the third, which is really an offshoot of the first two, is the structurally constrained notion of the subject that is inherent to both of these positions, and, if not deconstructed, would put an end to the narration of this Sonic Fiction. So, to get through this we, unfortunately, need to simultaneously build up a pair of concepts in order to tear them down again: Adorno's theory of the artwork and Stiegler's phenomenological conception of technology. Both of these are incredibly far away from pop and yet they illustrate many of the limitations in a great many of the discussions of it. To save on citational interruptions, everything in the following section is either from Adorno's *Aesthetic Theory* (2012) or Stiegler's *Technics and Time, 1* (1998), unless otherwise indicated.

Adorno believed artworks could contain emancipatory potential in a very specific way.

Stiegler's conception of technology is through the concept of techne, or the capacity for producing tools, which he argues is inexorably related to time and memory.

All artworks that are not merely commodities, according to Adorno, were produced in a dialectical motion between the expression of that which cannot ever be fully expressed, or content, and the means of making this inexpressible content comprehensible through socially accepted artistic forms, which inevitably produces a tension.

Stiegler's conception of time and memory is phenomenological and his concept of technology is as a tertiary form of memory or retention. Following Husserl, who posited that phenomenological retention could be thought of in two stages—moment-to-moment primary retention and the longer term, event-organized secondary retention—Stiegler adds the externalization of money in mnemotechnical objects (technological tools) as tertiary retention.

For Adorno, explicit political positions or arguments are not capable of producing genuinely emancipatory art. Such content cannot be dialectically synthesized with existing artistic forms as it is already reified and thus implicated in capitalism. The same is true of the fetishization of formal experimentation, which, without some kind of truth content, just becomes a practice of bourgeois fascination. Emancipatory artworks are what emerge after the synthesis of some kind of truth content that relates to the conditions of the world, such as Kafka's angst under modernity, and a form that can articulate it despite the inherent impossibility of this task, as seen in Kafka's unfinished, darkly funny prose.

Each of the levels of retention also produces a kind of anticipation, known as protentions. Husserl points to the way in which one can anticipate how a musical melody will progress from what came before to describe this phenomenon at the level of primary protentions and retentions. On the second level, one could think about deciding which piece of music they would like to hear based on what they have heard before. An obvious example of Stiegler's tertiary protention in action would be the autocomplete function of many search bars based upon the retention of previous tertiary retentions. Of course, there is no clear distinction between these levels. For example, it is at the primary level that we experience the recollection of secondary retentions, often while attending to material stored as tertiary retentions. If we consider the act of listening to a pop song in this framework, you would have used the same process described by Husserl for primary retentions, not just in relation to the melody but also the harmony, song structure, lyrical ideas, beat, timbre, etc. ... But at the same time, you have a biological archive of secondary retentions that relates the characteristics of the song to other songs or fragmented recollections and imaginings of them, which gives you a set of expectations about the song as a whole. And, if you were to be listening to this song on a tertiary retentional device, like a smartphone or even just music library software, you could quickly compare it to related pieces of music, and the algorithms of the software may produce a protention of what is to be listened to next.

There are, of course, a great many other criteria for Adorno's notion of what constitutes emancipatory art in addition to this dialectical process of particular kinds of form and content. Another element that is vitally important for his definition of the artwork is its uselessness. Adorno is suspicious of those who seek to elevate the aesthetics of that which is useful, like bridges or assembly lines. For him, these merely express the logic of rationalized society, referring back to the Crusoe creation myth upon which bourgeois society is based (Marx 1990, 169). Thus, the useful cannot be the beautiful, as such things have already been reified. That said, there still must be something of this unfree society in an emancipatory work of art, but Adorno finds this in the negative. The emancipatory work of art is the antithesis of society. It is in these artworks that the possibility of moving beyond the status quo is made manifest, though it must not fall into instrumentalization.

On another level, one could even consider the song itself as a type of tertiary retention, containing musical traditions and prior utterances. For Stiegler, it is safe to say the artwork is a tertiary retention, loaded with protentions.

***

In the years following the crash of 2008, Stiegler's interests moved from a tight focus on human/technological ontology, to something more political. In this project, he turns to once again reading Adorno (and Horkheimer) to produce his own criticism of what he considers the systemic stupidity [*bêtise*] of contemporary cultural production (and other forms of production) leading to a global proletarianization of consciousness (Siegler 2013, 22). Stiegler agrees with Adorno and Horkheimer's general point in their essay on the culture industry, that the cultural productions of capitalism are being used to stultify the masses, but disagrees with them about the mechanism. Here, Stiegler is quick to point to the daylight between their and his positions. Stiegler argues that there is an inexorable pessimism to Adorno and Horkheimer's argument that the reified goods of the culture industry are inherently oppressive. Stiegler points out that this is reactionary. Their mistake, according to Stiegler, was that they failed to conceptualize these productions as tertiary retentions, a notion that Stiegler first expounded in 1994 (some twenty-five years after Adorno's death and a little less than fifty years after the publication of *Dialectic of Enlightenment*), which meant they did not consider these productions with Derrida's reading of Plato's pharmakon, which appeared in French in 1972 (2016) (a mere three years after Adorno died). This is to say that, for Stiegler, the productions of the culture industry should be considered as a drug (that is to say a tool, that is to say a tertiary retention) that can be administered either as a poison or as a cure. That Adorno and Horkheimer overlooked this places serious limitations on their analysis, according to Stiegler.

But Stiegler's pharmacological view of cultural productions themselves and, by extension, art objects is strangely closer to the Adorno of *Aesthetic Theory*, who holds that certain kinds of artworks, constructed in a particular way, have within them a capacity for our coming to know that there is an emancipated form of life beyond the status quo. And there is an elegance to this understanding of an artwork. Stiegler's argument is simply that we need to learn how to use the tools (that is to say tertiary retentional devices) of the culture industry to engender this. Which, as an agenda point, would be where Adorno, were he still alive, would part company with Stiegler, because such instrumentalization of artworks would reify them entirely. To wit, Stiegler would then hit back that he is actually thinking in terms far larger than just artworks, reaching to the very systems of communication and externalization of memory themselves. Then, Adorno would of course counter this with the argument that these systems are nothing more than the mechanism for the production of mass deception ….

Where they agree, though, is very interesting. For both Adorno, writing in the 1940s, and Stiegler, writing today, their belief is that we are missing something that can help us snap out of our stupor. There are vested interests and systems of oppression that promise to fill this missing piece, this lack, and they are deceiving us, entrapping us in the production of value and the reproduction of capital. But, for Adorno and Stiegler, there exists something else that can help us to finally be free. The problem with this is that it presupposes a whole bunch of things about humans, about capitalism, and how these things relate to each other.

Shake It Off

If attention to popular music is not simply a question of the spectacle casting a fish hook into the eyeballs of the proletariat and dragging their focus to the power of the industrial might that oppresses them[5]; if it is not problem of commodity fetishism that can be addressed through the production of more worthy art objects or MP3s or "CD quality" Tidal streams, then what is at stake when we talk about attention to popular music? Well, Adorno and Stiegler are pretty close to naming it, if only in an oddly disavowed kind of way. What is at stake has always been lack: its manufacture, its pseudo-fulfillment, and its reproduction. Something needed by the subject, which is always missing. Something missing that the market addresses in that particular way that the market addresses all problems: with an eye to repeat business. Their diagnosis makes a great deal of intuitive sense, as does the follow-on point that if this lack needs to be fulfilled, then we should try to find better ways to fill it than with what the market provides. This is the practical synthesis of Adorno and Stiegler's work (allowing, of course, for the fact that such a synthesis would be an anathema for Adorno because it would be akin to the sort of instrumentalist reification that prevents art, under such conditions, from being in any way emancipatory and so on and so forth). But aside from the objections of negative dialecticians, there is something else troubling about this diagnosis and this fix: *making lack a natural need to be fulfilled makes emancipation little more than a state that can be retroactively defined from any ideological position that can produce something that fills the absence.* This is reactionary. It also ascribes to the productions of the culture industry some kind essential quality that corresponds to this lack rather than its merely being an emergent phenomenon contingent upon the cultivation of bodies. With all this in place, you'd have to dismiss pop out of hand. This is also reactionary. And contrary to these positions, our attention to popular music shows us that when it comes to the productions of the culture industry, we're not dealing with just fish hooks but with live bait.

Using the appearance of lack as the basis of a project to overcome capitalism has previously been shown to run into some problems (Deleuze & Guattari 2013a, 40–41). While this may seem like an all-too-old debate, and a debate that is stopping us from really getting into Taylor Swift's "Shake it Off" (2014), the pervasiveness of lack discourse in the analysis of cultural production can't be swept aside. And, despite the decades that have passed, it is still Deleuze and Guattari who are the ones with the best tools to move past it (not for good but for the time being). But we may be getting ahead of ourselves. First, we need to see this problem of lack in action.

A few years ago, I carried out empirical research into the kind of music that made up what was then contemporary, mainstream popular music in the UK (Holt 2012). What I found then was that, with very few exceptions, the UK top twenty was made up of two major musical trends: a sizeable minority of balladic songs by singer/songwriters and a majority of star-fronted electronic dance music (EDM) tracks. At the time that that research was carried out, it could be argued that the charts were becoming ever less representative of music consumption, as they only accounted for physical music sales that took place in disappearing boutique record stores and supermarkets (the negative definition of curation). This was more than a little out of step with the reality of streaming consumption. Checking in a few years later, and with this oversight now addressed (Williamson 2014), not much had changed. The only noticeable differences were that some singer/songwriters were now in collaboration with the EDM producers (e.g., "Bloodstream" by Ed Sheeran & Rudimental [2014]), while others have reestablished themselves as a fusion of the genres ("Love Me Like You Do" by Ellie Goulding [2015]) and some have made a self-conscious shift to danceable pop (a good example of this is Taylor Swift's album *1989* [2014]).[6]

The explicit content of these songs is, on the whole, pretty similar to that of the Black Eyed Peas' "I Gotta Feeling." Is the world stressing you out? Then, pursue a hedonistic release to solve all your problems. And with this, I think we are beginning to see the outline of what is missing. However, with this kind of data, sociologists would be well advised not to draw definitive conclusions about what this says about either this music's immediate audience or the culture on the whole. But, as we are a good long way being absorbed into a policy document, some speculation here might be fruitful.

When practitioners of TCT have attended seminars on the work of Jacques Lacan, they turn back to things like the celebration of hedonism found in pop music with a reductive use of an excessive label/concept: *jouissance.* This reductive use of a complicated label has led some music researchers, such as Robert Fink, to abandon the perspectives offered by this psychoanalytic concept (2005, 6). But this is a shame because it helps to chart the limitations of lack. So how should this be filled out? Jouissance is a concept that refers to a kind of pleasure that exceeds semantic comprehension and is often connected to sex, sovereignty, and/or property. The fact that it takes the subject experiencing it outside of the system of language should be of incredible significance to the study of music and enjoyment but instead, as Fink found, it's often just thrown out as a way to denigrate enjoyment. Really, though, it should be acknowledged for what it is: the capacity of the popular music shimmer to be so alluring and for it to feel that it could be fulfilling.

This is why we take up the products of capitalism to restore ourselves after suffering from the mode of production that is capitalism. There is no real paradox here since even the notion of exceeding the limits put on us by the power of capital can be converted into a commodity for the valorization of capital. We could even say that this commodity is encoded into the conditions from which capitalism emerged. At least if we follow the Freud of *Civilization and Its Discontents* (2004), we can. In this essay, Freud argues that civilization (which pretty clearly should be taken to mean Western civilization as understood from the perspective of the European bourgeoisie, and thus pretty clearly entangled with capitalism) exists as a bulwark against the base drives of humanity. These drives to fornication and violence are disruptive and destructive and are repressed by the laws and structures of civilization, creating tension that is displaced either through productive sublimations or pathological neurosis (19). These could both be considered as responses to lack. Jouissance offers a third option of response: transgression. In transgressing the laws of civilization that prevent people from pursuing their drives, jouissance allows for the experience of something other, a world imaged otherwise, but never quite escaping this one. Following Attali, in earlier social forms such transgression of the law may have required punishment, lest the law be represented as impotent. But in using the shimmer of pop hedonism to charge into a transgressive hedonism of excessive consumption and self-destruction, capitalism has placed a spigot on jouissance. Far from punishing transgression, capitalism is always trying to package new forms of it.

And, unlikely as it seems, this brings us back to Taylor Swift, a public persona that is more similar to a Gap commercial than Gomorrah, and her injunction that we "Shake If Off." There are consequences to the pursuit of jouissance. A social stigma that persists even if the dominant economic mode is happy enough to sell you everything you need to indulge in a bit of the ol' jouissance. "Shake If Off" (Swift 2014) is about grappling with this social cost of being perceived as hedonistic or transgressive by a conservative culture. "I go on too many dates, but I can't make 'em stay/At least that's what people say mmm mmm" (Ibid). Where does Swift align herself here? In casting these remarks as rumors and nothing but jealous gossip, she is asserting the moral force of the accusation. Even if they are entirely unfounded, unless these remarks carried some kind of weight why would one need to shake them off? This is revealing some something about the so-called rupture of jouissance: it can produce its own disciplining force. You either care about the rules or you care about breaking them, which actually means you care about the rules because they need to be in place to be broken. "Nothing runs better on MTV than protest against MTV" (Fisher 2009, 9). Lack persists in transgression, begging the question: has anything really been transgressed? The excess of jouissance still needs civilization and its discontents.

But wasn't this chapter about attention? Well, the logic present in the chastisement of jouissance coded as hedonism and the championing of transgression as jouissance is all derived from the Adorno and Stiegler, art-object-to-subject, model of attention, which is predicated on the notion of the reduction the human to an incomplete and thus completable subject, which presupposes an idealized telos. Experientially, this makes a certain amount of sense but limits what popular music and its enjoyment are, by treating them as a means to facilitate this broken subject's survival through access to an inner truth and definitive self-knowledge, which are themselves taken to refer to some natural manifestation of innate drives. This way of thinking all but ensures capitalism will always have some hold on us as subjective lack ensures a (libidinal) economy of scarcity. So to start to get out of this requires us to think of attention differently, which also implies a different kind of subject.

Deleuze and Guattari can now make a proper contribution to this discussion. Their Bergsonian time coding breaks them out of the trap of subjects' utterly blinkered perception of their phenomenological self. (Or perhaps maybe it just helps us think about doing that.) Whatever the things that can be thought to be subjects are, pop music shows they exceed the phenomenology of their perception. Phenomenological accounts, even allowing for memory, paint the act of listening to pop as if the subject were the first being ever to hear a pop song. But because that hearing of the pop song carries encoded in it a past of millions of hearings of millions of songs and any and every listening carries with it this implicit past, an inherent multiplicity and virtual futurity (Parisi & Goodman 2011, 167). Thus an attentively phenomenological listening subject is conceptually stultified, when it comes to describing this quotidian reality. Typing in search terms on a streaming platform and waiting for the algorithm to suggest which piece of posthuman, postsoul expression was searched for makes this obvious. This is a banal experience of distributed subjectivity, a notion of subjects as a folding of bodies and culture, of materials and signs, of technologies and biological processes, defined only in continuous relation to one another. Even if they experience it as such, they can never really be lacking because there is always too much and they (we) are part of it. It is in this constant indeterminate folding of things that phenomenology is revealed as a sluggish OS. This excessive reality imminent to experience makes the assertion of any particular moment as the present—as distinct from the past and future—a tricky thing to do. It is a kind of abundance that makes the lonely world understood through lack seem lacking in its explanatory capacity. Kassabian picks this up and put it to work on music:

> My basic thesis is this, put bluntly: *Ubiquitous musics,* these musics that fill our days are listened to without the kind of primary *attention* assumed by most scholarship to date. That listening and more generally input of the *senses,* however, still produces affective responses, bodily events that ultimately lead in part to what we call emotion. And it is through this listening and these responses that a nonindividual, not simply human, *distributed subjectivity* takes place across a network of music media.
>
> [...]
>
> Nonindividual subjectivity, a field, but a field over which it is distributed unevenly, over which differences are not only possible but required, and across which information, leading to effective responses. (Kassabian 2013, xxv)

This can all get pretty frightening once the figure of the non-individual raises its head(?) for the seemingly simple task of understanding attention to Taylor Swift and the Black Eyed Peas. It seems to make a great deal more sense for Childish Gambino, though it is hard right now to say why that is. But Kassabian has a fix for the identity vertigo that this kind of thinking can induce. For Kassabian, as it is for Deleuze and Guattari before her, identity is not some kind of fixed labeling of being but a becoming that is ever-emerging from the traces of affect that impress themselves upon a body, which is itself a process of becoming (xxvii). But what does all this mean? Let's think about Oswald again and his complaints of unbidden pop music sullying his consciousness. Before, this was almost like the infringement of the liberty of an individual, who should be spared such suffering. But we should consider that his subjectivity is itself a product of the same system of affective traces that produced him as an unwilling listener, the music imposed upon him and its ravenous fans. His suffering is not merely an unintended and uncared about epiphenomenon of commerce but something of a culture of which his is a constituent part. Oswald's experience of suffering through these tunes is not in some other category from its intended consumer's enjoyment. Criticism of culture is culture and so needs to place itself in the sludge. The limitation of the points of view of Oswald, Adorno, and Stiegler is that, as they present it, there are people for whom these cultural productions are *for* and those for whom they happen *to*. When, rather, it is an obvious fact that there is no happening. These cultural productions have always already happened. There is no restoring to a before, there is only moving through. If this isn't recognized and you continue the search for what is missing, all your cultural critique can produce is another iteration of the existing law with the pieces rearranged.

Nonetheless, the status quo remains insufferable. The bait placed before us still directs the movements of bodies and dictates the construction of desire in the service of the reproduction of capitalist realism, which reduces pop music to something that can only engage in transgression as a commodity. But we need better metaphors. We have already replaced the spectacle with the shimmer so maybe we should replace the subject with a field of distributed subjectivity, comprised of affects and desire. This would help us to see hedonism differently, as simultaneously a reified transgression of the law, but also perhaps as something unbound by that logic of transgression. Something that can also be a manifestation of sociality that could transcend the boundaries of control laid out by capital. But perhaps we can't get there yet. These things have to be held together because, despite all these ingenious poststructural deconstructions of the subject, in which our bodies have their attention directed like ripples through a field of subjectivity, the problem remains that there is no outside to subjectivity even in this extended definition. At least no outside that can also read this book. So, if there is no outside of this field of distributed subjectivity, we had better hope that pop can help this field to stretch beyond capitalism, because we are going to need its libidinizing virality to make something new happen. Our complete infusion into capitalist realism is not a reason not to change this, but instead a reason to be bolder in how we go about it. And we need to get to this emboldening immediately, because capitalist realism has no idealized past (political discourse might but capital doesn't), so it is already at work reproducing itself into the future. And we are always already implicated.

Vignette: Busking on the London Underground

Switching lines at Kings Cross tube station, I was witnessed to an increasingly rare sight on the London Underground: an unlicensed busker playing to a crowd of underwhelmed passersby. Slumped in an alcove along the walkway, the man in his late-thirties/early-forties, who appeared undernourished (although this is entirely conjecture), wore only an oversized leather jacket and ripped jeans; he had gold teeth, and knotted hair. He strummed the occasional a-rhythmic chord on his acoustic guitar and was, as I approached, singing the opening verse to Leonard Cohen's "Hallelujah" (2011). Ahead of me were a gaggle of older upper-middle class members of the metropolitan elite walking in the opposite direction to myself. As they passed the busker, the gaggle's conversation shifted to comment upon the appropriateness of the busker's location, at which point he reached and relished the line: "But you don't really care for music, do ya?"

I had been thinking for a while about the odd intrusion into a previously anarchistic musical practice of allowing and regulating licensed buskers to perform on either side of the barriers at tube stations. Previously, busking on the Underground was an illicit activity conducted through wit, guile, community, and negotiation. Performers would self-organize to circulate the best pitches and had to be ready to run at a moment's notice, should the authorities show up. For more than a decade, however, the practice has been professionalized. As busker, Wayne Myers, writes: "Since we don't have to be constantly ready to flee with all our stuff, we can use more equipment, and incorporate backing tracks and loop pedals. Amps, too, have made otherwise unplayable pitches – such as Canary Wharf, where acoustic instruments are inaudible – worthwhile" (Myers 2013). But Myers also mentions how the thirty-nine pitches seem to be have been placed arbitrarily; the low foot traffic at some locations means that a two-hour slot is barely able to cover the travel costs. In recent years, seemingly in conjunction with a drop in sponsorship since the election of former mayor, Boris Johnson, online slot booking has been replaced with a premium-rate phone number. The best slots are often snapped up before many performers have even managed to get through, all while the call charges tally.

In 2001, London Underground, as a part of Transport for London (TFL), took a peculiar initiative. They won a court decision giving the organization the right to "change the national law and the local bylaws to legalize licensed busking"

(TFL 2013). According to the TFL website, these buskers have a "unique audience of around 3.5 million Tube passengers every day" (ibid), which the press releases on the TFL website suggest would make it an attractive opportunity to the sponsors. Previous sponsors have included Carling, Coca-Cola, and Capital FM. Exactly what the sponsors sponsor is unclear. The scheme's website states the buskers "are not paid by London Underground and rely on the generosity of Tube passengers" (ibid). However, as the press release online notes, "The London Underground Busking Scheme has up to 39 pitches across 25 Central London stations, which are clearly defined by a semi-circular floor graphic and a backdrop advert on the wall" (ibid). Which for sponsors has the benefit that "[t]hese are highly visible and attract attention because of the professional musicians performing on them every day" (ibid). Presumably, then, if the buskers are paid for by commuters, then the sponsors pay for maintenance and management of the sponsorship scheme.

The buskers are used as a snare, a device to draw attention to the sponsored plots. They are unpaid and rely on donations from travelers. The latter part of this financial arrangement has been the status quo for buskers forever; however, that used to come with the freedom to choose the best location and to be free from exploitation. They have not previously been granted the permission to play on the condition that they draw the eyes of onlookers to the marketing material of a patron. Thus, to perform for the anointed pan-London mass transit user is, apparently, not something that can be entered into casually. Your craft must be up to scratch by the criteria of TFL judges; your appearance, demeanor, and sounds have to be assessed, and then, finally, you can be located. In these specific spots, the activity becomes productive of value for the sponsor, which is what legitimates the busker's musical utterances. This seems to be becoming a norm across a number of musical activities.

The most striking example of this phenomenon, for me, is found at the bottom of the escalator at Canary Wharf underground station. As you descend the escalator and become engulfed by the modern cavernous station, all high ceilings and imposing pillars, you see a tiny busker, often strumming a guitar and singing, emerge from the darkness. The busker is so alien to the besuited commuters around them, and yet so dependent on said same commuters' notional generosity.

From the skyscrapers on the surface, which some consider a prerequisite of a global city, a particular strata of white-collar workers are making their way home. Down from the offices, through the Jubilee shopping center and its jeweled window displays, weaving through colleagues and competitors and tourists, and finally past someone with a guitar. Someone who perhaps spent an hour on a premium phone line to win this slot to be able to perform for this strata of worker—to attract the attention of these commuters to the surrounding advertisements, some of which make use of socialist iconography—and is happy to receive any change thrown his way.

More than half a century ago, Adorno and Horkheimer wrote that music had lost its rebellious character within the culture industry. It seems, however, there may have been even more rebelliousness still to lose. In the formation of politically stagnant neoliberal subjects, public music becomes an inconvenience that must be justified in all its forms through utility if it is to be expressed. Especially if it is to interrupt the flows of the busy people engaged in value production as they traverse London. Otherwise, these individuals are free to simply listen to their personal music devices as they're on the go. As the TFL website states, busking on the Underground has been a lure to now famous artists (The Libertines, Julian Lloyd-Webber, Badly Drawn Boy) early on in their careers. But this was all before licensing came in. This should not be taken as a simple glorification of *the bad old days of busking*. The guy slumped on the floor that Saturday night was intimidating, but then he wasn't there for my benefit. He wasn't there to sell a product. He wasn't an entertainer. He wasn't on the first rung of the career ladder constructing a rags-to-riches narrative. He played music to pass the time and if you threw him some change, great. If you found him unpleasant, *c'est la vie*.

In its sponsored plot form, busking becomes a career move, though admittedly not one with many prospects for success. Under the present circumstances, however, it may be a necessary move as the value of recorded music approaches zero, as gentrified city centers legislate for noise restriction so as to not offend the sensibilities of highly valued renters, as each moment of the day that is not monetized becomes akin to luxury. This seemingly trifling thing is enmeshed in something systemic. And the only thing more terrifying than being subsumed by this system is the prospect of being cast out of it. Especially as the outside appears, increasingly, not to exist at all.

○

2

Complicity

Determined by Many Situations

There is clearly much more going on here than just being distracted by pop; more than simply having our attention misdirected.[1] The individualizing and alienating forces that facilitate the mechanisms of capitalism, that make it so oppressive, have to operate on something deeper than just misdirection or slight of hand. And whatever this "something deeper" is, can't be countered by a resistance that reproduces the same kind of individualizing, alienating motion. This is what's wrong with cultural critiques of capitalism that focus on the art object, i.e., traditional critical theory (TCT). Even as these objects are brought into a relationship with people and society, they present the overcoming of capitalism in the same terms as capitalism presents the good life: get the sanctioned thing (the commodity or the emancipatory work of art) and complete yourself. The best such frameworks can produce is some kind of subtle rearrangement of the forces of exploitation and maybe offer some kind of *alleviation* of a fraction of it. Nothing to be scoffed at but also nothing to spend much time championing. As long as the route of emancipation lies in finding some missing piece or pieces to complete a whole, alienation, and thus exploitation, will inhere within it. But we can chart another route through if we dissolve and distribute the subject. The likes of Deleuze and Guattari have told us this for decades and now Kassabian has applied this to popular music and ubiquitous listening, which can only function as they do because our world is built upon the actuality of distributed subjectivity. This is how capital works, and using capital's mapping onto our distributed field of pop subjectivity might be what we need to chart a route through this quagmire. But this means dealing with something uncomfortable: our complicity in our own exploitation.

Popular music was always already a commodity. Prior to this form, pop was just folk. Pop, as we know it, makes no coherent sense as a concept without recording, and recording makes no coherent sense, under industrial capitalism, without the profit motive. Popular music is the commodity form in the first instance, so much so that, in terms of value production, the commodity of pop itself is now more valuable than the recordings. It is a product that seems to chisel itself out through entrepreneurial verve with nothing more than a huge amount of structural privilege and/or luck and the tiniest amount of state support. To some it seems like a meritocracy or some such. The capitalist mode of production has its tentacles in everything, through the fluxing record industry, the international monopolies that control the marketplace and promotion of live music, the merchandise, and the synchronizations with products and events.

This mode of production has other odd effects on pop. That which was once deviance and degeneracy, now makes up the line-up of the British Royal Variety Performance. But this is just moving with the times, is how the dismissal of such a concern would go. Another way to think about this, which is more accurate, is after Deleuze and Guattari, that capital deterritorializes and reterritorializes. For all the horrors that such motions tend to produce, it has allowed for the wondrousness of witnessing the end of most of the conservative backlashes to pop. For example, the hard fought and hard won concession in the US to place a warning logo, "Parental Advisory: Explicit Content," on music that made reference to sex and violence (but mostly sex) became little more than a reasonably effective marketing tool (Thomas 2010). There is capital to be made in transgressing mores. Here we can see evidence of that under-explored rift in the political right between authoritarians who have capital but don't understand how it works, and those who have it and do. The latter group will sell music to you with any lyrics you desire. They will deterritorialize discourse to reterritorialize attention. Rage Against the Machine are (were) on MTV. After all, you have to get the message out there.

The capacity of popular music to promote "human flourishing" (Hesmondhalgh 2013, 10) is held up by its contemporary academic defenders, in response to the criticism this music received from TCT. This capacity was used as justification both for the study of pop and the often uncritical nature of these studies. The criticism leveled on pop by TCT is rightly considered to be the result of major methodological problems and a basic ignorance of the subject matter as it relates to its actual audience (Frith 1981, 45). Against this, by engaging with pop music at the level of actual audience experiences, some have been led to see the possibility of emancipation in pop (Small 2011, 6), where the Frankfurt school could see only induced passivity. The trouble with TCT emerges once again. There is an oddly unexamined individualistic and romantic component in its admonishment of passivity. It would seem that the subject, however it is to be constructed, is meant to be able to consciously engage with every demand placed on its attention, regardless of the impossibility of this task. But passivity is actually unavoidable, particularly under the contemporary machinations of the culture industry. By failing to grasp this, the TCT of Adorno and the post-TCT of Stiegler have overvalued the art object/cultural production, and require too much legwork, which could be thought of as a force directed towards emancipation, from these peculiar/familiar artifacts. More than this, in addition to not appearing to work, this perspective cannot fully grapple with the implications of the relational space in which the object can be said to exist. Yes, they can claim that the artwork is the social antithesis of society, or speak of networks of tertiary retentional devices, but the notion that there is something in the particular objects of this kind that is the key piece to the resolution of alienation haunts these notions. When listening to music, this abstract shimmer of pressurized air, it becomes quite obvious that this relational space is all there is to art's existence. What we find in an artwork is some kind of material reflection of the affects that course through us. Or perhaps we don't. In this field, passivity is baked in.

The way that Deleuze and Guattari put this is to claim that passivity is even baked into desire. The bodies that we have are guided by—"drives" is the wrong word—pulsions[2] that run into obstacles and possibilities, and that are over-coded by the structures used before the activation of our mapping processes[3] that channel the pulsions of those who came before. These pulsions are forms of desire, that desire precedes the existence of a subject who desires. Understanding a desire as being denied to us, not simply as yet unreached but actually denied, is an understanding on the level of the map, or the subject who desires. Experiencing this as lack is an active process of the map. Desire just flows, passively (Deleuze and Guattari, 2013a, 370), without a decision, without attention, without a destination. It can be otherwise but this is a capacity, not a necessity. The tributaries that guide these flows are defined by the world around us and a not too insignificant part of that definition is formed by capitalism, which is itself influenced by the pulsional force of desire. This is an irresolvable tension, a motion that cannot cease, lest it die like a stationary shark.

So what is the upshot of all this for our complicit pop? Back on the thread of recordability, the twentieth century saw more people experiencing more of the same cultural productions simultaneously than ever before. And these productions were more profitable than they heretofore had been. A new network of tributaries emerged from this new arrangement of the flows of desire; new imperatives could be formed and so too could the potential of a new lack. The distinction between what had been considered high-culture, and thus worthy of attention, and that deemed low-culture, and thus limited to the status of a mere diversion, began to blur as previously ignored desires were channeled by market forces, which found profitability in previously unprofitable formations of desire. From this chaotic interplay of forces, we arrived at a situation where, in 2008, pop producers like Will.I.Am orchestrate presidential campaign videos to accompany specially composed music (Will.I.Am 2008) and thus play some role to influence the flows of capital in global markets. "Yes, We Can" as an affirmation of social democracy. We might look at this as a moment of democratic potential, where the vernacular musics of the populous are able to play a role in the political conditions under which they live, but this would be an optimistic and naive reading.[4] But there are so many mechanisms of control that had to be negotiated to bring this song to the public. For example, the artist has to first prove they are a successful businessman before they can officially campaign for the nominally left-leaning candidate. So what makes more sense to explain the direction and investment of desire in the maintenance of the status quo? This an example of what Herbert Marcuse, a theorist who bridges TCT and the French men of the 70s and 80s, called "repressive desublimation" (2002, 75), wherein the motivations and pulsions that could be directed to the overcoming of the status quo are redirected and reinvested to enforce its maintenance. The pop song facilitates this as much as it facilitates the formation of communities championed by post-TCT pop music academia. Perhaps even it is because it can form communities so readily that it can also perform repressive desublimation. "Yes, We Can" is a call to action without an object. A political platform that promises nothing. The production of a political Will(.I.Am) to do nothing but "circulat[e] idiotically on the spot" (Fisher 2014a, 342). For all its faults, it has never been so simple as leaving TCT or the perspectives it offers behind. There is stuff in this theory that the contemporary champions of pop ignore to their detriment.

What we need to be careful of here is looking at or listening to anything in particular too directly. This is the problem with using the Will.I.Am music video as an example. The clarity with which it can be used to make the points made so far can give the impression that this mechanism of complicity operates through the communicative power of some of music's semantic content. One doesn't need fancy concepts like distributed subjectivity to make such an argument and, if you were to do so, such concepts would actually get in the way. Instead, we need to think this through differently. There is semantic communication in the song but this doesn't function without an archive of previous experiences to measure it against. More than just the complexities of language, this refers also to the concepts of pop songs themselves, where they are positioned in relation to politics, how pop has previously engaged in politics and an imagination of how it may in the future. This functions on the level of, what is poorly termed, the individual and the level of culture, or how the archive is shared and communicated. Each engagement with popular music, attentive or passive, is tangled up in this process, which means it is hard to understand any discrete example as the complete manifestation of anything in particular. All they offer is a window into the flows of desiring-production. Flows that are proximate both to the field of subjectivity and to capitalism. Flows that can help us chart our complicity.

Casually Cruel

It is difficult to account for the lived experience of globalization.[5] It has been a project since before the phenomenon had a name (Marx 1990, 931), but contemporary analyses seem to cover it either as an impending technocracy (Castells 2000; Moulier-Boutang 2011; Mason 2015) or as intimate dissolution and injustice (Spivak 2013). To draw these and the myriad other threads together, pop can be a cartographic tool; sonic uranium running through and illuminating the connections between the rare earth mineral trade, to shipping networks, to low-cost manufacturing, to marketing, to computing, to segregated and appropriative cultivation of culture, to consumption, to dancing, to imaginations and affects. This is largely because pop, due to its particular material contingencies, is currently experienced through the conduit of the smartphone.

Smartphones are a form of science fiction technology that we use to distract toddlers when adults need to talk about mortgages and then to distract ourselves as adults on commutes or while using the toilet. The operating systems that run on them often also feature an app with which one can check in with the rise and fall of international markets. At one point they were the repository of your favorite tracks but now, with the reduced cost of data packages and the increasing speed of mobile internet, they are the portable way through which you can access your streaming service account. Occasionally they are used to make phone calls. The phones featured in the heavy-handed but, unfortunately, not inaccurate Danish documentary, *Blood in the Mobile* (Poulsen 2010) appear today as if they are from the distant past. The way Frank Poulsen, the film's director, tries to characterize his and our dependence on mobile phones is in reference to sending to sending "loving text messages" (02:23) to his family back in Denmark. Today the primary way to express love via smartphone is through the judiciously playful choice of emojis and Snapchat filters. However, what these phones have in common is the need for rare earth minerals at the lowest price possible.

Much of the discursive focus on the evils of smartphone production has been placed on how these devices are assembled. This is because it is awful. And awful in way that translates well to narration. But still, the true horror of working in conditions that have led businesses to introduce suicide nets to keep their workers alive can really only be hinted at. "It's not desiring the fall; it's terror of the flames" (Wallace 2007, 696). To set the images of these nets against the images of turtleneck "geniuses" "changing everything" (but the dominant mode of production) makes for great moralistic television news. But to paraphrase how it was put in an interview with the Lacanian big Other, Slavoj Žižek, by the writer Will Self (2017): what are we to do with the coltan[6] in our pockets?

In Paulsen's documentary, Self's glib jab is made human and empathetic as the documentarian interviews the people victimized by the rapists and murderers that run many of the mining operations in the Democratic Republic of Congo (DRC). At the time of filming, the civil war in the country had claimed over five million lives and produced a buyers' market for rare earth minerals such as coltan, which allow for the installation of software that facilitates the streaming of "Cruel" by the incomparable St. Vincent (2012), an artist named after Vincent de Paul, the patron saint of all acts of charity. It suffices to say that the conditions of civil war have created market conditions for rare earth minerals in the DRC that are excessive even by the standards of many other examples of exploitative post-colonial trade arrangements. This makes things a little bit more complex. With Foxconn, the exploitation can be laid clearly at the feet of Chinese labor practices and the hypocrisy of an insufferable group of billionaires in Silicon Valley. The history of trade with post-colonial African nations implies more culpability on our part as consumers, and the way around this, given the fixed location of the minerals, would require far more revolutionary social change than moving a factory.

The seemingly insurmountable nature of this problem, and the complexity of its causes, leads to what a differently heavy-handed documentary maker, Adam Curtis, calls "Oh Dearism" (2010). This, in Deleuzian/Spinozist terms, refers to the over saturation of an issue with negative affects; affects that preclude the possibility of action and actively repel the mind from engaging with them. We can think of this as a mechanism of capitalist realism. The change actually required—the total overthrow of this mode of production and its replacement with something more egalitarian—becomes entangled with these negative affects and are made to seem both impossible and undesirable, when they are, in fact, neither. But they are pretty tricky. Thus we turn away and continue to casually contribute material resources to the maintenance of this cruelty. After all, a lack has been produced now, and there is money to be made in momentarily filling it. This is where we are with the desire to acquire formed into a void, which at first appears to be the negative image of the super-slim oblong of the phone, but this belies the nature of the device. What it really produces is the feeling that it was missing. And that it has now arrived as a conduit to plug into communicative capitalism (Dean 2009, 19), to feel connected to the network that can protect you if you join in sufficiently.

But is this connection not just a discursive trick? That is, I can write sentences that join together the pop hits of indie darlings and the atrocities of the Congolese civil war as seen from the perspective of an iPhone, but is that substantive cultural analysis? Or is it just a banal observation that we are all caught up in global systems? Can the inability to leave this arrangement of things really be considered as complicity? To this line of questioning, the only response can be that this is not a question of moral culpability but of actual culpability. Since Hannah Arendt covered the trial of *Eichmann in Jerusalem*, we have known that evil requires little more than indifference and self-motivation (Arendt 1978). Some have just been slow to fully appreciate what this implies. That we hold no malice toward those we exploit is no argument for our innocence. Malice may even make the exploitation less efficient and thus, perhaps, less damaging. But the fact that a line can be drawn and drawn accurately between the casually consumed commodities of Western cultural production and suffering on a global scale is more than just a guilt trip to inspire the signing of online petitions. It may offer us a way to consider the normalization of the cruelty with which we live.

Pop music has a tendency toward intensity. It is not a universal law. Bands like Pavement, who made but a few concessions to the norm of distortion in 90s American guitar music, seem to shirk the pursuit of intensity altogether. Unless of course, one could say they intensely pursued slacker aesthetics. But aside from these corners of obscurity, pop brings forth intensities of volume, of rhythm and repetition, of emotion, of consumption, and lets you imbibe it. This is definitional to the commodity as it needs to stand out in a market inundated with content, all engaged in an attentional arms race. This was the case before the present crisis of profitability that has been brought on by ever-increasing internet download speeds. But since these conditions have become a fact of the market landscape, the pop music mainstream has turned to the production of an ever-more refined commodity in pursuit of accumulating all of what little value remains in the momentary capture of attention. It's like musical fracking.

Popular music, like all other commodities, has both a use-value and exchange-value. What became clear in the previous chapter on attention was that the use-value of popular music can be located in its capacity to facilitate the imagination of the world as other-than-it-is. Maybe "other" means a state of fully automated-luxury-intersectional-space-communism; maybe it just means not having to worry about the price of Grey Goose; maybe it means the total deterritorialization of everything; maybe it just means feeling less alone. For our purposes, "other" is meant in a general sense. This imagination of otherness can be provided by other means, of course, but pop's materiality and means of distribution make it a particularly useful commodity with which to deliver this resource. What these commodities have in common, however, is the frame of enjoyment. These are things to be enjoyed, and the time in which they can be is earned through the time and effort of labor. This is something that TCT had a massive problem with, and in Adorno's essay on hobbies, "Free Time," he makes the reasons for this totally clear (1991, 190). Basically, the problem is that it relegates all non-economically productive activities to the realm of the unserious enjoyment of frivolous diversion. He has other problems with the way in which free time itself is only understood as a kind of negative counterpart to labor time, which makes it inherently unfree, and this is somewhat tangled up with the first problem. But this is still shot through with values that elevate the notion of seriousness and some kind of idea of right or correct enjoyment as if righteousness were, in some way, a way to counter capitalism. Alfie Bown (2015) helps to cut this notion down. In his exploration of the relationship between Candy Crush and capitalism, Bown argues that many who consider themselves to be politically radical, whether consciously or not reproduce this notion of good and bad enjoyment, albeit with the less problematic, but still utterly inaccurate, labeling of conformist and radical enjoyment. Bown argues that these labels fall apart entirely if they're considered more globally. The Deleuze and Guattari Facebook group (2015, 19) to which you belong may seem radical on a discursive level, when compared to following the LAD Bible, but on the level of user data and post engagement, your posting of photos of underlined quotes from *A Thousand Plateaus* (2013b) is as useful to the valorization of capital as the selfies of the "friends" that you judge to be so vacuous.

The only thing that can perhaps be said to be different here is the context in which these different modes of enjoyment are judged to be correct in relation to the production of what Michel Feher calls "human capital." This could be defined as the "set of skills that an individual can acquire thanks to investments in his or her education or training, [which] to put it simply, [...] impact on future incomes that can be expected from schooling and other forms of training" (Feher 2009, 25). This is uncontroversial enough, though it could be useful to open it out to human/social/cultural capital. If our labor power is a commodity under capitalism then, of course, our education and training shape those commodities exchange value. But, what of enjoyment? Surely this can be set aside. No? In the world Boltanski and Chiapello describe, in which the managers of capital are trained to consider their employees as creative individuals in rhizomatic networks (Boltanski and Chiapello 2018, 70), contextually correct enjoyment becomes human/social/cultural capital. This is always contextual to certain careers, however. A nurse in the UK in 2013 does not have to conceal his enjoyment of Mumford and Sons from his colleagues, with the exception of certain snobs, whereas a writer for *Vice* magazine is only capable of publicly admitting her enjoyment of the band ironically or to produce some kind of mildly controversial clickbait. Another example would be an academic with an enjoyment of pop, who must situate the expression of this enjoyment in an argument about the nature of desire and political economy. But conversely, a nurse who listens exclusively to experimental noise music may alienate her colleagues in the same way a *Vice* writer might inspire awe in the pseuds they work with by listening to the very same Puce Mary record. In all of this, we are trying to scale the aperture of how we are understood to desire and thus to imagine the world as other-than-it-is. Our tastes and commitments to certain aesthetic practices are something that can be modulated by our position in the market. And we see this most clearly in those with personal investments closest to capital.

In Bret Easton Ellis' novel *American Psycho* (2006), we find critical commentaries on the merits and demerits of diegetically contemporary (of the late 1980s) popular music from the perspective of the psychotic Wall Street yuppie, Patrick Bateman. Bateman applies a discerning ear and extensive knowledge of branding and media manipulation to artists like Whitney Houston, U2, and Huey Lewis and the News. He remarks on how he never really understood the popular rock band Genesis when they were led by Peter Gabriel, but with Phil Collins taking more of a central role, they made much more sense as "complex studies of loss became, instead, smashing first-rate pop songs that I gratefully embraced" (Ellis 2006, 128). Music is, for Bateman, a commodity in which he can invest or not depending on how it will affect the growth of his human/social/cultural capital. If at one point we could say, with confidence, that the use-value of popular music was to facilitate the imagination of the world as other-than-it-is, then the oddly reductive notion of individuality—as it functions in the "rhizomatic" network management we find in the new spirit of capitalism—has flattened this further. Now this music is a way to signal to others how you imagine the right things. In a world without economic coercion, we could maybe say this was only a way to build communities, but in ours this cultivation of taste is a mechanism through which to align yourself with those who can sanction the reproduction of your life. One must express, with no obligation to actually have, the "correct" opinions on popular music (as well as on political and social issues). For Bateman, and perhaps most of us, this is essential to maintaining social and professional life. We are not all psychos, but psychopaths like Bateman can perhaps help us to see what is actually at stake in the enjoyment we express. The outcome is the same. Murder and destruction abound a little further away from us than they do for Bateman. He just knows why he acts like this.

Interlude: Mumford and Sons (for Patrick Bateman and Huey Lewis)

Have you ever heard of Mumford and Sons? The band burst onto the UK music scene in 2009 with their hit debut full-length LP *Sigh No More* (Island, Glassnote) rocketing up to #2 in the UK charts with even greater success overseas, including a #1 position on the US Billboard. However, they really didn't come into their own, artistically or commercially, until their 2015 record, *Wilder Mind* (Gentlemen of the Road, Island, Glassnote).

Their early work was a little too folksy for my taste. The band seemed a bit too willing to cash in on the kind of nostalgia that is the stock-in-trade of the UK entertainment industry. This is especially noticeable on songs like "Little Lion Man," which strain to affect the feel of a well-known song from a country fair with a conspicuous over-use of archaic phrases like "my dear." Or indeed a song like "Winter Wind," where the close mix of brass and vocal sounded like little more than a direct rip-off of the Arizona band, Beirut, who themselves have moved to a more mainstream sound on recent records. This may have been a good tactic for making a splash, which is, of course, a necessary first step in the entertainment industry, but it could risk future earning potential by defining one's brand too narrowly. Still, on a song like "The Cave," with its deceptively simple lyrics that provide just the right amount of depth and sing-a-long choruses that make perfect use of the so-called "millennial whoop," you got the sense that they wanted to transcend this gimmick.

I was somewhat disappointed with their sophomore effort, 2012's *Babel* (Island, Glassnote, Gentlemen of the Road), as it still clung on to so much of that nostalgic iconography. Songs like the title track, "Babel," leaned hard on that same kind of folksy instrumentation and arrangements that were more proper to a standard in the public domain than an original multi-purpose piece of intellectual property. And the latter is really what the industry is demanding today. It didn't seem to hurt them commercially, though, but it did make their concerts feel a little too close to a novelty act to really get into. That said, landing an A-list actor like Idris Elba for the video for "Lover of the Light" was a great move for illustrating the potential applications of their sound. Indeed, the song itself is less dependent on its folk production than much of their previous work. And, were they to edit out an archaic word here and there such as "sanguine," they were getting closer to a place where they would no longer need the genre crutch.

There are no such missteps on the band's third album and masterpiece, *Wilder Mind*. With songs like "I Believe" and "The Wolf," the band have mastered the combination of setting a subtle gloss against a lyric left wide open to interpretation, sung by a fragile voice that is just crying out for synchronization with a climactic moment from one of the prestige shows that comprise our present renaissance of television drama. It is not so much that every song has the potential to be a huge hit, as today, in many ways, such a style of composition can actually place limitations on the available avenues for revenue.

The real stroke of genius, though, has been the marketing. Having done so many of the cute folksy videos, it was going to be tricky to suddenly switch gears on the audience. So, rather than releasing a traditional music video, they synched their new songs to fairly generic, but nonetheless compelling, kaleidoscopic night-time dashboard camera footage. These pieces of content were like hitting the reset button on the band's image and really opened them up for fans like me to appreciate them. But, more importantly, it opened the band up for other media engagements. The album's cover, an empty bench overlooking an illuminated cityscape, like the non-videos, declares to the producers of the world "fill our songs with your content." What to say to *Wilder Mind* dissenters in the long run? Even on traditional metrics, in this day and age, over a million records sold and climbing is something not many can top.

***

Is this not a way to say that, at least on this, Adorno's TCT had it right? It seems like music in the commodity form can't escape the fetish, a situation in which "the consumer is really worshipping the money that he himself has paid for the ticket to the Toscanini concert" (Adorno 1991, 37–38). If only this were still the case. There is ever less thrill to be had in worshipping our own cultural consumptive power; a Spotify membership and internet connection are too cheap, while the costs of education and living increases. The thrill needs to be understood more granularly as part of a larger project of human/social/cultural capital accumulation. There is simply not enough left in the single consumptive act to be a demonstration of power in itself as what was once considered attainable floats ever further out of view. As the dream of attaining a bourgeois lifestyle and its associated security becomes more difficult to grasp, we are willing to give up more of ourselves in our attempts to do so. Where before we may have sought the protection of capitalist power structures out of entrapment or desperation, by willingly shaping every grain of our identities to earn its protection, we end up closing the gap between ourselves, the system of capitalist exploitation, and the actions it carries out.

Perhaps this is still Marcuse's notion of repressive desublimation, but now it seems to be moving past what is left of what can meaningfully be called ideology to the parts of us we mistake for being innate. The common reluctance of many to interrogate why we like the music we like is an attempt to protect something of ourselves from the troubling and corrupting discourses that structure so much of our lives. But given the increasing fragility of our positions in the world deterritorializing techno-capital, we will hand this space over too to the algorithms and thus increase the demand for coltan. There is still no affirmative hatred here and yet, somehow, cruelty persists. Deleuze and Guattari can help us understand why this is by flipping the formulation we get in *Civilization and Its Discontents*. Culture, and in particular culture as constituted by capitalism, is not what keeps the cruelty of the impulse to violence at bay, it is what constructs it.

> Cruelty has nothing to do with some ill-defined or natural violence that might be commissioned to explain the history of mankind; cruelty is the movement of culture that is realized in bodies and inscribed on them, belaboring them. That is what cruelty means. This culture is not the movement of ideology: on the contrary, it forcibly injected production into desire, and conversely, it forcibly inserts desire into social production and reproduction ... (Deleuze and Guattari 2013a, 169)

There is something unbelievably tragic about this. The systems we have built to keep us safe, systems that precede capitalism but which capitalism has optimized, have also made our lives cruel; have left us feeling so precarious in our position. Whether we too could become the targets of this cruelty is an open question. Thus we feel we cannot imagine an outside to this arrangement. So we hand over every last ounce of inarticulable enjoyment to buy a little more time inside.

Anhedonia and Hip Ennui

Ultimately, in *American Psycho*, the barbarous acts apparently carried out by Bateman leave him unfulfilled. Perhaps because he did not carry them out at all, or perhaps because, in a world in which cruelty is carried out on the scale of global capital as a matter of course, the transgressions of those most closely identified with capital are without significance. While, for a time, he seemed to revel in defying the social order through his abstract in-depth knowledge of its codes, he is, by the end of the novel, bereft. They had not been transgressions at all. "THIS IS NOT AN EXIT" (Ellis 2006, 384). Bateman can be read as something of a social composite. "There is an idea of a Patrick Bateman, some kind of abstraction [...] only an entity" (362). A site at which we can recognize a combination of the barbarism inherent in global capitalism and its representation in mainstream media and political discourse; he is a veneer of bourgeois societal values, which conceal the horrors inherent to the means of production through ubiquitous consumption.

In this act of consumption, we see the motion that Deleuze and Guattari spoke of above: the forcible injection of production—capitalist production with its attendant logics and imperatives—into desire. While violence predates this process, cruelty is a concept intimately tied up with systems of signification, of meaning-making. Cruelty is violence that produces enjoyment. And however indirect, however fleeting, however disavowed this enjoyment may be, it comes from the enaction of the imperatives of dominant power structures. When Bateman believes he has murdered sex workers and his business rivals, he may be violating the laws that govern the explicitly stated values of the world around him, but the enjoyment of this transgression is facilitated by his proximity to the actual hegemony. From the perspective of capital, all Bateman has done is use a commodity he has purchased and eliminated some competition. His cruel enjoyment was in becoming the deterritorializing power of capital. The same force allows us to sanction the murder of children in the DRC if it helps us with our ease of access to some the beguiling songs from St. Vincent's third album. Nothing has been transgressed. Complicity is an unavoidable part of being in the community of pop, listener or producer. And stepping outside this to a sufficient degree to no longer be complicit is to be placed in a position of social death. The rejection of the dominant value system, even in matters of aesthetics and enjoyment, is something that carries risks. Risks that many are not in a position to take. The music professor can affirm their opinion of listening only to the music of the avant-garde on reclaimed vinyl, and while this is certainly a myopic attempt to exit capitalism, in attempting this exit their position protects them from many of the negative consequences of exiting the community of pop. But when you depend on a network of friendships and associations to reproduce your life, the social cost for disagreeing, even in matters of taste, goes up.

This inexorability of enjoyment through violence that is ultimately sanctioned is upsetting to the calculating Bateman, who believed he was outside of our petty morality. For those of us who are considered not to be psychopaths, it is even more unpleasant and it's here that we start to suffer. The psychoanalysts said that this was born of our destructive cruel nature coming into conflict with the rules that keep society safe and ordered. This is an idea that reads a lot like an attempt to produce a scientific theory of sin, and so has been largely accepted as palatable in the West. The neuroses that resulted from this arrangement are the price we pay for controlling the beast within.

What Deleuze and Guattari and Marcuse argue is that, while we may be creatures with the capacity for violence, it is the systems themselves that morph this capacity into cruelty. Systems that effectively define right violence, like that which reproduces the valorization of capital, and wrong violence, like that which inhibits it. All the while, this sits uneasily against the notions of social justice that stem from the discourses of democracy present in so many places around the world. But this system is of another level. A more superficial level that defers to the principle of valorization. We find a route through this conflict in the restriction of subjectivity to the norm—the midpoint identity from which all others are deviations—of the bourgeois individual (man). This is an incompletable subject riddled with neuroses and petty cruelties, but one that is at once able to affirm the kinds of discursive piety that is required for social acceptance under the most profitable form of social organization that has existed so far, liberal capitalism. A subject that is a yawning hunger, a lack that must, at any lengths, be filled, but cannot be. This is what is needed for contemporary cruelty. Deleuze and Guattari call this the Oedipal subject and point to how social organization down to the level of the family works to install it (Deleuze & Guattari 2013a, 123). But it also sounds a lot like Patrick Bateman.

All this is pretty heavy. To engage in socially prescribed methods of the validation of human capital, to pursue surplus value in a competitive environment—that is at the same time inflicting suffering upon millions—just to feel like you can survive is depressing. Especially because whatever rewards you can find are fleeting and many don't work at all. This is the abyss into which Ellis leaves us staring at the end of the novel and which he is reluctant to actually occupy or examine without the armor of psychopathy. This is the space that Wallace sketches out so well: the misery and suffering and impotence of inexorable complicity. The claim made in *Infinite Jest* is that a great deal of the entertainment, which constructs most of the cultural landscape of the United States, is structured by a profound anhedonia: a state in which pleasure is unattainable from actions or thoughts that would normally induce it. For Wallace, this is a defining characteristic of life at the end of history, in which liberal capitalism has won. The central character of the novel, Hal, reflects, through the narrator, on the tendency of his tennis academy peer group to identify anhedonia in others, but not in themselves, which is itself tied up in cultural production

> It's of some interest that the lively arts of the millennial U.S.A. treat anhedonia and internal emptiness as hip and cool. It's maybe the vestiges of the Romantic glorification of *Weltschmerz*, which means world-weariness or hip ennui. [...] Forget so-called peer-pressure. It's more like *peer-hunger*. No? We enter a spiritual puberty where we snap to the fact that the great transcendent horror is loneliness, excluded engagement in the self. Once we've hit this age, we will now give or take anything, wear any mask, to fit, be part-of, not be Alone, we young. The U.S. arts are our guide to inclusion. A how-to. We are shown how to fashion masks of ennui and jaded irony at a young age where the face is fictile enough to assume the shape of whatever it wears. And then it's stuck there, the weary cynicism that saves us from gooey sentiment and unsophisticated naiveté. Sentiment equals naiveté on this continent. (Wallace 2007, 694)

There is a self-defeating double motion to anhedonia. On the one hand, it affects a stance of detachment that allows one to pose in the knowing-how-the-world-works position from which cruelty can be inflicted with impunity. In so doing, one can attain the various pleasures associated with being accepted as a right-thinking member of society. On the other hand, this eventually ceases to be an affected stance but actually becomes a part of who we are, making the acceptance we seek meaningless because, as a tenet of the knowing-how-the-world-works posture, it cannot be trusted. From this position, all this acceptance is contingent upon what others hope to gain for themselves by accepting you. This makes the whole enterprise an exercise in spinning plates, causing any pleasure to be forever deferred by the consideration of the next strategic move. The connection is always secondary to whatever it offers the individual parties. What Ellis satirizes with the dead-end label of psychopathy, Wallace dissects as perpetual anhedonia.

There is a convergence here with Deleuze and Guattari's notion of the Oedipal subject. Wallace's bête noire in most of his fiction is the solipsism that he sees a pervasive part of life under neoliberal capitalism (Smith 2009, 269), a system that encourages and requires the conceptualization of people as discrete subjects and indivisible individuals. Deleuze and Guattari's critique of the entanglement of psychoanalysis and liberal capitalism in *Anti-Oedipus* also focuses in on this enforced limitation of experience. This creates conditions in which "the little ego of each person, related to its father-mother, is truly the center of the world" (Deleuze & Guattari 2013a, 304). This is a trap we should be desperate to escape. In the novel, Wallace wonders if that desire is possible by moving this criticism from the foundational texts of TCT to the cultural productions of even later capitalism.

Most of the characters in *Infinite Jest*, indeed the society depicted in general, are suffering from various intensities of anhedonia. This makes the McGuffin of the ostensible plot—a film so intensely pleasurable to watch it casts all its viewers into an inescapable state of catatonic bliss resulting in death—gloriously multifaceted. Rational self-interest—the vapid ideological statement of capitalist morality—says one must act to survive and pursue pleasure. But what if survival is only possible if pleasure is no longer possible? The film in the novel poses the question: Should survival be abandoned in favor of the possibility of pleasure? But below this heady ethicopolitical debate, Oedipus lurks. The eponymous film cartridge was produced by Hal's late father with the intention of freeing Hal from a persistent anhedonia from which he had been suffering since a childhood accident (Swartz 2009). Wallace scholar Marshall Boswell claims this has something to do with a critique of Lacan's notion of the mirror stage of child development (Boswell 2005, 129). To avoid too much exposition, this basically refers to how Hal's lexical prowess functions as a totem in the narrative for his being utterly engulfed by the symbolic order of the status quo (Wallace 2007, 12), which prevents any kind of interaction other than exchange, precluding both regular old vanilla pleasure and the pleasures of cruelty from being experienced. This is the site of precarity for capitalist realism to which the film points. A tantalizing promise of a pleasurable sensation that is other from the world that would also remove you from it. Once again the similarities between the promise of capitalism and its counter in TCT are made clear. Both promise to provide the missing piece to undo the damage, which, in the case of capitalism, it itself has wrought.

But this is all of a fiction. *Infinite Jest* the movie does not exist in our world. So, what of our world of actual, existing, capitalist realism? A world filled with X-Factor clones that limp on forever and superhero movies that sell tales of essentialist African monarchies as if they were tales of black liberation. Well, we are, maybe, not yet quite so numb as Hal in the tennis academy. Perhaps our present is, at least, not one of universal anhedonia. Fisher said we instead live in a time of depressive hedonia;

> Many of the teenage students I encountered seemed to be in a state of what I would call depressive hedonia. Depression is usually characterized as a state of anhedonia, but the condition I'm referring to is constituted not by an inability to get pleasure so much as it is by an inability to do anything else *except* pursue pleasure. (Fisher 2009, 22)

The misery of trudging through the world after the semiotic apocalypse that is the end of history that we see in Wallace's novel is only in the process of becoming our reality. Instead, we, complicit as we are, are in a frantic state pursuing constant distraction. The human capital of pleasure-seeking, and how it helps us along by investing in ourselves as sites of value production, can't be passed over. Music festivals, a site at one time, at least, of some kind of naive revolutionary dream if not potential, have now grown into grotesques of middle-class consumption; temporary tent cities that, today, seem like tasteless parodies of refugee camps. Production is constantly inserted into even the desire for freedom. The struggle is fake and cruelly enjoyed.

But is this not an updated version of the TCT rant? A vacuous indictment of pleasures that many in the academy have little contact with or knowledge of? Yes and no. Pleasure, as Bataille, and Deleuze and Guattari, and Lyotard, and Gilbert and Pearson write, has been written off for too long. But to say it should no longer be automatically suspect is not to say it is above suspicion. When the casual enjoyments that permeate our lives, that shimmer through intimate moments and public spaces, are built atop a cruelty in which we partake, suspicion is warranted. The key difference, between this argument around the anhedonic and depressive hedonia vs. the indictment of pleasure found in TCT, is that TCT rooted its objection to pleasure-seeking in the lowly status it afforded pleasure in comparison to revolution. For this analysis, the rapidly desensitizing effect of depressive hedonia becoming anhedonia is a cause for concern, in that it is not pleasure for its own sake. It is not pleasure for its enjoyment but pleasure so as be protected from what being without pleasure may let in. The pain of knowing that you are cruel and complicit. A pain that, if you're not a psychopath, gets you running to mask it with pleasures. Depressive hedonia is accelerated through ever-more cultural productions, injected into desire, until we become numb. And with numbness, there is the specter of anhedonia. The concepts begin to blur. Pleasure is defined by a feeling of satisfaction but capitalism abhors satisfaction. Is pleasure injected with this mode of production just the promise of future consumption? Can there be hedonia under capitalism if satisfaction is always deferred? Or is the best we can hope from our earbuds some kind of anesthetic?

In all this, pop rests upon particular strata. A way to delimit the concerns of geopolitics in a space of distinct separation from career anxiety. To let you know what should be experienced as a burden. To define what is sorrow and what is not. "Nothing compares to you" (O'Connor, 1990). It organizes what is to be meaningful, what is to be enjoyed and what can be effectively ignored. "Do they know it's Christmas time at all?" (Band Aid 1984) The sonic shimmer of pop is but one instrument of many that provide this form of affective organization. Some inspire awe, while others gently frustrate. Pop provides a continuous cloud of "novocaine for the soul" (Eels 2011). A feeling of deliverance, of resolution, of catharsis as an anesthetic.

O

Vignette: On "Bored in the USA" on Letterman on YouTube (Now Removed)

This video of Father John Misty, performing "Bored in the USA" (2015) on *The Late Show* with David Letterman was uploaded onto YouTube in November of 2014.[7] By the happenstance of the recommendation algorithm, I saw it in the early spring 2015. So, my viewing (along with I would guess about half of the nearly 470,000 other viewers) took place once the initial promotional ruckus had subsided. However, since I first wrote this paragraph, the official video has been removed from YouTube though copies and mirrors abound.

There is an idea of a Father John Misty, a Josh Tillman, a musician/artist/beard enthusiast/social commentator, but on YouTube this is some kind of abstraction. An abstraction brought to the fore in the particular mechanics of this performance. Because this piece of media, this little cut-up snippet of TV—thrown up online and used to promote a format that is becoming anachronistic—drags the expression, the aesthetics, the commentary on society, politics, and ennui that inhere in the song and its performance, into an ever-more dense tangle of images and representations; into ways and practices of sharing ideas and affects that simultaneously also produce distance.

This song is from Father John Misty's album *I Love You, Honeybear* (2015) and performs an overtly satirical function, largely due to its lyrical content. For example, the chorus:

> I'm just a little bored in the USA, Oh just a little bored in the USA,
> Save me white Jesus, Bored in the USA. (Misty 2015)

This is the hipster appropriation of Bruce Springsteen's working-class authenticity in his, willfully misunderstood, "Born in the USA," a song ostensibly about the post-Vietnam War disaffection with the American dream, so drenched in the irony of its upbeat arrangement that this absurdist tension goes largely unnoticed even by fans. With the opening lines of Tillman's song, he occupies a similar space to Springsteen. These lines fit with a totally sincere ballad lamenting a sense of possibility now lost. But the third line of this refrain makes clear that he is here to play. His direct delivery of "Save me white Jesus" is the audio equivalent of speaking directly to the camera in a realist drama. He wants his intentions to not be missed or misunderstood. He desires the pseudo-agitation, for conservative media commentators to pour scorn upon him. He wishes for their ire to come in his direction. But this will not draw their gaze.

There is also some pretty interesting stuff running throughout the song about marriage, chrono-normative relationship imperatives, and consumerism; staples of contemporary stand-up really. This is not, however, ostensibly a comedy song. It does teeter on the edge of becoming one, particularly with the line "Can I get my money back," as the song builds to the chorus, and the vowel sound of "back" extends into stratospheric ornamentation with ascending strings that lifts this banal sentiment like angels might in a 1940s Disney cartoon. And we are to believe that, lo and behold, the vacuous nature of the late capitalist notion of the "consumer as king" has been firmly skewered. Though, like the cultural vapor that these notions are, the notions of late capitalism are pretty much immune to skewers. It's just sort of like waving your skewer above a boiling kettle; you'll move the steam around, but it's still basically steam. As Deleuze and Guattari wrote in 1972, "[c]apitalism is profoundly illiterate" (2013a, 276), and I think this extends to the subtext produced through the ironic juxtaposition of form and content. But then, perhaps it's just that musical comedy is not to everyone's taste.

Often satire serves as a cathartic release for those who have already been, discursively, converted. A way by which they can confirm their own beliefs in the company of a like-minded virtual community and simultaneously ridicule their opponents, building a kind of problematic solidarity. Adorno claimed that catharsis was a mechanism used by the culture industry in the reproduction of capitalism. The "substitute satisfaction" of catharsis, Adorno argues, satiates the public's desire to struggle for change (2012, 324). And, for sure, you can certainly get that out of this song, especially from lines like "Save me President Jesus." Easy lines like this seem designed to flatter the knowing self-perception of certain segments of the "American left." If this is entirely the case, if satire only serves to relieve the experience of suffering but does nothing to dismantle its causes, then it must be an extraordinarily conservative pursuit. Yet, in the experience of such satire, the feeling that this cannot be true persists. This is especially the case as we notice that irony and cynicism no longer make sense in direct opposition to sincerity. The irony and cynicism, common to satire, would seem today to allow for the expression of sincerity in the particular conditions of our age. This can, perhaps, be constructive.

Tillman, with his hip beard, retro tight-fitting clothing, playing music that is sonically influenced by nostalgic Americana, is laden with the baggage of the painfully earnest. This could lead an ungenerous listener to dismiss the song as millennial whining, but in *The Late Show* performance, this assessment is gradually undercut. After the first verse, during which Tillman appears to be playing the piano, he turns away from the keyboard and reveals the piano is playing by itself. And so, we get some points for recognizing the artifice of the media event: the artificiality of whatever Letterman, and being on Letterman, represented. However, Tillman turns this gaze around once we reach the chorus. For here, Tillman laments his boredom, sat atop the piano like a lounge singer, before rising to his knees asking for salvation from "White Jesus," who's look Tillman seems to be emulating. He has now become the target of his ridicule. The satirical elements of the song are no longer directed solely at Tillman's ideological opponents but, beyond the textual self-loathing of the second verse, he starts to attack his own delivery of the message and the medium by which he is presenting it: the TV performance of the earnest social-commentary ballad.

This becomes even more complex as the performance moves to the bridge.

They gave me a useless education,
And a subprime loan, On a craftsman home, (Misty 2015)

In this section of the song's recorded version, canned laughter is mixed in, increasing in intensity with each line before becoming rapturous laughter and applause as the chorus returns; "Bored in the USA." This section becomes a set of one-liners from a hack comic. A comic for whom Tillman's very sincerity has become the punchline. This allows us to see how the power of these images can be instantly snuffed out by the mediated laughter of an audience with a ravenous desire for cathartic release. We hear clearly now the subsumption Adorno warned of would take place. In other live performances this laughter track is missing, but on *The Late Show*, it's right there. Regardless of whatever Tillman's original intention for the laughter (perhaps to get-there-first for cynical or ironic defense), this performance with recorded laughter allows us to witness the act of defanging a content-based critique. This laughter is not that of the studio audience; they can be heard separately at the end. This is the laughter of a virtual audience being played to the actual audience.

Since his first book in English, written in the late 80s, Slavoj Žižek has been rehearsing the argument that canned laughter helps to fulfill the duty of the cultural consumer to laugh at and enjoy the products of late capitalist entertainment (2008, 33); even if they are too exhausted to open their mouths or don't find them funny. Try watching *Friends* with the volume on low, so you can't hear the dialogue, just the laugh track. It is so much louder than anything said by the cast. The laughter is almost rhythmic. It's like it fits to a beat metric rather than the more organic subtleties of an actor's performance. It sounds more like the regulated subdivisions of a twenty-minute evening ritual than a depiction of friendships in the 90s. On "Bored in the USA," however, the laughter is literally rhythmic, drawing attention to the qualities of its artifice, the consumer's duty, and its supplemental function. This gets more interesting on YouTube. In this discrete form, this artifact itself contains both the canned laughter played to the studio audience and the applause and cheers of that studio audience. For us, the YouTube viewers, the audience we hear is the artifact. When we watch a clip of *The Late Show*, especially the one posted officially by *The Late Show*, we aren't watching *The Late Show*. We are watching a taster intended to promote the idea that it would be great to watch *The Late Show*. Listen to that audience: they're having such a great time. But then, we watch Father John Misty play a mimetic form of the audience's own laughter to them. We are the audience of that mediatized satirical loop. An iteration of media that contains a representation of its own mediation.

This is what makes me think that, in the instance of *The Late Show* performance, Tillman has done more than just cover his appearance of naivety and sincerity with knowing cynicism or irony. Rather, the potential exists in this mediation of the work for a more haunting kind of satire that can be brought to a wider audience as he beats them to their own ironic response. He is not covering up for his own desire to avow something; he is preempting our disavowal and defanging it.

This isn't going to change the world but it's interesting to see a subtle device of audience-critique that is usually left in the wilderness of the art world or art house films like *Funny Games* (Haneke 2008) on mainstream late-night TV. What we can see through this extra medial layer, as trad media institutions have now firmly arrived on the Google-owned YouTube, is perhaps the beginnings of the end of the cultural stasis supposedly ushered in by full saturation of mass media and the postmodern condition. This is not to say the internet will save us all; it is not a tool that has been designed with that purpose in mind. It is a tool designed by the military industrial complex to, among other things, defend capitalism. But it is also a tool that, in this case, allows us to see more in what media institutions produce than they perhaps intended. What we can see here, as the laughter kicks in and Tillman shrugs and sings with audible sincerity, is the opening up of a space where irony and sincerity can coexist. A space that adds complexity to a satirical expression such that it may move beyond mere cathartic functionality. But I don't know what that space beyond, fully realized, will look or sound like yet.

○

3

Catharsis

Feelin' Good

To be overcome by geopolitical guilt sucks.[1] It feels lousy. But even when you don't take in that grand scale, there are so many little, and not so little, things in the world that seem to be trying to grind you down. The rent is too high, the pay is too low, you have no free time, relationships, romantic and otherwise, are hard, and you can start to wonder who you even are in this, all too confusing, complex world. Now, on top of this, you need a new phone or you can't do your underpaid job properly, and also to prevent a kind of social exclusion that can occur when one can't be reached at every moment of the day; a purchase that will apparently implicate you in the murder of children. These problems seem to garner exactly no sympathy and, from a technical point of view, nor should they. These are the problems of people in a part of the world that has long been comfortable using civil wars, subversions of the democracies of others, hard and soft oppression, and indirect and direct violence to build up the so-called new economy of the digital age. Beyond this though, these are actually the problems more proper to a subset of these people. A group whose privileges—were its consumptive habits to be extended beyond its tiny enclave to the rest of the population—would see the world in ecological ruin within a year. But still, despite the validity of these points, there is something insufficient about the high-handed morality of this account. Carving out certain exceptions for the traumatic and horrific, suffering can be relative. And even when the experience of suffering lacks absolute justification, merely pointing this out is an approach that seems more concerned with winning on points than working through our present predicaments. One such predicament is the way the pop music created under these horrendous exploitative social relations of production has become a salve to heal us as we live within them. To purify us of the negative affects of moving through the world of capitalist realism. To provide catharsis.

We have long been fascinated by the connection between the sonic shimmer of music and our responses to it. And this fascination has not been limited to any particular discipline. Of course, when musicologists started to look up from their sheet music, it fascinated them (Frith 1981), so too for sociologists (DeNora 2000), psychologists (Juslin & Sloboda 2001), and media (Hesmondhalgh 2013) and cultural (Gilbert 2004) theorists. As noted by Tia DeNora, most of the literature on how music makes us feel, from Aristotle on, has been devoted to speculation on "what music may produce which emotion" (DeNora 2003, 84). A reasonable enough place to start, perhaps. The fact that music is seemingly able to *do* something, and that this something is hard to pin down, is an enduring mystery and likely the reason it has maintained and expanded its place and power over millennia in our ever-changing media environment. The odd thing, though, is that while this capacity for mysterious but strong emotional effects has been a foundational part of the answer to the question of *why talk about music*, there are some, like DeNora, who lament the fact that this capacity has not been explored more through empirical methods. There are some pretty straightforward answers for why this is the case. Music and emotions are too nebulous as terms to allow for properly controlled experimental conditions. And if you could narrow the approach down, the kind of data that would come from it would be either too general or too specific to tell you anything beyond the most banal of observations. For example, one might discover something like: *Many parts of the brain light up. It seems to have something to do with memory. Reactions are especially strong if the stimuli is a piece the subject is familiar with, particularly if it is from their youth. When they listened to music they didn't like the data shows the reaction was negative.* This kind of thing seems to be an exercise in justifying the existence of the humanities to those who both lack the imaginative capacity to ever come to grips with what these fields have to offer and have control over the sources of research funding. That being said, if one still wishes to see some numbers relating to the emotional responses to music, it would be worth following Timothy Taylor's approach and looking to the advertising industry (2012). Away from the glacial turns of the academy it appears, from Taylor's work, that an acute understanding of the mechanics of this particular capacity of music can be a particularly marketable skill. While profit margins may not be perfect measures, they are nonetheless significant.

But this is not really what this chapter is about. It's not the direction that this book has taken so far at all. No, rather than focusing on what music makes you feel and producing underpaid market research, it is more important, here, to consider how it can *stop* you from feeling. Which is to focus less on what your attention is being drawn to, and more on what it is being drawn from. Your personal problems, your geopolitical guilt, the feeling that even your problems are invalid, that you are "good for nothing" (Fisher 2018, 747). And in being drawn away from these feelings, your attention is also being drawn away from their origin. So, rather than following some kind of associative chain from musical stimuli to an emotional/aesthetic response, which is of course also at play, we need to listen out for what we are running away from as we turn to pop music for the anesthetic that allows us to wear the armor of hip ennui.

This idea might not seem totally new. Indeed, we can find partial articulations of it in TCT. As DeNora writes on the capacity of music to allow one to forget suffering:

> ... [I]t would seem to be part of the natural attitude (or, in Adorno's sense, the 'ontological ideology') to 'forget', paraphrasing Marx, that we are oppressed by the things we have helped to produce. This 'forgetting' is the cognitive practice of reification. (DeNora 2000, 40)

This gets at part of what is at stake. There is a pretty useful materialist conception at play in the notion of the use of cultural production as a way to forget suffering, which is, in turn, the cognitive practice of reification. This is the thing-ification of the self or, at the very least, its cognitive components that function, through affective and emotional care via commodities, to help maintain the worker as a thing of capital. But this needs some extra buttressing to deal with affective and emotional strain inherent in this mode of self-management that exceeds these commodities. If we are looking for a frame for this onto-ideology and a subject's relationship to it, capitalist realism would seem to be the perfect descriptor for the arrangement of this concept as it pertains to the contemporary consumption of cultural production. And in the formation of capitalist realism as onto-ideology, we could conceptualize the experience of this reification as a kind of purification, an unburdening, a process of catharsis. And it's with this troublesome and unstable concept of catharsis that we should understand what pop offers us in our compromise and our complicity.

Catharsis may seem an overly grand way to talk about the banality of much of pop. As texts, many songs are just affirmative declarations of good times to come through excessive consumption that never provide much in the way of consideration as to why this impulse towards self-obliteration is so strong. Beyond this we often find denouncements from singers directed at those who have done them wrong with little attention paid to nuances of relationship dynamics. This is the form. But it is not artistic grandiosity or subtlety that most readily lends itself to the capitalist production of materials for the management of affect. When we look at the practices of deployment in which we find these texts, there seems to be no better way to describe the shutting out of the world with earbuds on a crowded commuter train, the pouring of affirmative affect into your consciousness, than catharsis.

There are risks, however, with this formulation. It may seem perilously close to the condescending detached tone found in TCT; condemning the ways in which the masses are taken in by the productions of the culture industry and proletarianizing themselves in the pursuit of a little enjoyment. It seems to leave no space for spontaneity or the possibility that someone's particular engagement with even materials produced under exploitative conditions may itself not be mere exploitation. This is the criticism we find in the pop musicologist of the new left and it should be taken seriously. Frith's criticism of how the Marxists of TCT painted us all into a corner through our enjoyment is that this formulation seems more concerned with an elitist notion of how music ought to be engaged with while it neglects to think of the practical, personal, and communal ways in which such engagements are actually played out. On the ever poorly defined subject of rock music, Frith writes:

> ... rock is a source of vigour and exhilaration and of the good feelings that are necessary for the next morning's political struggle as for the next day's work. (Frith 1981 264)

But the question that goes unanswered in this rebuttal is, has rock produced these good feelings, or has it just pushed away the bad feelings? The answer is, of course, both. TCT practitioners such as Adorno miss that there is some potential in enjoyment because there can be a dis-alienation that instills a feeling of possibility in the person doing the enjoying, regardless of the conditions in which the object was produced. This needs to be recognized. But the new left musicology critique of TCT is too quick to discount the problems at play in this kind of affective management and how it connects to the material and ideological conditions in which it is performed. A feeling of possibility may indeed be produced in the "vigor and exhilaration" of rock music, but if our sense of the possible has been hemmed in by capitalist realism, then the horizon of the "next morning's political struggle" remains an impossibility. All that has happened is that we are made to feel less bad, while the conditions that produced bad feeling remain in place.

So maybe we could say that catharsis is different from what we have looked at so far. The vice or virtue of attention and complicity are contained not in the concepts themselves but in the objects to which they relate. One could attend to the actions that are complicit in the glorious enactment of the overthrow of capitalism, for example. Or one could attend to their complicity with the exploitation of Congolese mineral resources for the purposes of profit. Catharsis, though, always has something tricky about it. Catharsis does something but this something is extra to the circumstances it is directed toward. It seems as though it has made you feel better but has done nothing to actually address what made you feel worse. At best, one could say it has helped you to reinterpret what has gone on before and this can be more or less useful. But in terms of fundamentally changing circumstances, it does nothing. Worse still, if we go back to what this term actually refers to, we find purification and purgation, and there are few words more ideologically loaded than these.

When Aristotle discussed the term in his *Poetics*, this was the explicit goal of tragic drama "with incidents arousing pity and fear, were to accomplish its catharsis of such emotions" (Aristotle 1984, 2320), and, in *Rhetorics*, this notion is extended to the purposes of comedy and music. We see this idea that one should be unburdened by negative or disruptive emotion again as Dr. Freud attempted to devise what would become psychoanalytic therapy (Freud 1989, 254) or the "talking cure" (Breuer & Freud 1957: 30) as it was colloquially called. The intention here was that if patients were to describe past traumatic events, then they could relive them in different circumstances, come to a new understanding of the trauma, attain closure, and move past it. And from the analyst's couch, this term has migrated and mutated into common parlance; which is to say, it has become ideological. The stated intention of undergoing cathartic experiences is to attain some kind of resolution. Some way to compartmentalize the burden of a negative experience or situation so as to be able to move on from it and leave it behind. Aesthetic experiences such as therapy, tragic drama, and pop music can serve as triggers to start off and then direct a cathartic process, so that at the end, once the purgation has been completed, this new interpretation of past trauma is one of a particular nature. One in which the need for regarding it as trauma is no more and the subject is able to function normally in accordance with accepted social standards.

But the problem is nothing has actually changed. Of course, in many cases, it may be impossible to change things in a way that corrects the actual problems experienced by those seeking catharsis. If a loved one has died from cancer, for example, and in pursuit of catharsis you participate in a charity run for future research to combat the disease, this makes a great deal of sense. You cannot change the circumstances that caused your suffering so, instead, you sublimate your desire for this into an activity that may help to prevent future tragedies. The cause of your suffering has not been negated but, to carry on with life as normally as possible, you seek out an experience that can allow for the suffering to be recontextualized and understood differently. However, if the causes of suffering are not so specific and intense, if they are more diffuse and entangled in the reproduction of everyday life, then the pursuit of a cathartic release loses some of this justification. In short, if you're playing Muse's cover of "Feelin' Good" (2005) at full volume on your earbuds to drown out the subtle and crushing horror of your commute and the memories of a day being micromanaged at work, then the only thing you're getting from catharsis is the ability go in tomorrow and produce a future need for catharsis.

Hello Darkness, My Old Friend

Catharsis is for the management of the responses to harm.[2] Depending on what has taken place and any person's particularities, these responses are often disruptive, ranging from rage to melancholia, disassociation to depression. Catharsis can offer a way to draw any of these responses to something of a close and restore a degree of normalcy. Some kinds of harm and suffering are inevitable; for example, like the scene depicted in the cold open in one of the later episode of *Six Feet Under* (2009), when a jogger stops to catch his breath in a forest and is savaged and killed by a mountain lion. No amount of anti-capitalist activism on the part of his loved ones could have spared them their grief. This is what's appealing about it. When there is no possibility of the cause of your suffering being reversed, the pursuit of catharsis might be the only option open to you. The problem is when the cause of suffering could, in theory, be removed but has taken on the appearance of reality. In these circumstances, the insistence on the importance of catharsis becomes especially useful to those whose interests require the perpetuation of harm.

This is why it's useful to hold on to the TCT of Adorno. It stops us from trusting our feelings of release or resolution or enjoyment. Adorno sees a straight line from the conceptualization of catharsis proposed by Aristotle as a means of social control and its contemporary deployment:

> The purging of the affects in Aristotle's *Poetics* no longer makes equally frank admission of its devotion to ruling interests, yet it supports them all the same in that his ideal of sublimation entrusts art with the task of providing aesthetic semblance as a substitute satisfaction for the bodily satisfaction of the targeted public's instincts and needs: Catharsis is a purging action directed against the affects and an ally of repression. Aristotelian catharsis is part of a superannuated mythology of art and [is] inadequate to the actual effects of art. [...] Art, as a substitute satisfaction, by virtue of the fact that it is spurious, robs sublimation of the dignity for which the whole of classicism made propaganda, a classicism that survived for over two thousand years under the protection of Aristotle's authority. The doctrine of catharsis imputes to art the principle that ultimately the culture industry appropriates and administers. (Adorno 2012, 324)

Whatever problems I have with Adorno's super categorical definition of art when it comes to defining its universal qualities, I have no such trouble when he explores how the things that are called art are deployed by those in positions of power. Adorno, Aristotle, and the-powers-that-be are all pretty much in agreement that the kinds of things that we call art can help us to sublimate affects and emotions that could otherwise lead to destructive behavior, be it through violence or misery. Where Adorno and the others part company is over what form this sublimation should take. Adorno wants this sublimation to take the form of realizing the truth of the unfree conditions in which we live, and from there, in his wildest dreams, we might be able to envision some way in which to revolutionize these conditions. The charge he levels at the others, though, is that they want the sublimation to take the form of catharsis or a substitute satisfaction. The suffering of people under neoliberal capitalism has material causes, and the way in which to address them so as to prevent this suffering could, hypothetically, be enacted. However, those with the most power to do so would rather this not happen, and thus, either consciously or not, have taken a cue from Aristotle to construct an ideological understanding of art as something that should soothe this suffering by purifying the soul of the viewer/listener/reader and returning them to some kind of socially determined natural state, which can also be read as the most economically productive state. Catharsis as a mechanism for the refusal of the desire to change the world. Aristotle said as much himself. On the subject of music, his *Rhetorics*, as the name may suggest, reads as a wonderfully simple "how to" guide for sonic crowd control:

> The melodies that purge the passions likewise give an innocent pleasure to mankind. Such are the modes and the melodies in which those who perform

music at the theatre should be invited to compete. But since the spectators are of two kinds—the one free and educated, and the other a vulgar crowd composed of artisans, labourers, and the like—there ought to be contests and exhibitions as instituted for the relaxation of the second class also. And the music will correspond to their minds; for as their minds have [been] perverted from the natural state, so there are perverted modes and highly-strung and unnaturally coloured melodies. A man receives pleasure from what is natural to him, and therefore professional musicians may be allowed to practice this lower sort of music before an audience of a lower type. (Aristotle 1984, 2129)

The last sentence in particular reads like a classical assumption upon which political conservatism is founded. So perhaps it is not surprising that those conservatives today who appear to hold to that assumption have often dedicated their youth to the study of such classics. But conservatism is not capitalism. They have just enjoyed a period of mutual benefit by supporting each other in an uneven partnership. Reading this highly classist theory of human resources management alongside Adorno's critique and an awareness of the way in which art and music are often dismissed as just something to make you feel better, there is definitely something that needs our attention in the casual laudation of catharsis through art as a panacea. Being made to feel better is not only in your interests but also in the interests of those who don't wish to deal with you in a state of suffering and who have an interest in your functioning under conditions that produce suffering.

This is one of the best applications of the TCT approach to these kinds of issues. The kind of nebulous concepts such as art, music, emancipation, oppression, exploitation, the subject, that your contemporary post-post structuralist theorist would trouble themselves with pages and pages of intriguing but by no means definitive text exploring, can briefly be made to coalesce with TCT long enough for you to see the machinations of the system under which you suffer. It's the next move where things get tricky, because this motion on the part of TCT closes off so many avenues of possibility as it makes plain some of the problems. The same well defined and delimited conceptualization that had allowed us to define which subjects were being oppressed by which systems also placed limits on which practices could be defined as artistic and thus endowed with the capacity of providing subjects with the resources to break out of this oppression.

For Adorno, the definition of such an artwork, as mentioned in the discussion of attention, was something comprised of what can be called truth content, which exceeds the limitations of those forms available for its delivery at the historical moment in which it was produced. It is a dialectic. The formations of artistic productions are intimately tied to the power structures that define social reality, which are, in turn, geared toward the production of certain content as commodities. Content that can entirely be conveyed by such forms functions as the system intends and therefore cannot truly be considered art. Whereas, if the content strains against the forms that social reality has provided for it, then it is expressing something beyond this formation of power relations and has thus some kind of emancipatory potential within it. A song that seems to be saying so much more than a song can normally be said to say, could change your life. One of the ways in which Adorno claimed one could become aware that they were in the presence of such an artwork was the experience of what he called the shudder (Adorno 2013, 116–117); that ineffable but decidedly actual sensation when the aesthetic experience of something seems to push beyond the ostensible definition of what is taking place before you. But in the proliferation of aesthetic experiences that were being facilitated at the time of his writing by the culture industry, Adorno worried that even his prized shudder was becoming reified and thus akin to mere pleasure.

This is a big problem for TCT. Its conceptual categories allow it to construct and reason for incredibly compelling and theoretically sound claims. But as it engages in this process, it fails to consider its own position as being a part of the system it critiques. Adorno's shudder is better than the mere pleasure of others. Put another way, Adorno's denouncements of jazz, the pop of his day, are reminiscent of the moment in the movie *Manhattan* (2012) [1979], in which the protagonist meets a woman at a party who tells him that she had finally had an orgasm for the first time in her life, only for her therapist to tell her it was the wrong kind. His particular dislike for certain forms of enjoyment, on the one hand, allows him to discern certain things that may not be obvious to those in the throes of enjoyment, but this does not give him license to claim it is just some oppressive trick and not actual enjoyment.

In short, the conservative impulse to denounce pleasure has no place in an analysis of pop under capitalism as a tool of oppressive catharsis. For one, it just perpetuates the same motion of lack production that capitalism feeds off. Also, what is pop without enjoyment? Should such a thing be practiced at all? Why is it that pleasure must always be suspect while some state of post-cathartic purity is to be praised? And to whom is all of this happening? To examine this we need to view this very internal process at a more granular scale, with more attention paid to the permeation of power within the person.

Frontier Psychiatrist

Catharsis isn't just some kind of old-fashioned method of oppressive governance, it's also something that gets in your head.[3] Of course, there is not really a great deal of daylight between these two positions, particularly if we consider it in relation to mental health. Or, to put it another way, both Adorno and Freud read Aristotle but the latter didn't see much wrong with the old-fashioned Greek notion of cathartically purging the passions to promote civilizational stability. But despite so obviously having this political angle baked into the very formation of the concept of mental health and its administration, the mainstream institutions doing this administering seem more than a little reluctant to recognize it (Berardi 2015a, 3). One reason for this, aside from the clear entrenchment of power, and thus the lack of incentive to recognize it, is the way that the logic of catharsis in general, and as a method of treatment in particular, has a widely understood kind of intuitive appeal. And so the cathartic method, being understood as a way to return someone to a notional prior state of wellness without their individual maladies, serves as a kind of proxy justification that sees an individual as the locus of their own suffering. It is your inadequacies, it is your failings, it is your problem if you cannot function in the world without suffering. This framework doesn't leave a lot of space for the role that the systems we live underplay in the production of this suffering. Because if a subject needs to be regularly cathartically purified to the extent that it is able to function just well enough, then systems that implicate themselves in the very formation of that subject from the get-go should not be allowed to continue. Or, put another way, if wellness means functioning in the world as it is, the particularities of this must be concealed through the individualization of systemic problems, thus making it appear that to desire to be anything other than healthy by the standards of the system can only be understood as a desire for illness. This is why, as Mark Fisher writes, "one of the most successful tactics of the ruling class has been responsibilisation" (2018, 749).

As mentioned above, the psychological use of the term "catharsis," to mean "a release of emotions and tensions" (Strickland 2001, 116) has its origins in the work of Freud. And if there was anything his psychology attempted to promote, it was some normativity. Not uncritical normativity but certainly a conservative take on what wellness should be. We can read this in the stated aim of his cathartic method:

[T]o provide that the *quota* of affect used for maintaining the symptom, which had got on the *wrong lines* and had [...] become *strangulated* there, should be directed along the *normal path* along which it could obtain *discharge*. (Freud 1989, 13) [my emphasis]

Affect, here, is being used pretty much as a synonym for emotion, implying a certain engagement with the self as psychoanalytically conceptualized rather than anything more foundational. Most of what I have emphasized in the above quote only makes sense if we read affect as emotion belonging to a psychoanalytic self, because you need some kind of external authority or, in this case, social normativity, to determine which are the "wrong lines" that experience has taken. Added to this is the related idea that to posit resolution through discharge speaks of a culturally specific understanding of wellness, presented as a universal, that is inexorably tied up with the logic of patriarchal liberal capitalism (Deleuze & Guattari 2013b, 240). So, what we have here is a theory of mental health that is, if only unconsciously, ideologically constructed. And despite the fashionability among contemporary psychologists of denouncing Freud in favor of ostensibly more scientific methods, lines of his thought persist. Freud's cathartic method has gone on to form the basis "for all later forms of psychotherapy and counseling" (Launer 2005).

But this fact alone is not what is most damning. Talking to people to feel better is just a thing that people have always done. Venting to loved ones, talking the ears off your friends down the pub, and water cooler chats are common ways to share and perhaps half a burden. The curious thing about the adoption of catharsis by Freud and the adoption of psychotherapy by medicine is that wellness is defined by an authority. And such positions of authority, while not totally monolithic, are imbued with their power as long as they serve the overriding logics of the systems in which we live. To put it crassly, if you have a theory of mental health, then, in order for it to be authoritative, it had better serve productivity (Foucault 1998, 123–124). This is a rule of thumb, however, not a universal, though elements of this rule impinge upon the practice as a whole. Psychology, as a field, has interests that exceed making people productive members of neoliberal capitalism. It has researched conditions that make individuals with them physically unable to partake in this political economy, such as severe forms of schizophrenia, and has sought to develop treatments. However, as we have seen in the United States, following the closure of state mental hospitals under Ronald Reagan, the authority of this medical understanding runs out at the limit of productivity, with many untreatable people cast onto the street and criminalized (Torrey 2013). For less extreme cases, however, the reciprocal relation between medical authority and systems of political economy and subjectivization has meant that things like cathartic therapy have been instrumentalized for the purpose of maintaining the existing social order. This ties itself up in the world outside the clinic, becoming the commonsensical way in which we understand what is wrong with us. This comes with a great deal of baggage, as the way common sense works often causes it to approximate the most stupid formulation of the normative values of the systems that produce it.

In other words, while it is easy enough to state that our culture is causing people to suffer, notions of personal responsibility still abound when the conditions of those around us threaten to impinge on our neoliberal flourishing. As you start to hear someone muttering to themselves on the train, you turn up the volume of the music on your smartphone, to stop it seeping in. That feels better than risking contamination. To use the terminology of Lacan that Žižek is most fond of spouting, it is impossible to separate this kind of catharsis from the wishes of the big Other.

Interlude: You Are the Perfect Drug

"The Perfect Drug" by Nine Inch Nails, which is to say by Trent Reznor, was composed and released in 1997 as part of the soundtrack to David Lynch's film *Lost Highway* (2011 [1997]). I was seven at the time of this so didn't see the film in the cinema, and my subsequent attempts to see it have been thwarted by an unwillingness to pay for access and the low bandwidth of sites purporting to host it for free. I was well aware of the song long before I knew of the film, the director, or even the name of the band because, despite the weirdness of its structure and instrumentation, for two choruses it maintains a semblance of market-sanctioned hedonism that was perfect for commercial synchronization.

As Reznor declares to an object of desire that they are, "the perfect drug, the perfect drug, the perfect drug" over a rush of breakbeats and power chords, we're presented with the kind of mania that is often celebrated in neoliberal capitalism. The choruses in the context of the song simulated a mania that suggest a resolution that is always deferred as we are required to, seemingly, live in this loop forever. But they were so stable in this simulation that they could be stripped of the context that gave them this subtle significance. The frenetic dissonance of the opening was omitted and with it the semblance of struggle in the establishment of rhythms as the vocal becomes dislodged the further we get into the song ("how very little there is left of me" [Nine Inch Nails 1997]). So too were both pre-choruses, which speak to the dissolution of the self through the opening of a plaintive conjunction ("and I want you" [Ibid]), nestled amongst a radical drop in speed and an eerie choir whose only role is to add dissonance. The extended beat interlude was omitted not just from advertising synchronization but from the video edit of the track as well (Romanek 1997). It seems the Tim Burton stylized gothic setting couldn't cope with the horror of the eventual utter dissection of the song's identity into cultural referentiality as the song became an extended amen break. This is the point at which the cost of the appearance of functionality that we hear asserted in the chorus has been raised too high to be deferred any longer.

In the end, we are left without resolution. None of the original material has survived this process. The realization that whatever there was of a self was only possible in relation to another ("without you, everything falls apart, without you, it's not as much fun to pick up the pieces" [Ibid]). This is codependency as the constituting force of normalcy. But a moment earlier, it had been the soundtrack to an interstitial segment letting us know about the exciting programs that will be coming up on ITV this season, or something.

**

This isn't a new idea. There have long been objections to the medicalization of mental life. But one of the most sustained and overtly political critiques came from the (anti-)psychiatrist, R. D. Laing. Laing's experience treating schizophrenics led him to the conclusion that the cause of their suffering couldn't be reduced to poor upbringing, chemical imbalance in the brain, or physiology. Instead, by engaging with his patients' own descriptions of what was wrong with them, he reached the conclusion that their condition had a great deal more to do with the oppressive power relations that structured society than the psychiatry of the day was willing to admit (Laing 2010, 120). In Laing's analysis, this affected not just the circumstances of political economy but infiltrated every interpersonal relationship (Curtis 2007). Like the cathartic method, Laing was concerned with the process of having a patient explore and explain what is bothering them. However, he interrogates his role in this interaction to such a degree that this interaction is not geared toward some kind of discharge of negativity in the hope of being able to send the patient back to where they had suffered previously.

This was the most obviously problematic element of psychiatry for Laing. To send someone who was suffering back to where their suffering began, seemed to him as though the priorities of the profession were literally to keep people in their productive places. An obvious example of medicine in the service of power (Foucault 1998, 58).

In *The Politics of Experience* (1990 [1967]), Laing argues that psychiatric treatment, as it was practiced at the time, ultimately works to dominate individuals in the service of those in power. He suggested that by limiting the acceptable range of reactions that people were allowed to have to a given situation or experience, those in power could manipulate the way that people behaved:

> All those people who seek to control the behaviour of large numbers of other people work in the experience of other people. Once people can be induced to experience a situation in a similar way, they can be expected to behave in a similar way. Induce people to want the same thing, hate the same thing, feel the same threat, then their behaviour is already captive—you have acquired your consumers or your cannon-fodder. (Laing 1990, 80)

For Laing, any resolution that was offered by catharsis would automatically serve to return people to functioning within the existing social order and context and would be a corrupt and unjust manipulation of a suffering person. In his discussion of the slippery definition of schizophrenia as used by the psychiatric profession in the 1960s (1990, 80), Laing observed that the label has become a "social fact" (100) and that to be diagnosed as a sufferer of this condition becomes a "political event" (ibid) because the action taken allowed this diagnosis to be justified in the "maintenance of civic order" (101). What's more, this process invalidates anything said by someone labeled as schizophrenic as being the product of illness rather than an interpretation of a damaging experience. In doing so, the politics of their condition and experience is removed from discourse. Laing was not arguing that these ailments or conditions did not exist. On the contrary, his position was that the potential for these conditions always already exist within us in the psychic schism between our inner selves and what we project to the world (Laing 2010, 17–18). Instead, what he argued was that we are prevented from seeing that what is officially considered mental illness, and thus irrationality, might be the rational response to the experience of the violence and cruelties that are endemic under the enforced disparities and competition of capitalism. Laing claims that to understand this as a personal deficiency is incorrect given the circumstances in which we find ourselves. As Laing observes:

> We are born into a world where alienation awaits us. We are potentially men, but in an alienated state, and this state is not simply a natural system. Alienation as our present destiny is achieved only by outrageous violence perpetrated by human being on human beings. (Laing 1990, 12)

This position, taken together with Laing's notion of how power tries to limit the acceptable interpretations of experience available to individuals in a society, suggests that power is capable of acting in defensive or conciliatory ways. It doesn't just enforce itself on the world; power must also neutralize that which would denaturalize it; reveal it is arbitrary, contingent, and partial. Those who either do not or cannot conform are treated as individual aberrations to be contained and removed from politics.

Of course, as we saw in the discussion of cultural capital and complicity, under the ultra-competitive conditions of neoliberal capitalism, immense suffering is often the inevitable outcome of political decisions. The success of a few individuals requires them to have won out over and, put simply, defeated innumerable others. The argument simply goes that if a minority could succeed under these conditions, then the conditions cannot have been to blame for the failure of the others. There are individual failures and similarly individual successes (Berardi 2015a, 158). But what goes unsaid is that one of these conditions is that most have to lose out, so that what could have been distributed between us instead is awarded to the few that succeed. And this is before we take into account any of the material and historical imbalances at play. Far from the condition of neoliberal capitalism not being to blame for failure and suffering, these elements are a prerequisite. It is against this backdrop that we find the imperative to always be performing at our best, and the psychological strain this produces, and where we turn to music for the capacity to lessen that strain. Taken together with cultural capital, this action can serve a double purpose: catharsis, and valorization. And why not? This seems like the sensible thing to do. The risks of not addressing the strain you are under range from falling a little behind the pack to complete mental breakdown and with it social and political, if not actual, death. So why not engage with cultural commodities of rejuvenation like pop? It even comes with the added benefit of helping you accrue more cultural capital. And all the while you valorize money capital.

If all of this is taking place and the imperative for cathartic purging is a major reason for the flourishing of the culture industry under capitalism, as it seeks to redress the suffering induced by its systems of exploitation and alienation present even at the upper echelons of its hierarchies, then there may be more to discover by moving from the inhibiting mechanism of catharsis, to focus on what catharsis is meant to inhibit.

Where Is My Mind?

Because of the depths and complexities of debates between left-wing philosophers in the 1970s and the variously valid and invalid objections they had to each other's work, the significant affinities between the philosophical projects of Deleuze and Guattari and Laing can never quite graduate to full allegiance to one another.[4] Laing was an existentialist, meaning that, for him, the discussion of human suffering was very much a human affair. Deleuze and Guattari, on the other hand, rejected this anthropocentric framework in order to better enable an examination of "what is non-human in man" (Seem in Deleuze and Guattari 2013a, 6). Now this is, of course, more than a just a philosophical technicality. The way that Deleuze and Guattari conceptualize the human as something already utterly interpenetrated by all manner of non-human things has led to important developments in weeding out the latent fascist tendencies in anti-capitalist left-wing political movements, but also led to some novel developments of those tendencies (Land 2013). So, while it has its limitations, it is good to hold the experientially derived existentialism of Laing's approach in mind to keep pulling the focus of this dissection of cathartic pop under capitalism back to the question of how might things be better for us humans. With that in mind, I want to talk about Deleuze and Guattari's image of schizophrenia, which, while recognizing the suffering, they see very differently from Laing. Deleuze and Guattari understand schizophrenia as the "the exterior limit" of capitalism itself, and the conclusion of its "deepest tendency" (Deleuze & Guattari 2013a, 283). That being a limit beyond which it is no longer possible to force subjects to produce surplus value, as the schizophrenic subject cannot be directed toward this aim. This is really an abstract way of describing what Laing observed in his patients. But it also provides an implicit reason for medicalizing them. It is not just that schizophrenia is not productive for capitalism; for Deleuze and Guattari, it is capitalism's built-in destruction mechanism, against which catharsis is a brake pad.

The systemic structure of capitalism means that it operates through feedback loops (Land 2018, 295). The most famous of these is Marx's own M-C-M* (Money capital invested—commodity capital exchanged—more money capital valorized [if it is less it's not capital]) (Buchanan 2008, 54). As capital and the political economy of capitalism insinuates itself into every corner of life, the kinds of feedback its systems produce become more complex. For example, its insinuation into the bourgeois pleasures of the concert hall helped to stymie high culture as a route of escape. But, more significantly, its entanglement with more vernacular cultural forms like popular music help to give capital access to the production of imaginative possibility throughout society and detect when the frustrations of this are becoming dangerous. The difference from the Aristotelian despotic cathartic model is that while such despots may consider it prudent to deploy cathartic materials at particular moments, capital is able to automate this process and remove the need for decisions while precisely measuring out and administering micro-doses. Also built into capitalism's self-conscious recognition of the exterior limit of schizophrenia is the capacity for invisible ideological maintenance, which is best exemplified in medicalization. Thus, the notion that schizophrenia, depression, and mania, are problems resulting from a person's individual physical and mental deficiencies is enforced by the stigma of illness. But more than this, it is cast as an illness that is somehow deserved. For example, one could consider the stigma around depression or addictions as an attempt to deflect attention away from the influence that the structures of capitalism have over such conditions. This is described in a contemporary context in Franco "Bifo" Berardi's book *Heroes* (2015a), which presents the governing principles of neoliberalism as having nearly perfected the mechanism of protecting the exterior limit of capitalism as a place beyond the pale for decent humanity (50). What needs to be emphasized here is that this is performed for our benefit. The ideological constructions of these matters don't actually have any bearing on the mechanism of capitalism itself. Simply stating that the mechanism of capitalism produces the schizophrenic seeds of its own destruction holds no power over its continued operation. Because capitalism, as Deleuze and Guattari put is, "profoundly illiterate" (2013a, 276), which places it in a position immune to negative representation. If such representation causes material actions that affect its mechanisms, then perhaps something could change, but, while this is going on, feedback loops are already in place that will help capitalism to transform and shape its own representation. Perhaps the appearance of power and evil will suit it for a time, perhaps rights and justice, or perhaps artistic freedom.

This is to say that capitalism is a protean construct in Deleuze and Guattari's conceptualization; something that has emerged through a particular set of circumstances at the intersection of material reality, violence, power (and submission to it), and the frustrated desires of every being that thinks itself to be a subject (2013a, 257). So it is not a simple matter of the dislocating potential of schizophrenia produced under capitalism threatening us with suffering that we cannot endure. Rather, what can be found in schizophrenia is "not the identity of capitalism, but on the contrary its difference, its divergence, and its death" (283). For Deleuze and Guattari, this is because schizophrenia contains the potential to separate desire from the lack of that internal limiting principle, which motivates capitalist production. The world produced by schizophrenia would provide no comfort to those seeking to escape the exploitations of capital, but nor would it serve capital. This is what the CCRU heard in the inhuman speed of collective musical experiences like Jungle; what we hear in Reznor's descent into breakbeats through chemical self-obliteration, given permission to exist by its market-readable chorus, what today has been relegated to decidedly non-pop musicians like the traumatic industrial noise of Puce Mary (2016).

Pop cannot ever quite live here at the external limit. And it is not entirely clear that it should (though such normatives have no application in this schizophrenic space). It is a form that makes too many demands for structure. This makes it well suited to the cathartic processes of capitalism. But the question remains, can it be otherwise? If the engines of desire-powered capitalism tend toward the dissolution of everything, what pulls this in the other direction and allows capitalism to continue? What can resist that force? For Deleuze and Guattari this is the role of lack. Lack predates capital, but nothing is better at producing it. In some previous social arrangements, lack was produced by priests through the word of God. Words that were in disjunction with the bodies of desiring subjects who could thus not escape sinning against them (Deleuze & Guattari 2013b, 179). Today such figures play more of a managerial role, while capital itself uses a much more intimate mode of *lack* production to contain and direct desire. A mechanism that simultaneously maintains desiring-production while ensuring it will always be unfulfilled: Oedipalization. The "narcissistic ego is identical to the Oedipal subject" (Deleuze & Guattari 2013a, 305). This is not to say that under capitalism we behave like the tragic Greek king, but that, under bourgeois capitalism, we are made to want to but we are prevented from doing so. This is the structuring and limiting of desire along individualized and familial lines and the tying of wanting to feelings of shame, perversion, and transgression. Deleuze and Guattari's basic point was that Freud had it right when he found that people's familial relations under capitalism had warped their sense of self and sexuality, but was wrong to make the claim that this was an inherent part of human subjectivity. The claim that Deleuze and Guattari make is, rather, that under the individualizing conditions of capitalism, the only space of intersubjectivity becomes that family, and, as such, this sphere becomes the limiting principle by which desire is contained. But it is complicated. This isn't some libertarian conception of fighting for you and yours against a competitive world. Oedipal subjectivity is a collision of bodily learning, pleasure, and desire, but also violence and struggles for power. It is not just that Oedipus has a strongly negative reaction to finding out he has slept with his mother; he killed his dad too.

The emergence of pop music cultures since the 1960s has been utterly entangled in these structures. Even Deleuze and Guattari's book was very much a part of the same countercultural movement and moment from which what is considered popular music today was formed. The glorification of "sexual freedom" has been to some extent what pop is all about (Hesmondhalgh, 2013, 63; Frith 1981, 240–241). So too was the killing of the father, as each generation seemed to reinvent what popular music could be. But now we know this was a myopic understanding of what was going on. The sexual freedom on offer was something that was riddled through with patriarchal anxieties inherent to Oedipus, meaning little more than that straight men could indulge themselves brazenly, while the categories that haunted sexuality up until then still persisted and exploited everyone else. And the murder of pop's modernist father became a product to be sold again and again. The representation of an escape from a former prison became a form of commodified catharsis that ensured the bars remained as invisible as they are sturdy. The refusal, the rejection, the transgression are all too easily commodified to offer a way out.

Strange Currencies

Wallace's novel, *Infinite Jest*, is about Oedipal subjectivity persisting through the countercultural movement of the late 60s and 70s and finding itself reaffirmed in the crisis-ridden society of neoliberal capitalism, as seen through cultural production.[5] The argument runs through the novel that the addictions—be they to drugs, alcohol, or entertainment—of this near-future American society are rooted in the frustration and melancholy inherent to a capitalism allowed to metastasize long after "the end of history." The material suffering that results from systemic inequality persists and, at the same time, the only methods available to relieve this suffering are addictive and ultimately alienating and vacuous. And from what we have laid out so far, Wallace has a particular target in this critique of addiction, which could also be understood as a critique of catharsis.

The novel orbits around the hunt for a film, "Infinite Jest," which is said to be so entertaining that all those who watch it are thrown into a state of catatonic bliss. All the viewer/victims want to do is re-watch the film, and without intravenous feeding and other forms of personal care, they will die within days (Wallace 2007, 87). According to Marshall Boswell, and I'm inclined to agree with him, this plot device and its appended details clearly target the Lacanian psychoanalytic tradition and its focus on the unreachable desire of subjects for a "return to maternal plenitude" (Boswell 2005, 130) and ridicule it. The theory at play in such debilitating entertainment is that of the rupture caused by entering what Lacan called the mirror stage. This is the stage of childhood development at which, Lacanians argue, an infant recognizes him or herself as a subject, comprised of a self that is distinct from others around it. We can see this concretely exemplified when a child is able to recognize itself in a mirror. As Boswell puts it, "she acquires a subjectivity but only by becoming alienated from herself" (Boswell 2003, 129). Therefore, it is only by being able to consider yourself as somehow removed from what you are (ensconced in systems of economy, biology, language, culture, power, desire, etc.) that you can recognize yourself as a distinct identity. This is basically another formulation of the conditions that concerned Laing, which he saw as stemming from the condition of the modern world. Lacan also conceptualized a "'split subject' internally divided between self and other" (130) but for him, it is an irresolvable existential dialectic rather than a circumstance to be combated.

The film "Infinite Jest," in the novel, quasi-resolves this dialectic, with its particular content: an infant's eye view perspective, staring into the eyes of a beautiful, naked, and heavily pregnant mother figure, who tells the viewer/infant that she is so very sorry, in many insipid and saccharine variations. Wallace's argument, Boswell claims, is that the only thing that could come from this desire would be an infantile catatonia and the inability to ever consciously leave this space. In short, Wallace has it that the Lacanian gesture to point to this tension as the origin of all that troubles us internally is myopic, as the resolution of this tension can only be regressive.

This device, in and of itself, is not subtle. It can be read as a clear Adornian indictment of the sort of enslavement that entertainment can produce. However, its deployment through the novel both enables a real appreciation for the concern of the infantilizing power of entertainment and offers a subtle critique of this simplistic indictment. Because the film's maker is dead and those that have seen it are in no state to provide a response to any questions, all we have to go on are details emerging from rumors relayed by third parties, and thus the content of the film is never fully fixed. The sorts of things that might be in it, like the synopsis listed above, are scattered throughout the novel. Thus the final mechanism of resolution to the split-self dialectic can never be fully articulated. But this is then set against more concrete episodes in the novel, wherein different characters rely on televisual representations of idealized cultural norms for psychological emotional support. For example, one turns to the community represented in *Cheers!* (Wallace 2007, 834) to allow him to escape his abusive home life as a child, while another character recounts how their father becomes dangerously obsessed with searching for a greater cosmic meaning in *M*A*S*H* (639). These examples are both syndicated situation comedies, which are very much the art form of a previous time, and Wallace is careful to put that temporal distance into his character's relationships to the media. None of this stuff is strong enough anymore, apparently. We need to up the dosage.

The film, with its partial definition but concrete effects, reflects the way in which we engage with this kind of norm-reproducing media. In a discourse of empirical data, it can be difficult to articulate the influence such media can have on individuals, but within this novel, it is easier to see a relationship between the suffering that people endure and the dangerous medicine that entertainment can provide them. At the same time, Wallace does not present something clear-cut. The viewers of the sitcoms can't be allowed to get what they need. Those who get what the split-self subconsciously believes it needs—the return to maternal plenitude—don't become functional bourgeois subjects but instead end up as vegetables trapped in infantile satisfaction. Those in power in the novel—the president, secret services, media leaders—are those who are most worried about the film and the possibility of its being made available to the public. If everyone is satisfied, capitalist civilization is over. Thus, it becomes clear that the lack we experience has more to do with the construction of the self as it moves through the world, itself structured by capital and built out from a history of power's violent concentration in the hands of a few. The pseudo nature of this resolution to the problem of the split-self reveals the manufactured nature of its instantiation. But the problem persists, as just knowing that is in no way enough to overcome it. We are in too deep.

In the novel, this is discussed in the debate between a secret service agent and a terrorist turncoat who is undercover with the group planning to disseminate the film. The terrorists do not wish to broadcast the film as such. Instead, they merely wish to make it available for Americans to choose to consume. The double agent argues that if Americans were not so individualistic and focused on pleasure seeking, it would not be a problem to make available such a dangerous film. Instead, what is clear from the desperation of the American government and entertainment industry to recover the film from the terrorists, and their reluctance to allow the viewing of this film to be left open as a consumer choice is that the culture of the USA has produced a population whose subjectivities are so driven by the pursuit of pleasure and the ideological conviction that this should not be impeded that they would be all but compelled to see the film were it available. The terrorist remarks, "This appetite to choose death by pleasure if it is available to choose, this appetite of your people unable to choose appetites, this is the death. What you call the death, the collapsing: this will be the formality only" (319). In the end, Wallace is not attacking the media for being seductive but rather there is enough blame to go all around and back for generations.

This all stems from that feeling of separation that, whether it's Oedipal subjectivity or the split subject, we are faced with in a world that seems indifferent to us but for the pleasant distraction the market provides. Wallace finds this desire not to be existentially alone a valid and important one. But he also sees how that desire can make individuals who are easily manipulated. The conditions brought about by the film are a caricature of what happens when one looks for solace from pain and loneliness in an entirely individualized way; that is to say, as the resolution to an internal problem; alone in the attempt of dialectical resolution and completion.

This is catharsis as something that is hermetically sealed, which only serves to maintain the status quo. This may be the case for catharsis as such, as it is a process of purification that necessarily requires a defined vessel. A fixed, delineated territory, which matches well with bourgeois society's notion of the individual. This is where an *Anti-Oedipal* reading of the novel becomes useful, because it is clear that, for Wallace, turning inward is not how one addresses the suffering produced in the world left at the end of history. Indeed, that place where we may expect to find the most security (the family or home) is, in part, constitutive of the very condition that produced our sufferings in the first place. It is as Deleuze and Guattari have observed: the mommy–daddy–me triangle of the bourgeois household/unconscious. A cathartic process has, as its goal, a return to the same state/environment in which the suffering was initially caused, and in which suffering is perpetuated.

What this means is that if we follow (or catch up again with) the critique of popular music, from the level of attention to the complicity it engenders and to where we end up with the desire for catharsis, the ways in which popular music is oppressive become more apparent. In an environment in which security and relief are both imperatives and difficult-to-attain market commodities, popular music offers a simulation of them at a much lower cost. There are, of course, culturally contingent causes of this in the sound itself. But by far, the most substantial reason for this oppressive pattern of behavior is that this limited relationship has become so much of what we expect from popular music. So it is difficult to see this comfort, this affective limitation, as anything other than benevolence. However, as bell hooks writes on Beyoncé's *Lemonade* (2016), "to truly be free, we must choose beyond simply surviving adversity, we must dare to create lives of sustained optimal well-being and joy" (hooks 2016). This is where the constructive work begins, to build a relationship to popular music that can help us move beyond the cycle that causes us to use such music as a way to return to a home that capital built.

○

Vignette: The Stones

Standing in Hyde Park during "Barclaycard's presentation of British Summertime," I was immersed in the sonic shimmer, or perhaps it was the aura of the Rolling Stones. But despite not glimpsing the band or even passing through the entrance to the arena space, I can't help but think that my ticketless experience of the concert was perhaps more vivid than anything I could have gleaned in the gilded cage occupied by the paying crowd. In the park outside, I was bathed in this sonic aura, this atmosphere made thick by a Rolling Stones' artwork, and free of any referent or any of the disappointment of actuality.

Walter Benjamin's notion of the aura of a work of art expressed in his essay "The Work of Art in the Age of Mechanical Reproduction" (2008), has become a standard device for those interested in the culture industry. In the essay, Benjamin argues that the unique here-and-now existence of a work of art gives it a certain aura that is lost through even the most perfect reproduction. Despite his enthusiasm for the emancipatory potential he sees in the works of art that mechanical reproduction has made possible, such as film, the original, with its unbroken connection to some sort of originator, remains vitally important. Even from a materialist point of view, this idea seems pretty clear and demonstrable in relation to things like paintings with their chemical composition changing over time. But despite his anxiety about the loss of this aura through mechanical reproduction, for this idea to really have something to it beyond crass materialism, something of this aura must persist even through reproduction. Arguing for this was tricky enough with celluloid but has become even more complex, firstly with the kind of mass cultural productions Benjamin could have never imagined, like the Stones, and secondly in the inherently abstracting format of digital media. If we add to this copyright law, the notion of aura becomes even more difficult to grasp. With all this in place, we then have to identify the works produced by the band, who are legally allowed to be identified and trade under the name The Rolling Stones, as original Rolling Stones' works of art whenever they play together. Even if some of the songwriters are deceased, the legal entity of The Rolling Stones exceeds this crude biological fact. If this is the world we're in, it is then necessary to regard any performance by this legally defined entity as an original Rolling Stones artwork. But this is a pretty complex idea to hold to under the conditions of postmodernism that have co-produced this conundrum. Especially if we take the concept of aura as having some relation to signification, but we'll get to that.

The Stones were on stage in Hyde Park for two weekends in July 2013. This, the Stones playing songs on a stage, has happened perhaps thousands of times since their formation in 1962, and as such may seem a little quotidian for being originals. This means that they have produced tens of thousands of original Rolling Stones artworks on stage. But it goes much further this, because what is the stage show if not for the myth and the marketing? The Stones have had their images reproduced millions of times, broadcast from countless sources, and been packaged with countless commodities. During the more-than-half century of Rolling Stones artwork production, they, or at least their industrial framework, have sought to profit from the ephemeral and hard-to-access nature of the transcendent experience of had-to-be-there moments, with the quick and easy potential offered by the pop music industrial framework. The production of numerous concert videos, willing and unwilling photographs, and appearances in all forms of commercial media, have attempted to capture some of this ephemeral transcendence and transform it into discrete commodities through reproduction. In short, they are some of the earliest and most enduring examples of the rock 'n' roll mythology that has become an almost stale staple of the popular music industry. Manipulated and situated images and sounds, and fifty years of ecstatic anecdotes, are now far more pristine referents of the Rolling Stones than the admittedly impressive swagger of the elderly Mick Jagger.

When you attend a Rolling Stones concert, the crowd is enormous, and so the fight for position is fierce. For many attendees, some the same age or only a little younger than their idols, this fight is unwinnable. Here the crowd is so vast that if one arrived later than 7:00 a.m., even youthful eyes couldn't discern anything of a recognizable swagger from the viewing positions left available. The solution to this, here and at every other spectacular show of this scale, has been big screens. A whole industry has grown up around this problem-of-your-own-success. Strange time/distance sound-speed signal-transfer-delay types-of-things aside, the thought appears to be that the screen is less an obvious form of mediation than it is a magnifying glass. The tiny blur on stage becomes a close up on Keith Richards' rictus as he strikes a chord on his low-hung Telecaster. And this projection claims to get you closer to the band while maintaining the high status of these modern deities.

You know what really stunts this piece? It's the need you feel to touch the correct politically pious points throughout but reveal almost nothing about yourself. You're like an old-fashioned anthropologist, disguised as an English hedgerow in the Amazon. You were in love when this happened. New, intense, continuing love. That is why it stays in your mind. You had no money, still have no money, but you found a way to have pretty cool experience in London together anyway. Something you both shared and that stayed with you enough for you to try and write about it on at least three different occasions. To the point, now, where you have had to invent another persona to get out what you should have said from the outset, which itself is still a distancing tactic. I mean you are literally the second person right now. But here it is, the thing that could cut through a lot of the speculative spiraling in this book: music means more if you feel it is adding to the story you tell yourself about yourself. You don't particularly like the Rolling Stones. You like "Sympathy for the Devil" (Stones 2018) but only because it doesn't really sound like the Rolling Stones. This is not a deep insight, but it could be the start of one. Like, is it a problem that music has come to be a tool to allow you to think you're at the center of an experience?

Without paying between £50 and £400 for tickets, you can't experience the Rolling Stones engaged in the creation of a Rolling Stones artwork with readily available aura. It can, and no doubt would be, argued that this kind of exorbitant price all goes into the creation of a complete concert experience full of regalia. However, my being born in 1990, to a former hippy, has made the experience of the documentation of the Rolling Stones the way in which I understand their entire existence. The fact that some of them still live and perform is a curious afterthought to what I know them to be. Which is that they are less interesting than The Beatles. This is my primary referent for the band; the psychic resource I would use to understand the experience of seeing and hearing the band before me. And this has slipped seamlessly into our contemporary world of YouTube clips and streaming services. Whereas, my dad, growing up in Nova Scotia as a teenager in the 1960s, had such limited exposure to this media—now archived and accessible online—that his reference points were the occasional contemporary newsprint reproduction of photographs, album artworks and typography, and the way in which a vinyl LP can make the air shake. It seems from this that the Stones are, and may have always been, simulacra: an image without a real-world referent. But perhaps this is where we find their aura too. An interesting phenomenon for Deleuze and Guattari, and the end of the world for Baudrillard and Berardi. The postmodern complaint, expressed by David Foster Wallace in his self-critical account of his experience of 9/11, that "We've Seen This Before" is an all-too-common experience (2013, 140). A foil to excitement and the standard premise for the construction of commercials, movies, new media, and bands. This melancholic complaint needn't be the only way to experience such events, though, if the aura can be found in the simulacra. It could actually provide us with the resources to see past the corrupted authenticity discourse of corporate enterprise that surrounds almost all of our cultural productions.

I have never attended a Rolling Stones concert. My argument here is derived from attending other large-scale rock acts (Radiohead, The Smashing Pumpkins), who have begun or failed to create very different but similarly dense mythologies around their practice. Always, though, with some reference to what the Stones created. I doubt I'll ever see the Rolling Stones. Even if I attended, though, I doubt that I'd believe I had seen them. I'm sure I would, as I have done before, attempt to measure my perceptions against the culturally selected images and montages of sound that the media has used for half a century to stand in for the Rolling Stones. So, with the echoes of the concert blurring into the low-frequency distortion, as happens when sound emanates over open space, my mind was awash with images of pop culture experiments as my inheritance, but with no original article for comparison. I was in the aura of a Rolling Stones artwork. Without the distraction of the bizarre facticity of the event, I listened to the aura of "Sympathy for the Devil" in Hyde Park. Whatever was left of the artwork itself did not get in the way.

○

4

Home

Pop Music ... of the Refrain

Even more than going to pop music for the resources to imagine the world as other-than-it-is, under the conditions of the present, people turn to it for a specific formation of this resource: catharsis. This is the desire to be allowed to feel better through some sensation of resolution; a desire that the markets of capital are more than happy to meet, as people who feel better are more productive than those whose suffering manifests as paralysis. The part of this arrangement that goes unacknowledged is, however, the extent to which this capital-prescribed remedy is the medicine to a predominantly capital-induced ailment. But that is not to say that this mechanism is some kind of invention particular to capitalism. The contemporary deployment of cultural production as a tool of diffuse affect management for the masses is built upon the same intellectual tradition stemming from ancient Greece, which birthed Western conceptions of liberal democracy. Aristotle even makes this instruction explicit when he states that the simplicity of "lesser musics" can calm the savagery of the masses. But this is not the activation of some kind of universal cathartic resolution machine. This is the deployment of familiarity as a limiting principle entangled in the norms and values of the social order that was in no small part responsible for the feelings of corruption, burden, and suffering that it now seeks to expunge. However, to reject or discount popular music because of this gets us nowhere as this would be to fall into the same conception of reality held by those who reproduce the ideological components of this system. It would be to treat the hunger for cathartic relief as something trivial, a by-product to be managed through the surplus resources of production. What this myopic view misses is that the surplus has led to an excess in popular music that can go beyond the mere management of symptoms, and that the hunger for catharsis, to which it is applied, could, itself, rend this system open. Arguably, it is always already doing this. But to locate this opening we need to look beyond those initial attempts to escape this limiting principle of a cathartic return to purity (70s psychedelic counterculture or 80s consumptive excess), to something that was not merely based on the simple negation of these structures. Something that acknowledges that the existence of the cathartic mechanism is itself a failure of the overall structure; an expression of its own insufficiency and the incompleteness of its dominance that implies the possibility of its supersession.

To say that previous attempts to transgress this system of structural maintenance were mistaken, however, misunderstands what it is that reveals this weakness in the status quo. To be specific, the moment that we are living through has particular features that reveal the shortcomings of previous attempts to create a way out of capitalism. New media networks have allowed artifacts produced in the past to take on a peculiar atemporality as any mediated form of cultural expression that can be stored digitally can be theoretically accessed by anyone at any time. Its experience in the present, devoid of historical context, is only ever a correct search term away. Thus the archive has become largely invisible; all that can be perceived is the contents. There are obvious creative advantages to this. The influence of old material is not limited to its physical accessibility, and the capacity to engage with it directly as a creative material in itself is made all the easier by being in this quasi-universal format. This is perhaps the case for music more than any other form, and pop even more so. Dated visuals seem to resist becoming part of the present in a way that sounds, at least after 1970, can somehow bypass. There are, perhaps, notable exceptions in the early integration of digital instruments into music—which seems to remind many people of their own frustrations with the limitations of early home computing—but, by and large, songs like "Whole Lotta Love" (Led Zepplin 1990 [1969]) or "Thriller" (Jackson 2015 [1982]), with only a little remastering can slip seamlessly into a contemporary commercial. Attempts to do the same for visuals, like George Lucas' remastering of the original "Star Wars" trilogy (Lucas 2004), are often met with ridicule and derision.

But these networked archives of pop cultural history do not exist freely. They are subject to the same economic forces that shape culture more generally. This means that most of this content has become more easily accessible because someone is trying to profit from this accessibility, and thus the version that is often the most available is the one that is most commercially viable. (Apart from instances when, say, an unauthorized torrent can provide a higher quality version of something than that provided by the low bandwidth of a commercial streaming service, which just speaks to a lack of institutional imagination). This tendency can unmoor our perception of music's history. Trying to get a class of students to identify period-specific production techniques found in songs from the 1980s is confounded if the only versions that are now available have been digitally remixed and mastered. Fisher once remarked that upon hearing the Arctic Monkeys for the first time in 2006 he mistook them for a run-of-the-mill post-punk band he'd missed back in the 80s (2014, 9). But the same is true in reverse for younger listeners today. Someone in their early twenties listening to The Smiths for the first time could make a pretty compelling case for these aural qualities of "There Is a Light That Never Goes Out" (2017) being released in 2006 rather than 1986. This may in part be due to the particular production ideology of post-punk, but it is also because the rights holders want to use the updated version of the song on new media platforms to cut through the volume and sound quality of other contemporary productions.

Fisher's observation was that, where previously we could have perhaps heard the exploration of new technical and aesthetic possibilities over time, now due to the economic incentives to realize the commodity status of every piece of media that can be stored digitally and the way this has influenced the development of technology, the past sounds like the present and the future has disappeared (Fisher 2014, 10–11). To flesh out the implications of this, what we are witnessing could be a more fundamental form of the deterritorialization of time by capital. This is a move beyond the dislocation of the hold of biological memory and physical accessibility from the experience of music, which came about with sound recording, but in re-*producing* the media so that it is always of the present and making sure it is always easily accessible, the knowledge of context and history itself is devalued. There are upsides to this but, unfortunately, this is not to say we have been liberated from the chrononormativity or "reproductive futurism" (Hester, 2018, 34) of contemporary Oedipal capitalism. It is only that we have been denied the possibility of peeking into a future that could see us freed from our present conditions. Pop music is being used to keep us pinned to the same kind of domestic setting and routines that Laing has identified as so very damaging. The deterritorialization of time has become the reterritorialization of the internal limit to capitalism. Oedipus is no longer just in the family; he's on Spotify.

This needs to be unpacked a little more. At least discursively speaking, the commonplace rejection of Freudian dogma, which insisted that the structure of families, gender roles, and all human sexuality should be understood through the arbitrary templates of Oedipus and penis envy, is clearly progress. That said, such a rejection is an easy intellectual proposition to take but it has much messier real-world applications. If we make the fairly banal point that Freud's theories lacked the empirical rigor and diversity of cases necessary for something that claimed to be a universal theory of the structure of the human unconscious, we overlook what this perspective did offer an insight into. That being an insight into the structure of Western bourgeois desire in a crystalline form. There is no way in which we could plausibly claim that what Freud's patients described to him of themselves was a manifestation of some ill-defined human nature, because whatever these patients expressed and whatever Freud interpreted of this expression was steeped in centuries of norms derived from thousands of concrete but contingent particularities. Thus, claims to have uncovered some kind of naturalism are not just groundless but meaningless.

But what we can see in these accounts is how people experienced living up to the standards expected of them by a particular social order. So when the work of Freud is rejected, on the one hand, we reject some ungrounded and dangerous notions of human nature, but we also risk rejecting what the work might have actually revealed when read skeptically. That being that, the standards of bourgeois life, as the norms enforced by capitalism, were making people ill either by causing them to manifest some ailment or simply by designating them as sick. The danger of Freud's influence was the production of a positive feedback loop that has spread throughout society, shaping it through the persuasiveness and popularity of the description; but the danger of rejecting his work has been to ignore this loop.

So today, we find ourselves with two rejections: The rejection of the past *qua* the past, which renders the future meaningless, and the rejection of Freud in the particular way that makes the actual insights of his work invisible, while perpetuating the problematics of his normativity. These are deterritorializations in Deleuze and Guattari's language, and their scale is seismic and their consequences far-reaching. As mentioned above, what we are really talking about here is the dislocation of time and thus the future from the subjective experience of life under capitalism. And with this temporal dislocation, we lose the capacity for understanding that the pain of our frustrated desires resulted from how poorly matched they are with the social and economic imperatives that structure our lives, as the tools for thinking this have been concealed under ever more medical language. This is the foreclosure of the possibility that the world can be changed for the better, leaving us only with the desire to go home and forget the world for a time. And thus, this deterritorialization has opened the possibility of a new market reterritorialization. With the music of the last sixty years now digitally stored and remastered, the past, or the return home again that now stands in for it, has never been more marketable. Where previously what may have been called "cool" or "hip" was defined in opposition to the establishment—which would then become the establishment over time when new practices of "hip" would emerge—pop music has taken on a different role now as that very mechanism of constant revolution has been incorporated into its contemporary distribution. The rapture of the new itself has been commodified as some kind of nostalgia.

There has been a temptation to use pop as an object to theorize this process back to a positive possibility. Against the clamor of Adorno's ignorance of pop's qualia and with fresh English translations of Deleuze and Guattari to work from, the 90s saw an influx of attempts at this. In Ian Buchanan's article, "Deleuze and Pop Music" (1997), he argues that one of the strengths of popular music is that it can be conceptualized as a refrain. But his use of the concept to this end lets something unexamined slip through. He writes:

> [T]he refrain is composed of three functions. It comforts us by providing a rough sketch of a calming and stabilising [...] centre in the heart of chaos. It is the song the lost child, scared in the dark, sings to find his or her way home. The tune also creates the very home we return to, when our foray into the world grows wearisome. Home is the product of a very particular gesture: one must draw a circle around that uncertain fragile centre one is accustomed to calling home in order to delimit it. (1997)

This summary is an effective encapsulation of much of what Deleuze and Guattari write in *A Thousand Plateaus* over a couple of pages (Deleuze & Guattari 2013b, 262-263), but it's also a little rickety. When Buchanan uses the notion of "home" as a straightforward synonym for what the refrain could provide, the elision of the concepts excludes what is dangerous in each of them. That being, a Laingian reading of "home," which views Freudian theory as a synecdoche for social norms congealed by history and power, suggests that the respite home offers may also be the source of the suffering and lack in the first instance. Which then speaks to another problem in the notion of pop as a refrain. That by drawing this circle, as the refrain is thought to do, and attaching it to a place of such definition as there is in the notion of home, there's the production of an inside/outside binary reminiscent of the notion of purity championed by the structure of catharsis.

When Buchanan writes that the refrain creates "the very home we return to when our foray into the world grows wearisome," there seems to be some suggestion that the world is somehow left at the door. But this isn't quite so as you bring external "contaminations" in with you and sit inside with them festering. More than this, this thing that we call home and this feeling of being inside it has been made possible entirely by that which is outside of it. Everything that appears as if inside comes, originally, from out there. It is only if we're lucky or privileged that the constituent elements of this space will be flattened to such an extent that they can become a territory of familiarity and provide a safe respite from the suffering that life under capitalism can generate. If we think about pop music as a refrain with all this in mind, it becomes little more than a compensation system: a form of rest and relaxation between unwinnable battles.

But, as bell hooks intimated, if you're looking to plan a route beyond capitalism, then pop has to be more than just a consolation or some kind of milquetoast compensation system. As long as the primary reason to engage with aesthetic production is to recover through a return to a home territorialized by the logic of capital, post-capitalism will remain out of reach. And since we are in a world of ubiquitous pop music, which is to say ubiquitous calls to return home, finding other ways to engage with popular music is vital to escaping this reduction and insufficiency of possibility. This vernacular form of music is a diffuse point of contact with people and communities and it does have a real ability to foster a wide variety of social and personal bonds. But if we conceptualize our relationship to it as a way to return home as if this were some kind of inherent good and, beyond that, without deciding what this home should look like, then the capacities of pop will continue to be used as traps.

This is why, while it is easy to be skeptical of the optimism he expresses, Buchanan is right to point to this potential in pop:

> To my mind, it is its very amenability to "being heard again and again and again", which corroborates the claim that pop music is a refrain, for one of the defining features of the refrain is its inexpressiveness. Deleuze & Guattari say the refrain is pure content that awaits expression. Pop is like that; it too awaits expression. (Buchanan 1997)

So if we're going to go along with what is useful here, somethings need to be spelled out more clearly. The refrain is not pure repetition. Musicologically speaking, a refrain does not only connect one section of a piece of music to another. Additionally, even though the material of the refrain is *returned* to in the song, the content of the refrain is expressed differently in each iteration by virtue of its recontextualization. This is true of all repetition in music, and something Deleuze and Guattari recognize with their focus on differentiation as something more than simply *recognizing* difference but the actual *production* of difference (2013b, 393). However, working against this glimmer of unbridled optimism, Attali argues that capitalist societies and the music that they produce require repetition so consistent that it can appear as pure, and thus escape being understood as differentiating (Attali 2011, 187). And this notion does seem to hold up, particularly in the world of consumer tech; which is to say, contemporary music consumption technology. Here, we may see what appears as an innovation that breaks the cycle, but this is illusory. The technology of the next few iterations of the iPhone already exists but the market runs on keeping the release of these developments to a drip feed. Thus, innovation is sold in almost the same commodity as it was previously, only now there is a camera on the front and the processor can cope with the updated OS. All it does is infinitesimally purify the repetition of the flows of capital accumulation. This holds for Fisher's reading of the Arctic Monkeys and the covers of Mark Ronson just as well.

What is needed, then, is something subtle. A music, or a relationship to it, that can draw attention to the differences and changes inherent to its repetition as an engine of differentiation. Which is to say as a source of a sense that change is still possible but in excess of the world-other-than-it-is as capital would delimit it. As Buchanan states, in a Deleuzian formulation, "[t]he new is not 'the merely different' but differentiating" (1997). This provision would not be enough on its own for popular music to be an emancipatory force but it does provide us with a place from which a theory can be developed as to how it could be. However, to understand how to do this we really need to have sure footing on these concepts of home and a strong footing on the refrain.

The refrain is a concept that can't just be stuck to pop as some kind of quick and easy resolution, as there are refrains engaged in the reproduction of the entirety of social reality. Any slight changes such refrains may engender tend to deepen the perceived fixedness of the status quo. As Franco Berardi argues, the concrete effect of the refrain is conciliatory:

> The refrain is an obsessive ritual that allows the individual—the conscious organism in the continuous variation—to find identification points, and to territorialize herself and represent herself in relation to the surrounding world. The refrain is the modality of semiotization that allows an individual (a group, a

people, a nation, a subculture, a movement) to receive and project the world in reproducible and communicable formats. (Berardi 2012, 130)

For Berardi, it is what is comforting about the refrain that makes it problematic. This securing property of it is attainable only through an obsessive ritual that forecloses the possibilities beyond it. The ritual limits not only experiences that are available to us but also the interpretations of these experiences. This is how refrains in late-capitalism operate without limiting experience to the repetitive circuits that facilitate the system of M-C-M*, or the logic of capital accumulation, which would then put capitalism itself at risk.

Berardi sees this as the disciplining of society in a way that echoes Foucault—the refrain of factory work, the refrain of salary, the refrain of the assembly line (Berardi 2012, 131). The repetition of these refrains—a repetition that is very near perfect but for minor differences—mimics that of the environments from which it is derived. As such, these entirely contingent refrains begin to take on the appearance of a natural environment. And while this may seem merely an issue of representation that can be simply overcome, it is more than that. It is a congealing, an edifice of sedimentary construction that imposes itself not only of the image of life but also of the sensory field from which much of what we consider to be our lives is produced. It is the entwining of power with desire. However, we cannot simply do without refrains. To a certain extent, any society able to identify itself as such will engage in the activities of the refrain. And consistency is not, in and of itself, a negative. In Deleuzo-Guattarian ontology, consistency is a source of great potential. But this potential is complex and not without its dangers. The consistency that can provide a stable foundation on which to build can also become neurotic and produce suffocating restrictions.

So, when we think of the relationship between the refrain and its interconnection through power/desire to the construction of the concept of home, and if we want pop music to play a role in this, then we cannot assert it as an uncomplicated a positive. And, by extension, pop music cannot be relegated to this function alone; this safe, non-disruptive, undisputed good constituting familiarity and home in a culture wherein home is an uninterrogated mechanism of control. At the same time, the refrain must be thought of as exceeding this facet of its conceptual capacity. Instead, we should place emphasis on the capacity in the refrain and popular music for differentiation. And if we turn to our disavowed reading of Freud again, we might find the tools for this critical renovation of *home* in the underexplored elements in the structure of the uncanny.

FKA Twigs vs. Miley Cyrus: Or, How I Learned to Stop Worrying and Love the Uncanny

To explain what I mean by this abstract set of terms and relationships, I want to compare the work of Miley Cyrus and FKA Twigs and relate them to Mark Fisher's reading of Freud's concept of the uncanny. But we are not there yet. More abstract terms and relationships need to be fleshed out if we are going to be able to make sense of this comparison in a way that moves past the Adornian move of "good things are like the things I like." Or, at least, my instantiation of this move should come with the equivalent amount of complications.

There is not an unproblematic use of the notion of home. This may seem obvious as it is a term that stands in for an unexplicated relationship between certain norms and particular places of forced enclosure. To describe somewhere, whether this space is physical or metaphorical, as "home" is to rest upon unexpressed assumptions often pertain to the good; unexpressed assumptions wherein certain modes of oppression are able to situate themselves. From the accounts of some in queer communities, this can be a concrete problem of the home from which they come (Lewis 2019). Which is thus where we see the emergence of terms like "safe spaces" as an attempt to designate places where certain modes of oppression are kept at bay by making explicit the normative commitments of the space to force them out. This rhetorical move has undoubtedly had a great many successes; although, even with such designations, the evasion of external forces can never be entirely complete. As has been shown so far, in the cases of home in at least a Western context, neoliberal capitalism has been able to entangle itself within the home, building upon structures of oppression that predate this economic mode through its entanglement of power with desire. For Laing, Deleuze and Guattari, and Berardi, home had long been a sight of patriarchal dominance, but in this late stage of capitalism, this has been reformulated into the bourgeois family unit as described by Freud. And it is through this mechanism that capital is able to contain desire as lack in the service of the production of surplus value. In addition to this system, there also exists an ideological function that serves to strengthen this system through a feedback loop. The reification of a psychologically co-dependent family unit is discursively constructed in terms of possessive individualism, which, in Deleuze and Guattari's framework, is then made to reinforce the limited experience of the unconscious as a family drama constantly played out on a theatrical stage (2013a, 69–70). Discourses about family values, being a provider, and notions of the "ambitious family man" are instantiations of the limits placed on unconscious desiring-production and are constitutive of an inside and an outside. A space within the home to be returned to and desired, and a space outside that is to be feared and fled from despite desire actually drawing us to it. The tensions of these pulls upon desire are kept in check by refrains, which offer both security and their own maddening loops.

While there is a temptation to just do away with this structure, to claim that home and its refrains are inherently oppressive and need to be dismantled, would be myopic. To argue for this would be to reinstantiate the same illiterate logic of capital. Which is to say, a logic characterized by asignifying semiotics; that which rationalizes deterritorialization entirely in line with value production and nothing more. For example, we may wish to escape the patriarchal connections of the family and home that give it its implicit meaning, in order to produce new meaningful connections that have so far been prevented by capitalist patriarchy. But the kind of escape offered by simple opposition to such structures can't provide this as it can easily be reincorporated by capital. This is because the impulse or force toward the abolition of home and its refrains is similarly monomaniacal to the forces of capital, and can thus be fully engulfed by the mechanism of M-C-M*. This is to say, that while particular facets of bourgeois individualism lend themselves well to the containment of desire in line with the logic of capital, it is not unique in this capacity. Forms of social organization other than bourgeois individualism can also facilitate this process of accumulation. Some have been less successful, such as fascism or mid-century state capitalism in the form of the Soviet Union, though they were clearly compatibile with the logic of capital. But now, with the rise of a new articulation of state capitalism in China, the idea that bourgeois individualism had, at the very least, a monopoly on capitalist efficiency has come into question, opening up the possibility that the most efficient forms of this inhuman system may be something terrifying beyond our imagination (Žižek 2010, 156). But one form that is, nonetheless, easy enough to imagine is the simple abolition of these structures.

So if we can't claim home for ourselves and we can't just abandon it altogether, how can we see a way for this oppression to be overcome? To do this I would like to offer a *productive misreading*[1] of Freud's notion of the uncanny,[2] with a little help from Fisher. Put simply, the *unheimlich* describes a sensation experienced when something of a particular nature disrupts the established order in life (what we could call a "home state"). To explain this particularity, Freud writes:

> [T]his word *heimlich* is not unambiguous, but belongs to two sets of ideas, which are not mutually contradictory but are very different from each other — the one relating to what is familiar and comfortable, the other to what is concealed and kept hidden. *Unheimlich* is the antonym of *heimlich* only in the latter's first sense, not its second. On the other hand [...] the term uncanny (*unheimlich*) applies to everything that was intended to remain secret, hidden away and has come into the open. (Freud 2003, 132)

Of course, as we have seen so far, it makes perfect sense that Freud would conflate the notion of the *heimlich* with the comfortable and familiar, relegating any negativity that adheres in the concept to its antonym. But even as he does this, his conceptualization of *unheimlich* almost reveals the falsity of this distinction. This is to say that, to elide the two definitions of *heimlich* we have here, comfort in the production of secrets produces the potential for discomfort in their revelation. Within a psychodynamic framework, what qualifies as *unheimlich* is often something from a previous experience that may or may not have been unpleasant at the time but, for a variety of reasons often having to do with social norms, has been repressed, and its later reemergence produces the discomfort called the *unheimlich* (152). Put more clearly in Fisher's reading, "Freud's *unheimlich* is about the strange within familiar, the strangely familiar, the familiar as strange—about the way in which the domestic world does not coincide with itself" (Fisher 2016, 10).

The *unheimlich* is, in the first instance, an aesthetic issue (Freud 2003, 123). It is an experience derived from our experience of sensations in the world and our memories of them. The *unheimlich* is not pure horror in the sense of something like the Lacanian real, but instead that which is horrifying through a distortion of familiarity, which is to say already symbolically coded. This could be because it is the re-emergence of an experience that one had assumed one would not experience again. To be talked to in such a way as to re-experience the emotional turmoil of being humiliated as a powerless child, would be a straightforward example. But one could also be made to occupy a space connected to a particular occasion again, perhaps only owing to way the light diffuses on a particular day, or a scent on the breeze that reminds you of it. But what make this *unheimlich* rather than simple reminiscent is that this re-experience occurs in such a way as to be absent of nostalgic enjoyment of, say, a loved one who is now gone from your life.

The assumption that these experiences would not resurface, was held to such an extent that it was itself unconscious and thus it can be difficult to recognize what it is that has specifically produced the discomfort. This is how the *unheimlich* makes the familiar or commonplace unfamiliar; it brings back something out of place without awareness of the rationale for is removal and so also without the recognizable identity as the source of discomfort. Here it is also important to attend to the part of the *heimlich* that refers to the secret being safely contained, as the depth of this form of repression is such that even important reasons for concealing the act and repressing the secret can be disconcerting in themselves. This may hint at the fragility of both the bourgeois individualism that has been deployed to reproduce capitalism and the problematics of simply renouncing it.

If we work with the Deleuzo-Guattarian notion of a productive mechanistic unconscious, then putting this productive force to the limited task of deforming reality in accordance with the dynamics of a multi-camera sitcom conception of the bourgeois family drama creates tension. On the one hand, this is an extraordinary limitation to place upon a potential creative force simply to facilitate the valorization of capital. But, on the other hand, attempts to simply tear this down become over-coded in their negative definition. The actions of all, due to their investments in either the maintenance of the status quo or its destruction, can simply be recorded as different categories of consumers, as even in rebellion the potential of the productive unconscious is still directed to the internal limit of Oedipal desire.

Interlude: FKA Twigs EP2 (2013) and Eros; Or, Can We Still Read Bataille in the Age of Xenofeminism to Come?

FKA Twigs' music puts forth a multiply-directed Eros. Not repressed, but harnessed deliberately rather than arbitrarily (unless it would be more interesting to do so). A cosmic Eros. Her music is the feedback from a radio signal that reveals the underlying architecture within moments of desire, sensation, tension, and release. The question is not should it happen? The possibility of coercion and its associated moralisms comprise the distant past in this sonic universe. The question is now, how should we go about it? But this question is never so crassly verbalized as to force this encounter into the domain of liberal subjectivity (unless it would be more interesting to do so). The concerns of this puritanism, and even of escaping it, remain only in the vaguest memories of the dead. It is far better to play. After all, Georges says this could let us access the infinite (Bataille 2007, 13).

"How's That?" stretches out the moment of the unuttered question, the instant of physical contact over three and a half minutes, with each shiver of the shudder enunciated in a syncopated ripple. The digital homunculus melts on the first contact with the downbeat and thus time and space, while they still exist, have had the rules of their relationship opened up as bodies become topographies. Something is being transgressed that cannot be returned to, as this space is now open. The shudder is different now, closer to pain but, in the absence of actual threat, it never actually arrives there. No, "that feels good, so so amazing."

The swells that open "Papi Pacify" are synchronized to his fingers slipping down her throat in stark black and white (FKA Twigs & Beard 2013). This image, its light and dark contrast, is something that we, in the present of "pharmapornographic capitalism" (Preciado 2017), have been trained to view with a prurient suspicion. It is violent. Bodies are entered, the bass/kick is gaining confidence, and a shriek is stifled with a soft curve to its fade. Again, we are dwelling in moments over the course of minutes. The last remnants of trepidation are cast aside with the line "even if you choke" and the rumble of bass—the open-mouthed chant of giant alien creatures—forms a bridge between the body of the listener and the subject of their voyeurism. This is intensified all the more by FKA Twigs' eyes looking into the camera; a stylistic feature shared by music videos and pornography. The sour glissandos of the strings lets you know, however, that you are somewhere very much other than the commercial conformity of what passes for transgression in the pornography of capitalism. When you can feel the nerves of another creature—so much like you, but so importantly different—like stars of the imaginary sprayed over your skin, what can the petty thrill of the jouissance, a pleasure of acquiring property, still offer you?

Nothing. This is abundantly clear on "Water Me," a song in which the price to make love is both "too much in pound" but simultaneously "free." In fact, once she is asked to set the fee, his inadequacies on this metric become apparent. It looks like the pursuit of jouissance is only open to a few. Perhaps this is why it's better not bother with it and chase something else. She sings, "looks like I'm stuck with me," harmonized with pitched up vocals. Her eyes are oversized and grow even more after the bridge (FKA Twigs & Kanda 2013). The same is true of her pout. Is this just anime or is it hentai? The visceral nature of the ticking, brought out in the waves of the high-cut filter, answers: both and neither. It is the squandered potential of letting the operations of capital structure desire. Those attempts to shock a viewer to attention that are so boring. Oh well, "looks like I'm stuck with me."

There is development being made in "Ultraviolet." The opening is safe, lulling. Things are proceeding at a more quotidian pace. "Hold my hand in error." On the second repetition of this line, FKA Twigs drags the trepidatious lover from "Water Me" by the hand and wrenches them from the ego that required a price from her in order to make love. It doesn't go quietly, as it attempts to retain its connection to this pharmapornographic capitalist structure, which has always been so meaningful but that now is starting to lack definition. The ego is defeated as a matter of course. The wormhole is open and they step through and are now fully immersed in her universe; in her "ultraviolet rays." Things look very different here.

But this is just a projection from where we are now …

***

In his book *The Weird and the Eerie* (2016), Mark Fisher attempts to push past this homebound conceptualization of the strange that seems only able to justify or perversely reinforce the norms that be. With the two concepts from the title of the book, Fisher neither draws the curtains to shut out the outside nor simply burns the house down to destroy the inside, but instead opens the door. The weird: that which is there but does not belong (absent repression). The eerie: that which acts and affects but without discernable agency. These concepts are an attempt to push past the limitations placed on transgression by notions like the *unheimlich*. But given the radical alterity to our experience in what characterizes the eerie, to the extent that Fisher even argues that "Capital is at every level an eerie entity," we should perhaps to turn to the weird as a better tool for redefining the constitution of home. By this, I mean it is time to apply the differentiating capacity of popular music to the construction of the *heimlich* as something weird.

I want to do this by comparing an example of the *unheimlich* as seen in the work of Miley Cyrus,[3] and the weird as found in FKA Twigs (the musical act centered around singer/dancer/producer Tahliah Barnett). Despite, these artists broadly fitting within the category of solo female dance/pop acts, they are very different. FKA Twigs comes from a dance/artworld background and started in the underground EDM scene of London. Cyrus, on the other hand, is the heiress of an American music dynasty, though she is currently working hard to disassociate her current self-presentation from the Disney-controlled version constructed at the start of her career. However, both engage in explorations of hedonism and sexuality in ways that are at odds with normative cultural discourse, although not the activities of capital accumulation and the directionality of such desires.

First, let's unpack the uncanny as expressed by Cyrus. Cyrus unveiled, what could be considered to be, her transformation from Disney star to a more adult-themed pop act during the 2013 MTV video music awards. She performed with Robin Thicke on his hit of that year "Blurred Lines," during which she "twerked" (a dance move involving the rhythmic shaking of the ass while bent over) against Thicke's crotch. The stage was then flooded with backing dancers dressed as seemingly unhappy, perhaps merely intoxicated, teddy bears. This was explicitly an attempt to rebrand Miley Cyrus and it went about this by drawing out the uncanny in relation to Cyrus' previous persona, as a marketing tool in itself. Previous attempts had been made in Cyrus' career to move beyond her child-star fame as the Disney character Hannah Montana. Albums like *Breakout* (2008) and *Can't Be Tamed* (2010) had attempted to repress things that had once been familiar about her and her audience's milieu. This was moderately successful but it had limitations. The end result was a persona that seemed to embody a more adult version of a persistently Disney worldview. The musical equivalent of the pseudo-woke Hollywood trope of a strong young female lead. We see this in Cyrus' music videos from this period, through the straightforward repression of both genuine childlike silliness (in favor of a more age-appropriate pranky-ness), and anything but the most normatively acceptable forms of sexuality being kept away from the camera lest it be placed in uncomfortable juxtaposition with her previous persona. In short, the basics of what is expected of a bourgeois individual: to set aside childish things and to become responsible for meeting their own desires. A discourse we are all encouraged (enculturated, indoctrinated) to follow but that lacks the requisite novelty of a value producing cultural commodity in the twenty-first century. To escape this, some tension, some frisson, had to be brought out. And at the 2013 VMAs, the Disney identity Cyrus had attempted to leave behind re-emerged but in an uncanny form. The bears with half-closed red-veined eyes and swarthy grins, and her costume, reminiscent more of what a child might throw together to play pretend than what a professional wardrobe team would assemble, was placed within a song about the ambiguities, as perceived by Thicke, of sexual consent sung by a man who was dressed as the archetypical sleazy older guy. Childhood remembered through a mirror darkly in the club. The is a clear example of what was discussed above: a purely oppositional logic that draws more attention to the act of transgression itself rather than the space it could open. Cyrus' commodity, which had previously been a bland reminder of how one is ought to live, was now entangled in the jouissance of a transgressive rupture. A violation of the social, sexual, and psychological order that was at the same time entirely facilitated by the existence of that order.

While we might point to any number of stylistic details, it is this point in relation to transgression where we can say that Cyrus differs aesthetically from FKA Twigs. This is not to say that Twigs' work is without jouissance, quite the opposite as it toys so much with it, only that this enjoyment is not limited to the point of transgressive rupture but instead engages with an opening onto the weird. To consider an example, if Cyrus primarily makes use of the mass media spectacle as her mode of musical expression, then we could say for FKA Twigs her primary mode would be the music video. In the video for "Two Weeks" (2014), we see a slow zoom out from FKA Twigs sitting on what seems to be a throne in full Cleopatra-esque regalia, looking straight to camera, singing while engaging in slow gesture-based choreography. As the glacial zoom out continues, we see that she is surrounded by dozens of miniature versions of herself, performing structured dance improvisations. The music is somewhat atypical within the popular genre but could easily have been brought more toward the commercial center with the appropriate visual accompaniment. Instead, what we see is a full embrace of the aesthetics of the weird. There was no moment of rupture in this audiovisual world; at least not within living memory. While much of what we see seems not to belong in our world (at one point the central FKA Twigs pours what appears to be milk or water from her fingertips over a waiting receptive small Twigs), the notion that this experience of recontextualization can only be understood as traumatic is as alien to the world before us as the world of FKA Twigs is to us. Here, within this decadent palace that appears intended to, at once, evoke something of ancient Egypt but also something from science fiction, we can feel both a comfort and a thrill amongst things that, according to the internal limit of Oedipus, do not belong. In this setting, we are reminded of the glorious possibility contained within Afrofuturism, another attempt to move past the political and psychological limitation of the subject. There may be a point to come at which even the memories of escaping the structures of oppression that are so present now will become little more than a historical footnote (Eshun 2003, 287–288).

With the video for "Two Weeks" (FKA Twigs, Nabil 2014), Twigs seems to be playing with the psychological transgression that is expected of her. On the one hand, she seems to be inviting a psychoanalytic reading and, at the same time, she beats the viewer to it and thus illustrates its irrelevance to her work. The visuals are rife with a particular kind of sexuality; skin becoming clothing, musculature revealed through the way light falls on the slightest of perspiration. We can see master/slave (or top/bottom) dynamics expressed through the precise and complex movements of each dancing iteration of FKA Twigs, while the lyrics play with an oscillation between control over and submission to desire. At first, they suggest a certain romantic subtlety ("I know it hurts [You know] I'd put you first") before undercutting it with direct statements, semi-hidden in the production ("I can fuck you better than her"). This is a motion that invites you to see her attempts to contain something repressed in the unconscious, but when it is expressed it is actually a relief. At the end of the video, the camera pans down, below the water of the pool, and in the foreground we find another FKA Twigs alone, floating supine underwater. With a Žižek-informed Lacanian reading, we could say that this is her touching on the inaccessible *real* with all that is above serving as a representation of the symbolic and the imaginary. However, that this reading is so obvious (literally levels of experience governed by a queen-as-big-Other), it seems that the jouissance of this transgression into the real is decidedly beside the point. Unlike with Cyrus' VMA performance, where we can read the mechanisms of this theory fitting precisely into the symbols she presents, "Two Weeks" by FKA Twigs appears to have included a reading of the work in the work itself, leaving the viewer with no need to deduce it. In so doing, it is able to stand outside the normative laws that appear as the structures of reality but which are themselves merely objects within a larger field with which to play, rather than an actual limit.

This can also be found in the sonic qualities of the song itself. The disciplined use of a limited number of digital instrumentation and textures in combination with tropes like the pitched-down vocals that function to blur gender and even humanity, signify, in their timbral darkness, a lineage of this strain of beat-based electronica. This work evokes a conjunction between a form of artistic practice and the milieu in which it was produced that is densely entangled with contemporary geopolitics. Which is, of course, also an economic, historical, and countercultural conjunction. In addition to a sound toolbox indebted to the, problematically named, IDM (Intelligent Dance Music) movement of the late 90s (which itself was indebted genres such as Detroit techno etc.), these elements were formed through established genre conventions of music from various diasporic traditions particular to south London; namely the tempo and rhythms of dubstep. But here some of the sounds Fisher once hailed for their critical potential as expressions of a dilapidated "Afro NoFuturism" (Fisher 2014, 100) in the work of Burial, have been repurposed to imagine a future.

This is not to say that specific histories of cultures and social organization are not present in all musical practices, only that the significance of them to the practice in question varies depending on their proximity to the hegemonic structures of power. This is something we find discussed the post-Foucauldian analysis by the musicologist and philosopher Robin James (James 2017). James argues that the capacity to transgress normative structures and social taboos in the commercial music practiced in a Western pop context has more to do with the artist's capacity to be understood as adhering to certain white identity markers before proceeding to transgress, than any kind universal notion of artistic and cultural progress. Basically, this is to say that what may appear as a transgression of status through the embracing of cultural practices of those who may be considered other by those in a position of hegemonic power, may actually be little more than a way to adapt and incorporate such practices into this hegemonic position. We can hear this in an example of Cyrus' work that James has herself critiqued: the song "We Can't Stop" from the *Bangerz* album (2013). As in "Two Weeks," we find pitched-down vocal production as an important textural and structural element in the work. However, in "Two Weeks," this device is in dialogue with the aforementioned lineage of electronic dance music as a way to explore Afrofuturist posthumanism and the consequences of technological abstraction as a means by which to complicate the fraught concept of identity. Whereas in "We Can't Stop," it could be argued that it is an attempt to appropriate some sort of caricature of black male identity to add a hook to a relatively generic pop song (James 2015, 179). Far from the studios of the VMAs, the music of FKA Twigs, at least at the time of the release of the single, was more at home late at night in a small club than in a well-lit TV studio. In a sense this is a weird home beyond the *unheimlich*, letting in what had previously been kept on the outside.

This should not be read as an affirmation of some problematic notion of authenticity to be universalized, but an attempt suggests that this notion of an open-doored home is not universalizable as anything other than an abstraction. The same particularities that give the music of FKA Twigs the capacity to transgress the normative dynamics of transgression make it incomprehensible to many of those most proximate to that structure of power. This is an audience who will not miss that the work of FKA Twigs moves beyond the normative borders of cultural production but, for them, this transgression can only be experienced in the negative because the jouissance of rupturing norms is, for the most part, tied to the implicit reaffirming of their underlying structure. The reaction is the same as horror's use of the *unheimlich*, a usage that seeks to repress it again. Cyrus' work operates on the logic that excitement offered by the kind of transgression provided in her work should be universally comprehensible. Even more limited than the experience of the *unheimlich* proper, Cyrus' work offers merely the diminished anglicized version of the concept in commodity form. Which is to say, a form of transgression underwritten by the structures of power. We can see yet another iteration of this in her collaboration with The Flaming Lips on *Miley Cyrus & Her Dead Petz* (2015). The figure of Cyrus does, speaks, and refers to things that are not in the territory of a Disney star, i.e., taking drugs, having destructive parties, behaving promiscuously, while at the same time drawing attention to her more normative past: stoned teddy bears, Dead Petz, etc. Even the fact that this collaboration was with The Flaming Lips, a band who rose to prominence in the 90s by repackaging the historically acceptable cultural rebellions of the 1970s, serves to highlight the conformity inherent in her act of transgression. This is a babushka doll of white neoliberal patriarchal normativity.

Conversely, despite her deployment of sexually submissive imagery, the ways in which FKA Twigs complicates it is disruptive to norm-reinforcing modes of transgression. Where in her collaboration with The Flaming Lips, Cyrus attempts to portray some kind of loss of innocence through her involvement with a group of older men, such things are simply banal facts of desire unpredictably colliding with normative constraints in the work of Twigs. For example, the song "I'm Your Doll," from *M3LL155X* EP (2015), requires an audience who is comfortable with the baseline that an adult human female may well have sex of her own volition and have a complex understanding of her agency in those encounters. It is this that allows the chorus to dig further into the complex nature of desire and fetish:

> Dress me up, I'm your doll
> Love me rough, I'm your doll. (FKA Twigs 2015)

The lyrics set up a metaphorical framework of submission to paternalism (Wind me up/Dress me up) that is ruptured by the implicitly knowing injunction, "Love me rough/I'm your doll," much like we heard in "Two Weeks" (I can fuck you better than her). These lyrics are performed in a breathless falsetto, produced so thinly that is barely able to surface against aggressively distorted bass. Yet again, we are listening to an interrogation of the complexities of desire, sexuality, and relationships, rather than being asked to react, as puritans might, to the mere fact of these fetishes' existence. The music video adds further complexity to this. The lyrics alone appear as a declaration of the desire to be submissive, but the video highlights the manner in which questions of agency are at play in this declaration. In the video, an amorphous computer-generated shape inflates, which is revealed, after a time, to be a sex doll. This is then intercut with a slow zoom in on an overweight white man in a tracksuit. He is perspiring and drooling and looks nervous but excited. Eventually, we see FKA Twigs' head atop the body of the doll, alternating between moments of open-mouthed inanimacy, and frantically looking around the space as if in search of escape. We also see, presumably, the man's fantasy of the fully animate FKA Twigs dancing before him, before coming to kiss him. Here we have a discussion of the reductive nature of the male gaze, the complicity of women in its construction and the restrictions to agency and desire within patriarchy for all those involved. Further still, this is also contextualized through the way in which it relates, on a psychosocial level, to the very sense of the possessing of a self that can desire.

In the work of FKA Twigs, the uncanny explored by Cyrus is merely a part of a much broader field open for exploration. The transgression it represents is never normatively coded as a traumatic trigger. To do so, to focus on how to smash the rigid bourgeois notions of home and its associated behaviors, would give these structures the same boost that a smashed window at a protest does, as it valorizes the insurance industry. Instead, the normative coding of the home needs to be regarded not as the barrier that must not be crossed but as the particular fiction produced by historical and continuing restrictions on desire. Because transgression of the rules, structures, and norms are coded into their operation, such acts can only prompt a disciplinary action of their own. But if this conceptualization is possible via pop music, then it may be possible to transform these restrictions into tools to be manipulated rather than not merely transgressed and reinforced.

Burning Down the House?

Our saturation in popular music and its repetitions on the levels of the similarities between songs and styles, our hearing of these songs wherever we go over and over again, and the moment-to-moment recursive repetitions that are so common to the internal structures of pop should be thought of with Deleuze and Guattari's refrain.[4] Or perhaps Deleuze and Guattari's refrain, in all its complexity and ambivalence can only be made to make sense if we think of it through popular music. This is to say that to think of pop as a refrain cannot be regarded as exposing something of an inherently emancipatory capability contained within it, but merely the recognition of an abstract mechanism that it shares with other forms of social organization that can be empowering and oppressive. Home is an example of such a form of social organization similarly entangled in the refrains of life, and one that shares, with pop, a certain ambivalence with regard to emancipation. It is both a site of recuperation and comfort and a site of pain and anguish. It both protects us from the world outside and denies us the full freedom of untethered exploration. It is both a shelter from capitalism and, as it is commonly formulated, a foundational element of it. But the distinction that we can make between pop and home is that pop manifests itself through the motion of the refrain and home is a threshold point of affective and material accumulation in this process.

But what does this mean, when it comes to popular music's capacity to help us escape, if not capitalism, at least capitalist realism? It means that as the kind of creatures that we are—creatures that require, for the moment (Crary 2014), sleep; that require, despite the economic incentives, some sense of connection to others; that require, despite the technological tendency to flatten everything to a search bar, some kind of space in which the projection of our identity can be reflected back to us—we cannot simply do away with home. To do so is to simply make ourselves more amenable to the logic of capital and to dive even deeper into capitalist realism. We see this in the conventional moves of cultural transgression, which seem to create more consumer desires even as they cast off traditionally oppressive structures. Instead, it appears we may have to reposition this threshold of home and reconstruct it through the production of new refrains, many of which will be entangled in our engagement with pop.

But to do this we need to come to terms with our involvement in this situation. When we look at a commercial for a piece of wearable tech that utterly failed to catch on featuring FKA Twigs, are we to consider her transgressive gestures as being just as interpolated into capital as those of Miley Cyrus? In a banal sense, yes. But when people exist in the conditions of capitalist realism, whatever sustenance their work may provide to those with a desire to escape from the systems in which we live, the force of capital will always be present. This is the reason why this problem is so vexing as Mark Fisher writes, for Deleuze and Guattari capitalism must be understood:

> … as a kind of dark potentiality which haunted all previous social systems. Capital, they argue, is the "unnamable Thing", the abomination, which primitive and feudal societies "warded off in advance". When it actually arrives, capitalism brings with it a massive desacralization of culture. It is a system which is no longer governed by any transcendent Law; on the contrary, it dismantles all such codes, only to re-install them on an ad hoc (Fisher 2009, 5).

So when we see and hear the uncanny escapes of Cyrus, what we are seeing and hearing is the ad hoc re-reinstallation of laws of old. Many of these laws we may well be glad to see the back of but others may have offered different avenues of escape from capital. This is why, even in her material complicity with capitalism, the work of FKA Twigs still pushes past this trad transgressive refrain. Her work, in the sense meant by Fisher, is expressive of the aesthetics of the weird, which operate through a differently constructed refrain. If that which the law understands and deems to be outside itself is not actually outside, then Cyrus' escape and transgression of her Disney childhood is but training for her audience in the new form of mass consumption, with the end goal of reproducing new Disney childhoods to be escaped in the future. The refrain of the uncanny and the constitution of the *heimlich* and its shameful secrets. However, FKA Twigs' work does move beyond the *unheimlich* into the weird. Whatever kind of refrain it engages in, it is not merely the return of the repressed but a return home that brings with it something that is truly of-the-outside. And in this outside is where we find the eerie and capital. When Twigs advertises for Google Glass, it is not the disciplining of the internal limit that capital has recognized in her, but that part of capital's own outside force that pushes it towards schizophrenia.

In his own terminology, Fisher claims capital itself to be "at every level an eerie entity: conjured out of nothing, capital nevertheless exerts more influence than any allegedly substantial entity" (Fisher 2016, 11). FKA Twigs' desire to escape brings her and us into contact with the eerie of capital, that space which is paradoxically beyond the disciplinary inertia of capitalist realism. The eerie and the outside that contains, but is not synonymous with, capital. Nonetheless, capital is eerie. It is not at all clear that humans can fully inhabit such an outside, eerie space and nor is it clear that to do so would be desirable. But it is within the refrain of the weird that we find artists like FKA Twigs, who incorporate something of the outside into the reconstruction of our homes. Perhaps with this we can at least move beyond capitalist realism and construct new sonic fictions. Beyond the insufficiency of a world so starkly delimited materially, aesthetically, and affectively by the internal limit of capital. Capitalist realism is the manifestation of Oedipus, and pop music can move through it as a conjunction between this internal limit on desire and the external limit of capital. With the price of music falling closer and closer to zero, perhaps the opportunity exists to split popular music from the logic of capitalist realism's internal individualizing limit—the music in your headphones on your commute—and move beyond to a conjunctive network of weird refrains. If this can be achieved, perhaps the open-doored homes of the weird could start to be built.

○

Vignette: One of Two: Carly Simon's New Boyfriend

I tried to sit, and write about a feeling I had had when I was younger. But it took some time and effort for me to go back far enough. The teenage years are the obstacle as this was a time when the discursive structures that surrounded me in my limited social circles were becoming more evident. These structures to which I could attach myself openly, structures that served as my means of communication with others, a means of exchanging signs. But the origin of these structures, or at least my understanding of them, precedes the signs with what could perhaps best be understood as shapes. These shapes themselves referred to feelings I had had years before, when the records that were played in my home were without context and without my curation. To me, the sounds they made were as near pure to sensations as anything I can remember; shot through with possibilities in the sodden, but quickly solidifying, projection of what I understood then to be real. A real that was, and always is, all around me but also always so far away.

So I arrive at this project, a thesis, now a book, to make sense of it all and to put these sensations in a political frame. But I am still blocked by that later entrance into the discursive structures and identity construction, into the field of social capital. The jargon of authenticity that the "white noise" of guitar music thrives upon flows out of too many of my tributaries. I should make clear here that I am not trying to claim some sort of psychological repression, or that it is only in childhood innocence that such feelings can be accessed. So many similar sensations can be reached in so many ways, and music has only ever been one particular infinite set among an infinity of others. What I have been trying to do over thousands of redrafted, rearranged, referenced, and rejected words is break through to a sensation felt before it could rest on these discursive crutches that can so quickly transform it into disappointment. And of course, limitations spring up instantly in the act of description. Each detail I add subtracts as it communicates.

I go back as far as I can remember to my first memory of being powerfully affected by music. There is an image in my mind of me dancing around the living room, only a little older than a toddler, to a particular piece of music. I think part of why this memory is clear is perhaps because something of this was filmed on VHS tape, but I'm sure I remember some points of view that would have been impossible to capture on tape. I don't know the name of the song or the artist, but I remember it was a woman singing and, from my present vantage point, I know the song was rife with the generic conventions of American 1980s pop. But I also remember the chorus. I type it into Google, but it is a common phrase for anxiety searches, which slows me down a little.

It turns out this formative memory was inspired by the song "My New Boyfriend" by Carly Simon. I don't think I have heard this song for twenty years and it was ten years old then. The song's video is at the top of the search results and I, of course, clicked to watch it just before writing this sentence. At that moment I had never seen it before. But as the video begins, I am instantly made aware of why this particular song has not made its way into becoming a dominant part of the narratives of our pop cultural history. The music is ok, and I recognize those elements that have been so heightened in my memory, and I try to work out if I can rationalize their defense, cliché ridden as they are. The lyrics would likely be considered problematic if the song had retained cultural relevance. But the main reason this song has not made its way into the media packages of nostalgia programming that fill TV schedules, which have done so much to ossify our ideas of our recent cultural history, is that much of the video is racist. Not racist in the sort of spectacular way but more as the result of a sort of pathetic negligence that is characteristic of so much media.

This is all an act of willful corruption on my part. As I use the skills of listening I have developed over the decades since I last listened to the song, what was once a mystery is revealed to be something eminently solvable. The power of what I felt to be so many voices I can now identify as the product of the burgeoning art of studio wizardry. I now hear the echo on the drums not as unknowable rhythmic thunder but as hack production. I now hear what were once thrilling alien textures as the inevitable result of performing with the sounds of a sampled instrument through the volume envelope of a keyboard. Most unfortunate of all the lead vocal, lyrics aside, have now been stripped of their previous excitement, as the sensibility of my present-day ear hears a singer of such competence that the pop limits of this song allows nothing to be at stake. The shapes of the melodic lines imply a dramatic potential that cannot manifest itself as the peaks are well within Simon's capabilities. The technical safety of everything in this song could be a synecdoche for an Adornian manifesto of all that is wrong with pop.

To be confronted with all this is in some ways disappointing, and this disappointment was only ever a few well-placed search terms away. But this is the trap of nostalgia; what memory can do to sense data and what reality can do to memory. There is the temptation here to dwell in this disappointment and claim that the view of this work offered to me now by the knowledge and faculties I have cultivated over the years is the superior position. After all, this view offers ready access to discursive truth content, which is what places me among my peers. At the same time, the nostalgist would hold that the place that the experience of this song holds in my personal narrative should be prized above all else and that only empty pain awaits the rational and knowledge bound.

I cannot find a reason to honor either of these positions, however. One appears to want too much of the song and the other too little. And on different criteria, vice versa. The problem is that these positions are a part of structures that serve something else. Something outside of the experience or the memory of the experience. A narrativizing machine into which these memories and experiences can be inserted and so meaning can be coherently attributed. This is not bad in and of itself. What is bad is to mistake it for the final analysis of reality, rather than what it is: a partial description of processes of perception. This is not to say judgment is impossible, only that it, to some extent, betrays another position. In addressing this song, I may have to betray these positions that would attempt to imbue it with meaning. But then what would I be getting at?

○

5

Conjunction

More, More, More

What the previous chapters have shown is that pop music is haunted.[1] It is haunted by a capacity for absorption and attention capture that cannot even be fully contained in the notion of the spectacle. Rather, it's more akin to the shimmer in Netflix's version of VanderMeer's *Annihilation*; something that does not simply mask the nature of reality but refracts it through the force and flows of capital and desiring-production. Pop music is also haunted by its complicity with capitalist desiring-production and through this we can discover ourselves as haunted by this complicity even as we use these sounds to help define ourselves. Nonetheless, we encode onto pop another new desire to be free of this complicity, to be unburdened and granted catharsis from both the corruption produced by our complicity and the suffering in the world that we have helped to produce and reproduce. But what is this unburdened state we wish to return to? Is that not the very imaginary place from which this process began? The home that pop built is also the home of capital and of Oedipus. But such is the entanglement of this haunting that we cannot simply cast these concepts or this music aside without merely reinforcing all that is problematic about the arrangement. A rupture of the laws and structures of our desires that are tangled up in pop can only serve to expand their power as they derive material resources from the commodity of comprehensible novelty that makes a rupture apparent and provide succor to an inevitable backlash. That said, more subtle works that play with the formal capacities of pop in such a way as to illustrate the trivial nature of transgression may lie just outside the vernacular that allows the designation of such music as popular to be meaningful. In short, the manifestation of other forms of desire that push against the origins of the form in the desiring-production of pop's interior limit, are themselves limited in reach and comprehension. We saw this in the works of FKA Twigs, which attempts to operate in a field wherein the act of transgression is merely one object amongst others instead of serving as the ruptured pseudo-absolute boundary that only produces transgressive novelty as a commodity. There is perhaps some oblique potential herein, but this work lacks the comprehensibility to be properly experienced as pop, despite its innumerate points of conformity with the form.

To lament this is to simply reproduce the critique of Adorno on the hunt for emancipatory artworks, like Goldilocks sampling porridge. Pop cannot be thought of as a form that one can get "just right." The potential it has to exceed itself is rich with creative possibility but risks the cost of making the popular part of the label vestigial. However, due to pop's iterative nature, in other words its abstract mechanisms as a refrain, there is also the potential for something more immanent to pop proper. Something else that has haunted pop just as capital accumulation has haunted all previous social systems and permeated and confounded desiring-production. Something haunts capitalist realism too. To uncover this we need to think of pop differently. We need to throw out conceptions of it as either pure commodity or aesthetic artifact. We need to rely less heavily on understanding its tangential capacity for community, alienated consumption, libidinal investment, or isolated headphone listening defense mechanism. Instead, we need to see it as the unstable point of conjunction between these and countless other flows of social, political, libidinal, and economic forces, which are themselves comprised of fluxing conjunctions of their own. And it is in this conjunction that we may be able to find the amplifier of pop's desiring-production and seize the potential of the distortions of its drive to concoct shimmers of different patterns of refraction and better sonic fictions.

And (1) and (2) and (3) and …

So, what is meant by conjunction? This term is used by Deleuze and Guattari in *Anti-Oedipus* directly in relation to the production of desire (2013a, 103) in the form of a synthesis, the last of a series of three that allows a subject to produce desire. Before the conjunctive synthesis there is the connective synthesis, during which the body becomes aware of things with which it can interact, which is to say the possibility of desire, and the disjunctive synthesis, where the body becomes aware, in a similar way to the Lacanian mirror stage, of what it is not, which is to say psychic separation. The difference between this and the mirror stage is that, for Deleuze and Guattari, this is not enough to produce a subject. Becoming aware that there are things in the world that you are not the same as or immediately proximate to can't provide the force required to produce the experience of lack, which Lacanians consider to be definitional to subjectivity, because, for Deleuze and Guattari, it is not sufficient to produce the subject who would perceive and experience it. These first two phases create an awareness of the flows of desire via the realization of the body's capacity to follow these flows and the experience of not being synonymous with them yet being able to plug into and disconnect from them. It is in the immediate aftermath of this that these two syntheses create a tension. The connective synthesis allows for the experience of the infinite and inherent desiring-production of reality, while the disjunctive synthesis places subjective limits on this desire by asserting the separation, distinction, and multiplicity of the body, bodies, others, and other things. This tension, between the infinite that inheres in reality and the finite nature of reflective perceptional positionality, is then processed through the conjunctive synthesis, which is an attempt to resolve the contradictions of these syntheses. However, they cannot be resolved fully. This process of an attempt at a conjunctive synthesis produces a residue, comprised of a combination of Eros (desire as possibility) and psyche (psychic separation). It is this residue or excess that animates the desiring subject. In Deleuze and Guattari's formulation, the subject is not some authentic creature of unrestricted connective desire that is always already there, nor are they totally cut off from what they desire and made to awaken as subjects of lack. Instead, they are what is left over after the synthesis of conjunction; the desiring subject, which is characterized not by "either/or" but by "both/and" (2013b, 116).

This then maps onto Deleuze and Guattari's ontological conceptual framework of the rhizome—the actual and virtual heterogeneous multiplicity that cannot be fully apprehended and which all human systems of knowledge reduce and constrain in their attempts to explain elements of it. This framework allows for the social construction of subjectivity whilst offering material explanations as to both why it experiences itself as separate from the world and why it is, in fact, not. But why bring up the weeds of this 1970s hippy philosophy, yet again, in the discussion of pop in our contemporary moment of capitalist realism? Well, if you continue to bear with me, it is because it is with this remark from Deleuze and Guattari that Franco Berardi begins his book, *And: Phenomenology of the End* (2015b):

> A rhizome has no beginning or end; it is always in the middle, between things, interbeing, intermezzo. The tree is filiation, but the rhizome is alliance, uniquely alliance. The tree imposes the verb "to be," but the fabric of the rhizome is the conjunction, "and ... and ... and ..." This conjunction carries enough force

to shake and uproot the verb "to be." [And to] establish a logic of the AND, overthrow ontology, do away with foundations, nullify endings and beginnings. (Deleuze and Guattari 2013b, 26)

Berardi uses this to argue that previous systems of meaning production have been, if always in a limited and incomplete way, oriented to producing semiotic chains that more resemble the conjunctive nature of the rhizome. However, under the emerging technical, economic and social regimes of neoliberal capitalism there has been a cultural shift away from "conjunctive concatenation to a model of connective concatenation" (Berardi 2015b, 11). Where previous social formations may have had cultural, aesthetic, and political concerns that would supersede the demands of the market, at the time of writing *And* in 2015, it appeared to Berardi that the concerns of capital accumulation were placed above whatever else anyone might think to do with these resources. Meaning had been placed in 1:1 correspondence with capital accumulation, that which would valorize was the right thing to do. Arguably, in recent years we have seen a strong countermove to this from the ethnonationalist right, though it is doubtful this will lead to any immediate damage to the connective semiotics of neoliberal capitalism. In music consumption, this plays out in a way that may seem smaller but is perhaps indicative of what is being lost. Keeping well clear of any kind of reactionary argument that would boil down to "well-it-was-better-in-my-day," it seems significant that the story of how one may stumble across any particular musical recording has largely been reduced from complex engagements in the world and perhaps with other people, to the search function on the software client of a streaming service paid for automatically by subscription. Whatever possibility for the production of difference may be contained in the audio itself is being flattened by contemporary models of content distribution that make each new discovery ever more similar to the last.

For Berardi, this has significant effects on the production of aesthetic experience and, ultimately, ethical and political activity (11). This is because there is something of an isomorphism between the syntheses of Deleuze and Guattari's formulation of the desiring subject and, for Berardi, the culturally available forms of semiosis and their relation to meaning. To express this, Berardi proposes three figures: that of the artist, the engineer, and the economist. He considers the first two of these to be the figures that comprise the contemporary general intellect:

The artist is the creator of new concepts and percepts, disclosing new possible horizons of social experience. The artist speaks the language of conjunction. In artistic creation, the relation between sign and meaning is not conventionally fixed but pragmatically displaced and constantly renegotiated. The engineer is the mast of technology, the intellectual who transforms concepts into projects, and projects into algorithms. The engineer speaks the language of connection. The relation between sign and meaning is conventionally inscribed in the engineer ... (196)

Both of the general approaches contribute different intellectual resources to culture. The engineer can use the language of connection to create technology that, in Berardi's terms, facilitates the refusal to work that is the precondition for the development of human intelligence (192). Subsequent to this, the role of the artist is to reap the benefit provided by this facilitation of the refusal to work and, in so doing, use the language of conjunction to expand the field of the possible. In other words, to diagram new potential modes and resonances of meaning on a field that cannot be readily reduced to a 1:1 relationship. This then feeds back to the engineer who can uncover the new kinds of connections in this newly expanded field of possibility that further allow for "the liberation of time from work" (198). But it is the economist in this formulation that Berardi sees as a threat to the production of meaning and thus social reality. The "fake scientist and the real economist who has been charged to reduce the combined power of the artist and the engineer into the established rules of capitalist accumulation" (196). For Berardi, it is more proper to think of these economists as the priests of capitalism, rather than the status they claim as scientists. They perform the role of desire management that priests did in feudalism under the conditions of instrumental enlightenment. Their role is to discipline the desiring-production of the general intellect in line with the teleology of capitalism. Thus economists make imperatives that serve the interests of capital, limiting the connections that the engineer can make by casting the conjunctions of the artist off as meaningless.

What strikes me as odd, sifting through these old texts of desire revolution and the newer ones about semiotic anxiety, is that it seems that the figure of the pop musician could be said to be all these figures in one. And as such she perhaps represents a conduit, through which we may find new lines of flight through and, hopefully, out of capitalism. This is not to say that the answer lies in some vague and mystical power of a piece of music, but that it may be in our relationship to this work and the affects this relationship emanates out into the world. The way pop captures attention, brings us into complicity and offers us catharsis and home may be configured in such a way as to help to disentangle us from the machinations of Berardi's economist while simultaneously being implicated in them. We could open up new ways of hearing and feeling popular music if we can experience it not only as the expression of semiotic conjunction but perhaps also subjective conjunction, wherein those kinds of subject formation most inclined to reproduce capitalist realism are brought into an unstable relation with those who desire it to be torn down. But it is not enough that a select few achieve this. So, if this argument is to work, we need to find this conjunctive configuration in the material that constitutes our cultural atmosphere. In a sonic shimmer out of which almost no one can step.

Lemonade

There are no other contemporary artists in popular music who have, or have had, the same level of prominence, influence, or commercial success as Beyoncé. Since her rise to prominence in the late 1990s with the girl group Destiny's Child, Beyoncé (the stage name/public persona of the person Beyoncé Knowles) has transcended the designation of musician, to occupy a space more akin to the role of an (inter)national treasure. In addition to a string of hugely successful solo records, viral music videos, and coinages entering the popular lexicon (for example, "bootylicious" is now a term that the Google Docs spell check can recognize), Beyoncé is also one half of a music industry power couple with her husband the Hip Hop artist, Jay Z, who, like her, is also something of an entrepreneur. At the same time, Beyoncé has built a brand beyond music, attaching her image to various product endorsements and clothing lines. In many ways, she could be seen as a clear example of the American dream coming true, which today should be understood as the central narrative of neoliberalism and capitalist realism. Indeed, by operating in so many fields, she is able to make full use of the mechanisms of virtual futurity that valorize capital in cultural production today (Parisi & Goodman 2011, 167). This has rapidly moved her image toward the state of simulacra, which makes it all the easier to separate two elements of Beyoncé as a cultural phenomenon: Beyoncé as desiring-production and Beyoncé as phenomenological experience. This is to say that of course, as Robin James points out, Beyoncé's persona and work are resistant to simple explanations (James 2015, 115). While, phenomenologically, there are certain points in Beyoncé's career that could be pointed to as supporting the racist patriarchal power structure of American capitalism, for example her song "Video Phone" with Lady Gaga (ibid), and her clothing line,[2] at the level of desiring-production, her recent work has been disruptive to this simplistic political understanding.

In the first half of 2016, Beyoncé released the single "Formation," which caused controversy due to its lyrical content, the accompanying music video, and her performance during the halftime show of *Super Bowl 50* as they were interpreted in the media. However, this was merely a teaser for the release of her visual album *Lemonade* in late April of the same year. The elements that made this work controversial could perhaps be characterized, in the terms suggested by James, as an engagement with a hegemonically understood "bad investment" in *black masculinity* (2015, 114). In that, the album's narrative is a story of betrayal and eventual forgiveness purportedly made in response to her husband's real-life extramarital affair. In other words, in our white supremacist cultural narratives, black masculinity must be understood as a dangerous other, which black women must reject to be accepted by the power structure. This was confounded in the redemptive element of this album. However, it could also be argued that *Lemonade*, rather than simply resisting this cultural narrative, unpacks this notion of *black masculinity* and exposes it to be a synecdoche. Which is to say that this notion is, in fact, a coded defense of the current neoliberal ideology that allows capitalism to function by relying on the hegemony of bourgeois white masculinity as the norm. A norm that, in order to maintain market relations, must illustrate their liberal credentials and so celebrate those of other non-white ethnicities who work to adopt the norms of bourgeois white masculinity as a precondition for entrepreneurial endeavors. This is something James calls MRWaSP (multi-racial white supremacist patriarchy) (12). This normative position is keen, not only to let others conform to it but, also, to appropriate certain practices of *the other*, in such a way as they no longer threaten the status quo. What is curious about Beyoncé's *Lemonade* is that it skirts this line effectively. The album affirms the neoliberal value of the individual overcoming adversity whilst at the same time affirming those parts of black culture that are anathema to the ideological foundation of capitalist realism, though perhaps not capital accumulation itself. In simpler terms, Beyoncé's success on this album is in part to do with the deployment of novelty that was, at least at the time of release, unable to be appropriated by the status quo and was thus, for a time, actually dangerous to it.

Interlude: Beyoncé's "Formation"

"Beyoncé's 'Formation' is a battle cry," says a fan's blog, probably. A conservative blog attached to an ostensibly respectable media company, which has never mentioned her before, calls the video/song (Matsoukas & Beyoncé 2016) a declaration of war. History looks different to some. Has the war that was feared for so long finally started or is this just another battle? Perhaps this conservative blog may have mentioned Beyoncé before. If they have, it would have only been to connect her to the Illuminati. So, in the first line of the song she addresses this blogger directly, calling them "haters," calling them "corny" with their references to the Illuminati, from the top of a police cruiser sinking into a flooded New Orleans. A horror that the powers that be did nothing to prevent. The flooded suburb is an arresting image, but it also looks more like an elaborate magazine spread and less like a stagnant pool of death resulting from institutional neglect.

This sample is not pop, though, and it is not stopping. It's a guitar filtered through a creepy cartoon, broadcast late at night on some obscure cable channel in the 90s and now available all day online. "My Daddy Alabama, My Ma' Louisiana, You mix that negro with that creole make–a–Te–x–a–s—Ba-maaah" (Beyoncé et al. 2016). The event of Beyoncé's birth has literally shifted the flow of time. The creepy sample goes on just as steady but at a new rate of iteration, and with all this change it's becoming more familiar. Against this, the bass stumbles but intentionally; always righting itself again by its rounded form. There is something about the world outside this song that makes the motion of the bass seem to be an impossibility. But we can still hear it.

This is, of course, a sales pitch; a teaser trailer. This does, of course, *slay*. This does, of course, take him to Red Lobster. She just might be a black Bill Gates in the making. Meaning, this video will be played in every home with an internet connection this year. Odd then to see the police as a force monopolizing violence as opposed to just "protecting property rights." And this is next to Southern gothic, from which we are to infer the subtext. We see retro 90s denim cool. And the face of Martin Luther King. Beats didn't sound like this when VHS blurred like this. Beyoncé exists outside of time, or maybe she owns time? "I work hard/I grind 'till I own it." (Ibid)

She sings; "Ok Ladies, now let's get in formation." (Ibid)

She sings; "Ok Ladies, now let's get in formation."

The last line she sings is: "Always stay gracious, the best revenge is your paper," and the video/song opened with a sample: "What happened after New Orleans?" The subversion of this juxtaposition can be missed because this is, of course, a sales pitch. What seems like a crazy collage is actually a force to mobilize something. Does the little boy, dancing in front of the police defeat them or buy himself time? Is this the same time that Childish Gambino is spending as he's running in the sunken place? Should you fight if losing is a certainty? Perhaps it will help to change something. It will make Beyoncé richer and, of course, the best revenge is your paper. Is this self-serving or just a way to avoid absolute defeat? There is a mug in my kitchen cupboard in Copenhagen that belongs to my flat mate that reads; "What would Beyoncé do?"

***

Lemonade transgresses the boundary of material ready for profitable appropriation. However, as we saw in the previous chapter on FKA Twigs, the transgression itself is not the point. In fact, the transgression, as with FKA Twigs, is only noticeable to those without the cultural vocabulary to interpret the conjunctive significations that it unfurls. There is an audience ready to embrace the complex structures of meaning communicated in *Lemonade*, but this is not everyone and nor should it be. Here, we might be able to offer that as something of a provisional axiom: *transgressions against the dominant power structures/discourses/modes of production, can only actually alter these structures if their enjoyment is not rooted in the act of transgression but in the space that has now been opened up*. Which is to say, a necessary quality of norm-expanding transgression is that it only appears as a transgression to those who disapprove of it or want it to be stopped.

To see such an axiomatic mechanism in action, it is necessary to step away from the nuance and subtly of intersectional feminist musicology and poststructuralist French thought and spend some time looking at the reactionary opinions on right-wing blogs. To them, who are at once outside the semiotic system and inside the hegemony of MRWaSP, a lyric such as this example from the song "Don't Hurt Yourself," is nothing more than a grammatical error followed by a clear message to young girls to "use sex as a weapon to possess and to gain revenge" (Walsh 2016):

> Who the fuck do you think I is?
> You ain't married to no average bitch boy
> [...]
> As I bounce to the next dick boy
> And keep your money, I got my own
> (Beyoncé 2016)

While of course, these elements are not absent from the text, to insist that this is all that is going on is a position that mostly displays the ignorance of its holder. Indeed, to frame it as advice demonstrates Berardi's point about how much of contemporary discourse is restricted to a mere semiotic connection. This is the story that is told by an economist. One can blame pop singers for their influence on young people but to make such conservative critique at the very least coherent, the view would have to be broadened to incorporate the individualistic hero worship inherent to the contemporary ideological framing of capitalism. Which, of course, is almost never brought in.

But if we read this through semiotics of conjunction, these lyrics tell a different story, which would itself also offer only an incomplete reading. As mentioned above, *Lemonade* is widely considered to be a concept album building from a supposed affair had by Beyoncé's husband, which then spirals out to encompass an exploration of struggle in general and for black American women in particular. The truth of the initial kernel of the affair is both unknowable and unimportant, and the recognition of this basic hermeneutic fact is the first move toward being able to engage with conjunctive semiotics. With this conceptual frame, the lyrics above can be viewed as a part of the narrative's construction by starting to flesh out a character in a particular situation. This distance can be heard in the first line of the song, making use of an idiomatic feature of Black American English, as the first person becomes the third person ("I is"). The album is not, as even some of its most ardent fans would argue, a set of instructions for how to react to romantic betrayal, but an exploration of the experience of betrayal as situated in a larger historical, political, and cultural context. The listener is confronted by a definite claim that turnabout is fair play. The confrontational affect of this position stems from the boundary that enforces the sexist ideas that do not consider women to be agents in their lives and in the world, and, even more so, in the case of sexuality. But what we see in "Don't Hurt Yourself," is a desire to be able to move into a new space outside this boundary. To spend time there and assert agency. While the conservative blogger can only comprehend the transgression.

It is because of this need to hold focus on the transgression that it is difficult to find much in the way of serious conservative critique of Beyoncé, so here we are forced to make do with contemporary clickbait journalism (in this case from the conservative commentator Matt Walsh, but another prominent and similar example can be found in the journalist Piers Morgan, whose prominence in this kind of thing precludes the need for citation). In short, the intellectually vacuous nature of these positions stems from the need for the transgression to overdetermine the material. Thus, they operate on bad faith as the conjunctive semiotics of the artwork (or even those of a cultural commodity) are slouched off to connect *Lemonade* to a discussion on the boundaries of propriety. With Cyrus' music, the boundaries of propriety were the point, as was the criticism it received, so it was always already appropriated. But with *Lemonade*, there is much more going on, in such a way that immediate appropriation was not possible at the point of release and so the work needed to be diminished to reinforce capitalist realism.

Popular music can express more in three minutes than political discourse can in 300 pages, which is just another way of saying what Eshun already has: "you don't need any Heidegger, because [George] Clinton's already theoretical" (Eshun 1999, 190). In this way, I would say that the shimmer of *Lemonade* highlighted certain things that were only just emerging in political discourse. The views of Walsh and Morgan, as set against the entrepreneurial project of Knowles, highlight what was then an under-explored schism on the right between its neoliberal and traditionalist wings. And, more worryingly, it showed a certain convergence with some strains of the radical left. This was, in fact, how I found Walsh's critique of *Lemonade*. A friend of a friend on Facebook posted the piece cited above. Their intention was to voice an arguable point of radical feminist indignation at what they saw as the uncritical celebration of a problematic mainstream work of pop music. Which is to say, they understood *Lemonade* as a work that promotes the weaponization of sex and the pursuit of material wealth. Such was their frustration with the unqualified celebration *Lemonade* was receiving from most of the liberal press that they reposted the piece without noting that the author assumes that young women are completely lacking in agency. Indeed, these women only exist in relation to a (presumably male) parent, as the title reflects: *Beyoncé is Destroying Your Daughter, Not Empowering Her* (Walsh 2016).

Herein lies a problem for both the political right and elements of the left. For the right, the traditional alignment of capital with established power has been coming unraveled with the unchallenged advance of neoliberalism under the conditions of capitalist realism. Deleuze and Guattari would describe this as the outcome of capital's capacity to deterritorialize power relations, only to reterritorialize them in forms more conducive to the flow of capital (2013b, 345). Berardi would point to a consequence of this in the way meaning is being reduced to simple connection rather than more complex conjunctions, i.e., 1:1 rather than and and and and. And this is where this project needs nuance in the mission of escaping capitalist realism. There is a tendency on the left to reject any of the freedoms that capital produces as being tainted, and in so doing to abandon the project of emancipation in the future in favor of desiring to return to an imagined past in which things were somehow more pure. Of course, it is right to be wary of any supposed freedom produced through the mechanisms of capital, but to reject them en masse outright forecloses the future as a space of possibility in the same way that Fisher argues it has been cancelled by neoliberalism (2014, 8). Such a view casts capital as an undefeatable, unspeakably evil foe and whether or not that is the case, to operate with such an assumption is the end of any emancipatory politics.

With this in mind, it should also be made clear that *Lemonade* is not a leftist project. The last line of the example above hints at a theme that runs throughout the album: Beyoncé's capacity to make her own money and accumulate capital in order to attain power over others. We see this theme made more explicit in the lyrics to the song "6 Inch Heels," which is an archetypical example of the "look, I overcame" narrative James claims is indicative of neoliberal pop (2015, 78). The song features a long bridge that appears to tell the story of the persona Beyoncé has adopted:

> Stars in her eyes, she fights for the power, keeping time, she grinds day and night, she grinds from Monday to Friday, works from Friday to Sunday (2016)

Here, beyond the necessary economic activity for material survival, we have the lionization of hard work for economic gain as the path to personal fulfillment. We could call this the first ideological move of capitalist realism (the second being that "there is no alternative"). This is a seven-days-and-sleepless-nights a week grind she enters into not only of her own free will but, it appears, in pursuit of the libidinal pleasure of this investment. In what seems like a page from Jean-François Lyotard's *Libidinal Economy* (2015, 124), there is apparently more pleasure in self-destructive capital accumulation than in any material commodity. The goal here is the power afforded by capital, or at least proximity to it. On one level, this is a neoliberal fairy-tale in which hard work and force of will can raise anyone above the circumstance of alienation. However, this fairy-tale must always disavow the unavoidable fact that, for this to be possible for some, it must not be possible for others, and in fact it is the latter who comprise the vast majority if this accumulation is to be meaningful. But to leave it at this is a mere connective reading.

For a more conjunctive critique of *Lemonade*, we should consider the response of the theorist, bell hooks. Although, it is of course still incomplete.

hooks opens her analysis by noting that *Lemonade* is "capitalist money making at its best" (hooks 2016). Some have seen this remark as a pointed barb, and to an extent it is, but it is also an ambivalent Marxian recognition of capitalism fulfilling its potential in an effective way. For the case in point, hooks refers to the visual album's opening, which sees Beyoncé in a designer hoodie—the "the controversial hoodie" (ibid), as hooks calls it. This garment is a complex symbol. Taken with the scene later in the visual album, in which the female relatives of black men murdered by the police sit holding photographs of their dead, this appears to be a gesture of solidarity and perhaps even defiance. But hooks immediately undercuts this in the parenthetical statement "[s]peaking of commodification, in the real-life frame Beyoncé's new line of sportswear, *Ivy Park*, is in the process of being marketed right now." This is a complicated intersection because, as hooks is quick to remind us, "Beyoncé's audience is the world and that world of business and money-making has no color." So, we have this hoodie as a statement of solidarity with the recent increase in social and racial justice activism and a simultaneous cynical ploy to capitalize on it. It is conspicuously a commodity in search of its USP. But the analysis can't stop there because, as indeed hooks does, it could be argued that, in the complex assemblages of images and sonics, "Beyoncé and her creative collaborators make use of the powerful voice and words of Malcolm X to emphasize the lack of respect for black womanhood" (ibid). Thus, this provides the questionable but real resources of representation to a group who have been marginalized both in terms of representation and material power. Simultaneous with their marginalization, black women also comprise a group who, under the conditions of patriarchy, often have a great many economic responsibilities and little structural support. As hooks notes, representations that recognize this situation are worthy of celebration.

At the same time, however, hooks asserts that the version of intersectional feminism that Beyoncé puts forth is a fantasy, because it suggests that liberation is possible simply by surviving the adversities of economic, racial, and gender oppression, rather than by moving beyond the material circumstances and arrangements that produced them. If mere survival is put forth as the highest goal, then all that one can do is maintain the conditions of suffering and inequality. To reproduce capitalist realism. For some, it may be possible to escape certain facets of oppression through acquiring material wealth. However, to attain this wealth, which is something that bears no relation to any social order that could be considered just, means maintaining a system of inequality. And while this system may claim to now be just about the money, to have moved on from the bad old days of slave labor facilitated by the codification of racism and sexism, it is still willing to deploy these modes of oppression whenever they can help facilitate the process of accumulation (James 2015, 12).

This all being said, there are limitations in hooks' reading as she reproduces an oddly limited understanding of music as the kind of ubiquitous relational phenomenon as we have seen it to be in previous chapters. Which is to say, she sees music as a way to facilitate your continued participation in the status quo by understanding it as promising to provide the missing piece to complete the subject rendered incomplete or damaged by capital, rather than considering the relationship between music and listener as the site of potential perhaps facilitated by capital but always in excess of it. This is not only insufficient for an emancipatory politics, but it might actually work against it. hooks' position appears to be that, while it is laudable to expand the mass media representation of black women, the work in question, overall, is little more than an exercise in the valorization of capital. And thus, despite the nuances she adds, the final view provides a banal and almost definitional observation of a piece of mainstream popular music. This point of view, while infinitely richer than the conservative critiques,[3] still fails to give Beyoncé the license that is extended to other songwriters. And, as such, it fails to account for the affective potential of this music as a relational phenomenon, or as a site of conjunctive concatenations. Even hooks, due to Beyoncé's identity, reproduces the false notion that there is necessarily a 1:1:1 correlation between what it is that is sung, who it is that is singing, and how the meaning of that singing is received. Only now it is not the specter of black womanhood and sexuality here to disrupt the development of teenage white girls as the conservatives fear, but instead the figure of the entrepreneur offering false hope to the proletariat, while becoming rich from their admiration. And while it is true that certain artists make the gaps between these communicative steps more overt (for example, Father John Misty (2015) uses his real name in the title of the song "The Night Josh Tillman Came to Our Apt.," thus highlighting the artifice of his musical persona) and Beyoncé is playing more closely to some notion of traditional authenticity, it doesn't excuse the paucity of critique that can't get beyond this romantic notion or attend to the commercial and aesthetic value of the artist using it as a tool. This deforms the affects and desiring-production that inhere in *Lemonade* into something like a straightforward manifesto rather than as a point of semiotic and aesthetic conjunction.

The clearest example of this conjunction is the song "Pray You Catch Me," co-written with James Blake, which invites interpretations of internal subjective multiplicity that would be flattened if we were to attend only to the official PR narrative. The opening, comprised of syncopated vocal layering, forces the main vocal to appear as merely the momentary coalescence of a subject articulated through sensations rather than a fixed or fully defined individual. In addition to this, the jazz-influenced harmonies of the synthetic keys introduce a type of dissonance that is out of keeping with much of Beyoncé's best-known work. Whereas the dissonance in songs like "Diva" from *I Am ... Sasha Fierce* (2008) asserts something consistent and aggressive, these chords seem to point to something insidious and destabilizing. This is not to say it is uncontrolled, but rather it is suggestive of a subject position that is used to being close to the mechanisms of control but now is in conflict with persistent destabilizing sensations that are alien to it. This plays into the interestingly self-destructive subject matter of "Pray You Catch Me," wishing to be caught eavesdropping on a lover's betrayal rather than revealing the discovery of the betrayal in a more confrontational manner. This is an expression of a momentary and subjectively disruptive feeling, not the depiction of a purely wronged subject, sketching the project of revolution from the moment of betrayal. It is a study of the sensations themselves as they are experienced from a particular position.

None of this is to say that a piece of music should not be analyzed from a narrative standpoint, nor that the facticity of what they contain should not be combed through for data points. All that is being argued is that when one does this they are not engaged in a process of uncovering what is truly there but rather one of creation, based on the decoding and over-coding of affects and semiotics entangled with their own production of subjective desire. So if we are to try and see what made *Lemonade* so exciting to so many, which should be of interest to those who wish for some kind of universal human emancipation, we have to consider what it is that it might do, rather than just critique the brute facts of what it is.

This is at the heart of sociologist Zandria Robinson's celebration of Beyoncé's recent output. Following the release of "Formation," in February 2016, Robinson published a celebratory analysis on her blog, in which she considers the work to be:

> ... a different kind of resistance practice, one rooted in the epistemology of (and sometimes only visible/detectable to) folks on the margins of blackness. [...]

> Formation, then, is a metaphor, a black feminist, black queer, and black queer feminist theory of community organizing and resistance. It is a recognition of one another at the blackness margins–woman, queer, genderqueer, trans, poor, disabled, undocumented, immigrant–before an overt action. For the black southern majorettes, across gender formulations, "Formation" is the alignment, the stillness, the readying, the quiet, before the twerk, the turn-up, the (social) movement. (Robinson 2016)

For Robinson, it is the initial step of expanding the understanding of what constitutes knowledge for her audience that makes Beyoncé's recent work important. This is not necessarily the first step toward emancipation, but it is nonetheless a necessary one. However, at the same time, as we read in hooks, such a step is always partial and incomplete, compromised, and limited. Though, this only adds to the need for such things to be brought forth.

What is put forth in *Lemonade*, both in the semantic meaning of the lyrics and the musical lineages it references, are not the means by which we will be able to emancipate ourselves from the oppression of capital. Instead, *Lemonade* offers a point of aesthetic conjunction to those with the patience or inclination to decode it. And due to the particularities of its formal condition in the popular music vernacular, much of the communicative work has already been done. We can read in Robinson's analysis of epistemic resistance an articulation of a very contemporary form of W.E.B Du Bois' notion of double consciousness (Gilroy 2007, 126). That being that, the particular experience of being black in America is of being both aware of who you consider yourself to be and who you appear to be to the white majority. The concept originated as a description of life in the Jim Crow era but we can see how it permeates Beyoncé's work in a subtly mutated form on *Lemonade*. Whereas for Du Bois double consciousness was about understanding how going about your business can be understood by others to be a provocation, *Lemonade* draws attention to this bifurcation as an important tool for capital by at once criticizing it and playing its game even when the deck is stacked against you. We are presented with the way in which what is called "black culture" is commodified as a novelty and used to valorize capital and how the idea of a straight on resistance is a luxury position mostly enjoyed by those who will actually do nothing. This was also the case in Childish Gambino's "This is America," though it brought a little more of the Jim Crow definition back to the concept and perhaps a little more irony, or perhaps cynicism.

The wide ranges of expression of black femininity in *Lemonade*, praised by hooks, are the tools of epistemic resistance that Robinson celebrates. They open up a space and the possibility of discourses that the industry often seeks to tightly control when rendering the presentation of blackness. This is particularly the case for black female musicians who are made to appear as some kind of reductive, exotic deviation from the white norm, which could also be a description of parts of Beyoncé's earlier career. Expanding this frame of reference of the knowable runs the risk of simply producing new commodities of novelty, but it cannot be reduced to this. In James' parlance, this kind of blackness continues to be a risky investment for capital. Indeed, even if capital is able to find some way to absorb this kind of expression, it remains to be seen if capitalist realism, as we know it, composed of an uneasy alliance between neoliberalism and conservatism, will be able to survive the depth of deterritorialization that such an inclusion would require.

We should have no illusions about this. It is a problematic compromise. This is however, all that the figure of the pop star—as the combination of the figures of artist, engineer, and economist—can provide. It is fantasy feminism, and fantasy anti-racism, and "capitalist money making at its best," as hooks describes. Artworks and albums in themselves are not the source of emancipatory potential. And nor are they merely a healing salve. But what they can do is provide a point of conjunction that allows us to uncover the structures of connection and disjunction that are usually hidden. They allow us to experience the affective potential and the possibilities of action and desiring-production. This form of epistemic resistance cannot be pure because it is about what can be done and letting the greatest number of people know about it. It is, in the Deleuzian and Spinozan sense (Deleuze & Guattari 2013b, 300), a question of ethics that is pre-political. For this, we need the knowledge that complexifies our understanding of ourselves and of the world. Because it is in this complexity that we find the source of ethical strife and ambiguity, but also a position capable of understanding, decoding, and sharing these conjunctive significations.

It's the End of the World as We Know It (And I Feel Fine)

It is not possible to know if Beyoncé's claimed involvement with feminism and the fight for racial justice is genuine or not. To suppose it is would rightly seem naive.[4] To suppose it is not would require a level of cynical speculation and arrogance of which we should be wary. While authorial intent is, of course, not the locus of meaning, let alone the emancipatory potential of an artwork, it is an energetic force that amplifies the conjunctions often denied by the dominant discourse surrounding the experience of pop. A simple synthesis of these two positions on the matter would also be wanting as it leads to the conclusion that the album is merely the folly of good intentions when lacking in rigorous class analysis. A conclusion that is patronizing to both the entrepreneurial strategy of Beyoncé and to the desire produced in her fans that she might just hold some key to saving the world. Perhaps it is not that we are to resolve this contradiction at all. Perhaps it is more that we should attempt to work through this dissonance—isolating the frequencies of resonance and breaking down the molar wholes so that we can reconstitute what any of this means.

In *Infinite Jest*, Wallace suggests to us that cynicism and naivety are not mutually exclusive. He then goes on to demonstrate this in ways that are often heartbreaking. This is particularly true in the strand of the novel that follows the reformed burglar and recovering addict, Don Gately. Aside from the abuse he suffered in childhood, we also see an unresolvable contradiction in the ways in which he engages with the rituals of Alcoholics Anonymous (AA), the only thing that is presently allowing him to keep going. We see this most clearly in the step of relinquishing his will to that of a higher power. Gately does not believe in any sort of God; in fact, he finds the notion ridiculous, but every day he is on his knees asking the ceiling to relieve him of his will (Wallace 2007, 467). Such moments of knowing and cynical surrender to naive notions are presented as being in some way necessary. Especially by the crocodiles, the older members of AA, who have a standard answer to a question they are frequently asked by the new members about how AA works. They respond "just fine" (350). None of this is to say we ought to buy into the quasi-mysticism of this approach. All it is to say is that *knowledge as such* is not enough. This is why the notion of conjunction is powerful. When faced with a 1:1 explanation of any facet of the world, conjunction will always point to some kind of empirical excess that complicates the existing schema and expands it into epistemic spaces previously considered outside. This is also why it is right to see popular music in terms of conjunction, because it allows the contradiction to be explored not as something in need of resolution to fit the schema but as something that allows the schema to be modified beyond recognition. It asks the ethical question of these apparent internal tensions: what can be done with this? And it allows for provisional answers to emanate and mutate into all of the other processes and practices in which we engage.

Something about this appears deeply unsatisfying as a response to the problems discussed throughout this book so far. In truth, AA makes a dubious claim regarding its effectiveness (Grey 2012) and Beyoncé has enriched herself greatly, in part through her association with a recent upsurge in media interest in social justice. And still, the dilemma above persists. To consider the attempts of pop to grapple with the injustice and insufficiency of the status quo as naive performs a similar move to the neoliberal foreclosure of the future. The same could perhaps be said of the cynical reading too, though it comes with perhaps more blinkered arrogance. Similar to the discussion that has run throughout the preceding chapters, both responses appear to be too negatively defined by the structures that they ostensibly want to resist. Naivety is too willing to accept that some things produced knowingly by the system of power can somehow be a threat to that very system of power, and cynicism is hopeless as it tacitly accepts the immovability of the system and, eventually, even looks to benefit from it (Žižek 2008, 25).

Throughout most of his work, Wallace struggles with these positions. Knowledge of the world and intelligent modes of engaging with it seem to lend themselves to a default insufficient cynical stance. And for this reason, he is, at times, too uncritical of the impulse to adopt the naive position, which can often lead to the denial of the knowledge necessary for life to function. However, a way through this can perhaps be found if we attempt to disentangle his use of the terms "cynicism" and "irony." Wallace has a habit of using these terms interchangeably when critiquing the postmodern condition as found in the media landscape after the end of history. However, Berardi argues that such a conflation is a mistake, and the distinction between these terms is vital to overcoming our present predicament with regards to a larger program of emancipation. He writes:

> The common starting point is that both the ironist and the cynic suspend belief in the moral content of truth (and also in the true content of morality). They know that the True and the Good do not exist in God's mind, nor in history, and they know that human behaviour is not based on respect for any law, but on empathy and shared pleasure [...]. The cynical person bends to the law while mocking its values as false and hypocritical, while the ironic person escapes the law and creates a linguistic space where the law has no effectiveness. The cynic is someone who wants to be on the side of power but does not believe in its righteousness. The ironist simply refuses the game, and recreates the word as an effect of a linguistic enunciation. (Berardi 2012, 20)

We saw this motion at play to some extent in the works discussed in the previous chapter. With this frame, one could say that Miley Cyrus represents the cynical position (a breaking of the law that illustrates its power) and FKA Twigs the more ironic position (an ignoring of the law). That being said, irony shouldn't be mistaken for a virtuous position because such virtue would require a system capable of bestowing something recognizable as virtue upon it. In actuality, these positions may be correctly considered as evil in relation to the systems they are within, as there is something duplicitous about them. They do not heroically stand against injustice; in the case of cynicism it reproduces it, and to an extent irony disregards it. So, if we accept that the manner of resistance necessary to overcome our present impasse may well not be free from the corruption of capital, then perhaps we need to make sure that we remain ironic rather than cynical? This remains unclear. But what the cynical and ironic modes illustrate is the manner in which the system strives to compensate for that which it has not yet been able to be appropriated. This is why FKA Twigs was offered the opportunity to sell the now long forgotten commodity, Google Glass, and why establishment figures like Michelle Obama rush to celebrate *Lemonade* (Young 2016). What is needed, then, if we are to be able to make use of irony at all, is to find ways to use these contradictions productively rather than simply considering them to be abject betrayals. Because an ironist cannot be betrayed.

In the conclusion of *And*, Berardi explores the quasi-mythical figure of La Malinche (Berardi 2015b, 331). La Malinche was an Aztec woman, sold as a slave to the Mayans shortly before the arrival of Cortés and the early Spanish colonizers. With her knowledge of the languages of these two native cultures, she was employed by Cortés as a translator and later became his lover. Many considered her to be a traitor to her people, both the Aztecs who sold her and the Mayans who enslaved her. Berardi argues that she owed these people, who had made her a slave, nothing. Hers was an ironic position in relation to these systems, because she knew she could expect nothing of the societies from which she had come and to whom she been sold. To her, the injustices of Cortés to come were abstractions compared to the injustice she had experienced at the hands of both the Mayans and the Aztecs, and thus she operated without faith in the existing systems from which she had come and the systems of meaning that constituted their worlds. But through her acts of translation, a betrayal does occur. Berardi uses this story to illustrate how "a world ends when the signs proceeding from the semiotic meta-machine grow indecipherable for a cultural community that perceives itself as a world" (ibid). He argues that the translations provided by La Malinche facilitated the destruction of the semiotic systems that enabled the Mayan and Aztec worlds to exist. He then draws parallels between this destruction and the present destruction of conjunctive codes by the automaton's connective worldview (336) and asks if it is possible for humans to find new means of conjunctive language in our new technological paradigm. His conclusion is that there is something in the process of betrayal in which La Malinche engaged from which we must learn if we are to survive the transition from our present semiotic paradigm to the next.

While there is a troubling nostalgia that runs through this particular section of Berardi's work—a hunger for a bygone age when things were more meaningful—the recognition that one cannot simply return to an imagined preferable previous state, combined with the notion that the only way through this is to sacrifice any semblance of purity, offers a way in which we might be able to think of pop as tool of emancipation. The type of knowledge that can be derived from popular music contains something of the nature of our actual conjunctive reality; a reality that is composed of material exploitation, the enjoyment of excess, gendered, and racial exploitation, the libidinal investment in identity, unjust and just violence, and violence as a brute fact, the thrill of rhythmic intensity and the re-temporalization of time, the communicative ecstasy of semiotics, the ease and convenience of reduction and the expansive vistas of seemingly infinite resources, the drive of capital to create, and the unacknowledged cost of assets stripped and appropriated to make this all possible. Much of this goes into the production of capitalist realism, but much of this cannot be contained by it. Pop can serve as a conjunctive bridge between these worlds

The experience of conjunction and the media that produces it relies on indirect signification and it is without a fixed system of signification to rely upon. Therefore, if it is to be experienced as such and not reduced to connection, it requires those undergoing such an experience to engage in the creative act of reconfiguring these capacities through the intensive network of the affects that produce them. So, not only is this more difficult than the 1:1 connections contemporary culture demands, but its outcome, in practice, is always uncertain. Indeed, what is certain is that the practice will reveal, and perhaps actually enact, the corruption of any project of emancipation. For example, it is a simple statement of fact, at this historical moment, that the route out of racial oppression that is championed by Beyoncé and the political culture in which she is an icon is not available to the majority of those suffering it. Beyoncé may enunciate the desire for a project of black female emancipation, and all the while perpetuate a conservative notion of gender roles and profit from a system that has helped to restrict others access to this project. AA will tell you to renounce yourself and your will to a higher plane to get sober, but declares, like neoliberalism, that it is you, the individual, who is to blame when this fails. Popular music, even of the most vapid and banal sort, has the power to transport you to an intimate position of pure identification with the mechanism of economic control and oppression under which you suffer, and causes you to enjoy the experience and even invest in it libidinally. It is not the job of a theoretical text such as this to redeem popular music. It is irredeemable but it has also never been in need of redemption. It was never a missing piece misshapen by capital, but a point of convergence through which we have the capacity to integrate with capitalist realism or act otherwise. There is no point in giving Beyoncé notes on how to improve her feminist anti-racism. There is only an opportunity to uncover previously unknown deficiencies that the apparent corruption of her approach reveals. These corruptions create new conjunctive networks as we continue on this infinite task. As Robinson argues, what is needed is a resistance rooted in epistemology, but this cannot come from Beyoncé. It can, however, come from the proliferation of conjunctions, like the intersection of Beyoncé with Robinson, which allow us to hear more in the music than we could before. The moments when Robinson finds the expression of something in "Formation" that has escaped her previous attempts to articulate it is such a conjunction in action. The question is: Can we follow this methodology as far as we may need to?

What might this look like? Back in the chapter on Fisher's *Capitalist Realism,* outside of this book within a book, I tried to dig into the misunderstanding of the oft-touted truism that it is easier to imagine the end of the world than the end of capitalism. Fisher, of course, understands this to be the function of capitalist realism, itself producing an endless chain of dead-end connective significations that seem only to mock the concept of meaning and the hunger for it by providing, instead, only glimpses of the rapacious monstrosity of capital accumulation and the horrendous affective oppression of contemporary life. But a clue as to pop's power to help us escape from this state of blinkered imaginative horizon is given by Fisher in his tragically curtailed *Acid Communism* project, in his focus on the potential for psychedelic collectivity in The Temptations and the manipulation of time that their music injected into the capitalist machine of pop (Fisher 2018, 767). This was a manipulation of time that could destabilize the symbol systems of, then emerging, capitalist realism. So, with everything that I have listened to so far, I am left to wonder if perhaps we should just pursue the path of least resistance first? Perhaps we should imagine the end of the world as a way to bring capitalist realism down with it?

If the problem is, in part, rooted in the effect that capitalism has on the production of meaning, and the world as it is only exists to the extent that this system of meaning remains coherent, comprehensible, and applicable, can we not imagine the end of capitalism by imagining the end of the world? After all, we see this kind of imagination at work in Eshun's future African archeologists, subjects who examine artifacts from our world long after its end. In our world—a world constructed by capitalist realism as informed by the intellectual tradition of MRWaSP—the very subjectivity of these African archeologists is inflected by the fact that the concept itself was constructed to exclude them. After the end of this world, however, these archeologists are able to explore the ruins of our primitive culture unburdened by our myopic semiotics.

This project to bring about the end of the world is no stranger to black studies. The desire to bring about the end of the world built by capital accrued through the deployment of anti-blackness is foundational to the position of afro-pessimism (Wilderson 2017). When surrounded by a system of meaning-making and exploitation that was built upon the plunder and destruction of black bodies that continues in other forms to this day, the notion that there is nothing of this system to which one must necessarily remain loyal may come more easily to those whose bodies have been actively disavowed by this system than it does for those with white bodies for whom the social ontology of capitalist realism was explicitly created. I'd argue we can hear this ironist status in what gets called "black music." I'd argue that the conservative tendency in the musicology of old to denounce rhythm as animalistic was a pre-capitalist check brought into the twentieth century to defend against the encroachment of signification systems that conflict with meaning-making that established the bourgeois norm (Gilbert & Pearson 1999, 42). I'd argue that to claim one has published a comprehensive musical analysis of the last seventy years of popular music through scientific means and to neglect rhythm, is the result of capitalist realism performing a version of this function today (Serra et al. 2012). And it is here that we see the schism between the system that produces meaning, and the world we know, which is capitalist realism, and the unnamable thing that has haunted every human culture that is capital. While capitalist realism, which takes MRWaSP as an ideological tool, may seek to minimize the semiotically destabilizing force of blackness, capital flows to territorialize new potential markets. We see the unease with which this epistemic expansion is met in the response to "This is America," and in the response to "Formation"; we even see this semiotic anxiety in response to the appropriation of blackness by Miley Cyrus.

But this confounding of the codes of capitalist realism has always been present in pop because it was through the blues that the form we know today as pop emerged. We can hear this in music that could be regarded as the pinnacle of entitled male white whine: "Closer" by Nine Inch Nails (2004) owes much of its success to the syncopated bass line with its extreme wah-wah timbre that was clearly inspired by the keyboard of Stevie Wonder's "Superstition" (2000 [1972]). Moreover, the pulsing beat in that song is what keeps it at the intriguing level of bodily sensation rather than being a mere disquisition on sexual frustration a la 90s hip ennui.

This should not be mistaken as being a call to some kind of black Jesus (Misty 2015) to rescue the world from capitalism. It is not some evocation of an authenticity essential to blackness that is somehow powerful enough to overcome capitalism. It is merely a demonstration of the fragility of the codes that hold the world of capitalist realism together when we take a view that refuses the limitation of its particular (post)modernism. And in the specific case of pop, it is a claim that we can hear in this music the kinds of difference, differentiation, and conjunctive codes that we should be listening out for when it comes to thinking about what world should replace the one that has started to disintegrate around us. In pop, blackness, or more accurately given the need to de-essentialize this concept, "afro-modernity" (Weheliye 2005, 19), is one such set of confounding codes. But so too is queerness, as is the recoding of the body's capacities in ways distinct from those demanded by capital. It is also a claim that the flows of capital and desiring-production have brought this about as the promise of valorization forms the deployment, through pop music, of codes problematic to capitalist realism and threatening to render it incoherent as a semiotic world. But this is not to claim that this mechanism is enough to overcome capital or capitalism. I still have trouble imagining that, as the range of hoodies available from Ivy Park is ever expanding.

It is still easier to imagine the end of the world than the end of capitalism. But if we can attend to that first task, betray our allegiance to this world and become complicit in the expression of the codes of a new world, a new home, it might be possible for our songs to offer a little more than cathartic compensation for the suffering inherent to the status quo. We can start this by understanding pop music as a space of affective and semiotic conjunction that drags with it all the potential and problematics that inhere in both its production and consumption. From there, it is just a question of sculpting this resonance, compressing its intensity, and amplifying the right frequencies to bring what it can help us to imagine out in the mix.

◐

Vignette: Two of Two: On Xiu Xiu and Mixing

Before I learned to play guitar, I often did not know what I was hearing when listening to music. Since learning, there are many occasions when I miss this particular capacity for ignorance. I recognize that some of this stems from nostalgia, but I believe there is something else to it. It was an ability to experience sound not absent of signification but not filled with the conventions of the established signifying chains.

A long time after having learned to play and record, I was pretty good at mixing for about a year. In the creation of pieces of music from recorded and sampled material, I had arrived at an aesthetic sensibility and developed the capacity to manifest it technically. I have since allowed this to atrophy, though I don't think it would take more than a little practice to get some of the feel for this back. The question is finding the opportunity to put the time in.

When I was mixing at my best, it captured something of my younger self's ignorance. It brought mystery back to music. In the sensibility I was cultivating it was not so much the case of bringing out the sonorous qualities of instruments but detaching these qualities from instruments. An adjective used to describe what I had stumbled into could be blurry. Though if it went so far as to become a wash, I had overdone it and my technique would not hold the piece together. For me, the goal seemed to be that everything would have its place but there would be no way to identify a point of separation between them. It would be in some ways comprehensible but also an utter mystery.

My relation to genre had similar qualities. My work was not so original that it defied genre convention. It was gloomy noisy guitar music. But the idea of knowing in advance what qualities were required to articulate genre conventions, prior to writing a song, repelled me. On some level, it still makes me uncomfortable. Each instance of recording seemed so variable in terms of outcome that to know how to cope with this in advance, when the material could—if only on a micro level—be so indeterminate, seemed a painful limitation. But this was not a position of intuitive wisdom as my fumbling around to find new ways to cope with each new set of samples and recordings made a mountain out of each project. This was a paralytic that, in part, led to me losing my touch, such as it was.

Despite clinging to particular artifacts in my practice, which for someone like me charted routes of signification so trodden they led directly to cliché, the notion that I should direct my work in line with particular conventions frustrated my ego. The goal was to make something that moved past conventional frames of understanding in which a sound was reducible to an instrument that had a lineage of signification. However, unlike many other forms of expression, in music making this desire is frustratingly attainable. The non-melodic, unformed, arrhythmic, and low-fi can take your work straight to incomprehensibility and it still might be performed, if only for an audience of two. So, at the same time, I had no desire to enter the realm of abstraction that had been expanded by modernism. This abstraction came with its own particular signifying networks, which also held little interest to me.

What I wanted to make, if I were to give it a firm comparison after the fact, was the music of Xiu Xiu. A California indie-noise-art-rock band, built around the multi-instrumentalist singer and songwriter, Jamie Stewart. This band had provided a sensibility that haunted the development of my practice. I first came into contact with them when I was sixteen or seventeen, on the MySpace page of a girl that I had found compelling when I had met her at a party. When her profile page opened, the automatic music player loaded and began to play the song "Boy Soprano." The song opens with aggressive irregular hits of a shrieking distorted, maybe, organ, before a pause and then dropping into something else: at once guitar music and eight-bit and cohesively organic. However, when Stewart's voice enters, breathy and fragile yet aggressive, the world this song had produced cracked along its tectonic plates:

> Look at me, nothing bad is ever going to happen to you again,
> Although you are a solid pile of hate you're still pretty like a cake (Xiu Xiu 2006)

I had no idea what this was. Even with the internet at that point, the world of my small-town music community was structured on binary definitions. Music was pop or rock, serious or comedic. But the confluence of elements at play here in the construction of some jet-black humor started to swirl in such a way as to produce contradictions that seemingly both resisted and did not require resolution. The fact that this music was saturated with a particular queer sensibility would escape me for years to come until I escaped the narrow view of desire limited by the nerdy "nice guy" martyr complex; a point of forking roads that can lead as easily to misogyny as it can to loneliness. In short, I was, although I didn't know it, listening to an expression of the ironic in the terms laid out by Berardi. A way of engaging with the complexities of existence and experience that did not succumb to the logic of existing power structures that would attempt to limit them.

Instinctively, this spoke to me, but within the scenes of exchange that I lived then and for the years that followed I could not communicate why. This is not to say that no one would understand me. It is more that I couldn't work out how to take on the risk of investing myself in this mysterious, this other, way of expressing the inside's entanglement with the outside. So, my attention drifted. Years later, with some grasp of a variety of theoretical tools, I can label elements of this experience with concepts that attach it to a rich history and extraordinary communities, but this still feels insufficient. I can produce thousands of words that attempt to articulate an experience of connection, disjunction, and conjunction that is radically at odds with so many others and so many other ways of talking about it, but still, this sensation has not been described or even adequately pointed to.

I didn't listen to Xiu Xiu again for almost a decade. This was not a conscious choice but rather the upshot of not knowing how to incorporate their work among the vast majority of experiences that were more readily comprehensible and communicable. All the while, however, blindfolded I chased this incomprehensible, incommunicable sensation that I felt could produce a difference. I pursued it with my ears through the computer, attempting to train unruly sound sources in such a way as not to bring out their origin but to transform them into something new.

I came into contact with Xiu Xiu again recently, which is what shaped the confluence I am now attempting to describe. It was at a festival in The Hague; the tickets were a gift from my girlfriend. She did not know the band, and I was surprised to see that they were headlining. They closed the final night of the festival in a gothic cathedral performing their interpretation of the soundtrack to *Twin Peaks*. Few combinations of established artworks and practitioners could have worked so well. Regarding expression, *Twin Peaks* could be thought of as the inverse of Xiu Xiu, as both produce an unsettling combination of the darkness and absurdity that motivate so much of human desire and agency so often disavowed by the cultures of capitalist realism. But these artists balance these qualities well in subtly different proportions. Importantly, common to both is that they dwell in this space beyond the boundary. They investigate its contours, its edges, and surfaces, the constituents of its atmosphere, and present it back to the very structures that would disavow it.

In the final piece of the concert, after a spoken word performance by the band's now former keyboard player, Shayna Dunkelman, who gave a haunting reading from the diary of Laura Palmer that she had kept to cope with and, perhaps, normalize the abuse she has suffered in the series, Stewart, off mic, breaks into "Mairzy Doats" the nonsense novelty song that Palmer's father, abuser, and murderer sings once he has recovered from the shock of his daughter's murder. Again, I feel the plates shifting as things that appeared to be something particular are revealed to be becoming something else. Again, I feel everything has its own particular place but I cannot tell where one ends and another begins.

Notes

PART 1

Chapter 1

1   A compound neologism of hyper- and superstition that describes an idea expressed in the present that can bring itself into actuality in the future.

Chapter 2

1   Boring dystopia was Fisher's wry formulation to describe some of the defining aesthetic and affective components of capitalist realism. It was based on the observation that, despite all the technologies of self-surveillance, the expensive pricing of services that should really be cheap or free and the liminality of public space controlled by governmental or corporate power, the trains don't run on time, the cash machine is out of order but charges you anyway, and Google maps has taken you to the wrong side of town. For a short time, Fisher attempted to use this concept as the basis to construct a Facebook community around this idea. Fittingly enough, Fisher eventually had to shut it down, as the dynamics of social media played out on that forum as they do everywhere else. (Kiberd 2015)
2   In the presence of such an AI, please ignore the rest of this book.

PART 2

Chapter 1

1   This section's heading is a reference to a lyric (Radiohead 2009).
2   See *Global Culture Industry: The Mediation of Things* (2011) by Scott Lash and Celia Lury.
3   "All popular music is (as is folk music by definition) essentially, if not legally existing in the public domain. Listening to pop music isn't a matter of choice. Asked for or not we're bombarded by it. In its most insidious state, filtered to an incandescent

bassline, it seeps through apartment walls and out of the heads of Walkpeople [...] Difficult to ignore and pointless to imitate: how does one not become a passive recipient?" (Oswald 2008 [1985]).
4. "This wise old whiskery fish swims up to three young fish and goes, 'Morning, boys. How's the water?' and swims away; and the three young fish watch him swim away and look at each other and go, 'What the fuck is water?'" (Wallace 2007, 445).
5. This section's heading is a reference to a lyric (Swift 2014).
6. All of these examples were gathered from BBC Radio 1's official UK Top 40 Chart for the week beginning 5 April 2015.

Chapter 2

1. This section's heading is a reference to a lyric (Bikini Kill 1996).
2. Basically, this is the kind of word you arrive at when you try to avoid using the word you're defining in the definition. This passage is a description of how subjective desire emerges from pre-subjective desire. A more straightforward word could be "drives," but it is loaded with meaning from previous uses. The way around this that Iain Hamilton Grant found in his translation of *Libidinal Economy* by Jean François Lyotard was the term "pulsions" (Grant in Lyotard 2015, xvi).
3. "Map" is used here in the sense that Wallace does in *Infinite Jest* (2007, 202), as the organization of things by which we understand our own personhood to be constituted, which it definitely seems like he is borrowing from *A Thousand Plateaus* (2013b).
4. Though not far from how it was viewed at the time (Michaels 2008).
5. This section's heading is a reference to a lyric (St. Vincent 2012).
6. A mineral that is used in the manufacture of computer components found in smartphones.

Vignette: On "Bored in the USA"

7. The reason for the parenthetical addendum to this title of this vignette is that between writing the first version of this piece in 2015 and now, the video I refer to in this section has been removed from *The Late Show* YouTube channel; however, some pirate versions can still be found online. This may be due to the show being retooled with Stephen Colbert as host following the retirement of David Letterman.

Chapter 3

1 This section's title is a reference to a lyric (Simone 2013).
2 This section's title is a reference to a lyric (Simon and Garfunkel 2001).
3 This section's title is a reference to a lyric (Avalanches 2001).
4 This section's title is a reference to a lyric (Pixies 1989).
5 This section's title is a reference to a lyric (REM 2016).

Chapter 4

1 According to Žižek, this is key to any real philosophical advancement (2004, ix).
2 For the clarity of this argument I'm going to use the German word *unheimlich* for the next little bit, to be closer to the cumbersome literal translation of un-home-like.
3 Though now I'm going to move back to the anglicized "uncanny" as the interplay between the German concept and the resonances of the English translation capture more accurately the commercial strategy of Cyrus.
4 This section's title is a reference to a lyric (Talking Heads 2006).

Chapter 5

1 This section's title is a reference to a lyric (Andrea True Connection 1997).
2 Which, while it has been shown to be the paying some of the highest wages for sweatshop labor in the world, still employs sweatshop labor (Oppenhiem 2016).
3 Simply by understanding it as a commodity of pop music rather than advice provision.
4 This section's title is a reference to a lyric (REM 2016).

References

Adorno, Theodor W. 1991. *The Culture Industry: Selected Essays on Mass Culture*. London: Routledge.

Adorno, Theodor W. 2012. *Aesthetic Theory*. London: Bloomsbury Academic.

Adorno, Theodor W. and Max Horkheimer. 1997. *Dialectic of Enlightenment*. London: Verso.

A.P. Møller—Mærsk. 2018. *About*. www.maersk.com/about (11/12/2018)

Arendt, Hannah. 1978. *Eichmann in Jerusalem: A Report on the Banality of Evil*. New York, NY: Penguin.

Aristotle, & Barnes, J. 1984. *The Complete Works of Aristotle: The Revised Oxford Translation*. Princeton, NJ: Princeton University Press (Vol. 2).

Attali, Jacques. 2011. *Noise: The Political Economy of Music*. Minneapolis, MN: University of Minnesota Press.

Ballard, J. G. 2014. "Fictions of All Kinds" in *#Accelerate #: [the accelerationist reader]*, edited by Robin Mackay and Armen Avanessian, 235–240. Falmouth: Urbanomic Media Ltd.

Bataille, Georges. 2007. T*he Accursed Share: An Essay on General Economy. Vol. II. The History of Eroticism. Vol. III. Sovereignty*. New York, NY: Zone Books.

Baudrillard, Jean. 2001. "Dust Breeding" in *CTHEORY*, a095. www.ctheory.net/articles.aspx?id=293 (13/12/2018).

Baudrillard, Jean. 2012. *The Ecstasy of Communication*. Los Angeles, CA: Semiotext(e).

Beller, Jonathan. 2006. *The Cinematic Mode of Production: Attention Economy and the Society of the Spectacle*. Hanover, NH: Dartmouth College Press.

Benjamin, Walter. 2008. *The Work of Art in the Age of Mechanical Reproduction*. London: Penguin Books.

Berardi, Franco. 2012. *The Uprising: On Poetry and Finance*. Los Angeles: Semiotext(e).

Berardi, Franco. 2015. *And: Phenomenology of the End: Sensibility and Connective Mutation*. South Pasadena, CA: Semiotext(e)

Berardi, Franco. 2015a. *Heroes: Mass Murder and Suicide*. London: Verso.

Boltanski, Luc, Ève Chiapello, and Gregory Elliott. 2018. *The New Spirit of Capitalism*. London: Verso.

Boswell, Marshall. 2005. *Understanding David Foster Wallace*. Columbia: University of South Carolina Press.

Bown, Alfie. 2015. *Enjoying it: Candy Crush and Capitalism*. Winchester, UK: Zer0 Books.

Breuer, J. and S. Freud. 1957. *Studies on Hysteria*. New York, NY: Basic Books.

Buchanan, Ian. 1997. "Deleuze and pop music," *Australian Humanities Review*, No. 7, 1–5.

Buchanan, Ian. 2008. *Deleuze and Guattari's Anti-Oedipus: A Reader's Guide*. London: Continuum.

Cage, John. 2008. "The Future of Music: Credo" in *Audio Culture: Readings in Modern Music*, edited by Christoph Cox and Daniel Warner, 25–28. New York, NY: Continuum.

Castells, Manuel. 2000. *The Rise of the Network Society*. Malden, MA: Blackwell.

CCRU. 2014. "Swarmachines" in *#Accelerate #: [the accelerationist reader]*, edited by Robin Mackay and Armen Avanessian, 323–331. Falmouth: Urbanomic Media Ltd.

Collins, K. Austin. 2018. "Donald Glover's 'This Is America' Is a Stylish, Ambitious Provocation—But What Is It Actually Selling?," *Vanity Fair*, May 2018. www.vanityfair.com/style/2018/05/donald-glover-this-is-america-review (13/12/2018).

Crary, Jonathan. 2000. *Suspensions of Perception: Attention, Spectacle, and Modern Culture*, Cambridge, MA: MIT Press

Crary, Jonathan. 2014. *24/7: Late Capitalism and the Ends of Sleep*. New York, NY: Verso.

Cuboniks, Laboria. 2017. "Xenofeminism: A Politics for Alienation" in *Futures and Fictions*, edited By Henriette Gunkel, Ayesha Hameed, and Simon O'Sullivan, 213–230. London: Repeater.

Cybernetic Culture Research Unit. 2017. *CCRU Writings 1997–2003*. Falmouth: Urbanomic Media Ltd.

Dean, Jodi. 2009. *Democracy and Other Neoliberal Fantasies: Communicative Capitalism and Left Politics*. Durham, NC: Duke University Press.

Debord, Guy. 1977. *The Society of the Spectacle*. www.marxists.org/reference/archive/debord/society.htm (13/12/2018).

Deleuze, Gilles. 2011. *Difference and Repetition*. London: Continuum.

Deleuze, Gilles and Félix Guattari. 2013a. *Anti-Oedipus: Capitalism and Schizophrenia*. London: Bloomsbury Academic.

Deleuze, Gilles and Félix Guattari. 2013b. *A Thousand Plateaus: Capitalism and Schizophrenia*. London: Bloomsbury Academic.

Deleuze, Gilles, Hugh Tomlinson, and Barbara Habberjam. 2018. *Cinema 1: The Movement-image*. London: Bloomsbury Academic.

DeNora, Tia. 2000. *Music in Everyday Life*. Cambridge, UK: Cambridge University Press.

DeNora, Tia. 2003. *After Adorno: Rethinking Music Sociology*. Cambridge, UK: Cambridge University Press.

Derrida, Jacques and Barbara Johnson. 2016. *Dissemination*. London: Bloomsbury Academic.

Dick, Philip K. and Eric Brown. 2016. *The Man in The High Castle*. London: Penguin Books.

Ellis, Brett Easton. 2006. *American Psycho*. London: Picador.

Eshun, Kodwo. 1999. *More Brilliant than the Sun: Adventures in Sonic Fiction*. London: Quartet Books.

Eshun, Kodwo. 2003. "Further Considerations on Afrofuturism," *CR: The New Centennial Review*, Vol. 3, No. 2, Summer 2003, 287–302.

Eshun, Kodwo. 2018. *First Annual Mark Fisher Memorial Lecture*, http://tle.li/~tle/mark-fisher-memorial-lecture/(11/12/2018).

Fantzen, Mikkel Krause. 2019. *Going Nowhere, Slow: The Aesthetics and Politics of Depression*. [S.I.]: Zer0 Books.

Feher, Michel. 2009. "Self-appreciation; or, the aspirations of human capital public," *Culture*, Vol. 21, No. 1, 21–41.

Fink, Robert W. 2005. *Repeating Ourselves: American Minimal Music as Cultural Practice*. Berkeley, CA: University of California Press.

Fisher, Mark. 2000. *Flatline Constructs: Gothic Materialism and Cybernetic Theory-Fiction*. University of Warwick. PhD Thesis. https://web.archive.org/web/20101123101648/http://cinestatic.com/trans-mat/Fisher/FCcontents.htm (08/08/2016).

Fisher, Mark. 2009. Capitalist Realism: Is there no alternative? Hants, UK: Zer0 Books.

Fisher, Mark. 2014. *Ghosts of My Life: Writings on Depression, Hauntology, and Lost Futures*. Hants, UK: Zer0 Books.

Fisher, Mark. 2014a. "Terminator vs Avatar", in *#Accelerate #: [the accelerationist reader]*, edited by Robin Mackay and Armen Avanessian, 335–346. Falmouth: Urbanomic Media Ltd.

Fisher, Mark. 2016. *The Weird and the Eerie*. London: Repeater Books.

Fisher, Mark, Darren Ambrose, and Simon Reynolds. 2018. *K-Punk: The Collected and Unpublished Writings of Mark Fisher (2004–2016)*. London: Repeater.

Freud, Sigmund. 2004. *Civilization and its Discontents*. London: Penguin.

Freud, Sigmund and Peter Gay. 1989. *The Freud Reader*. New York, NY: W.W. Norton.

Freud, Sigmund, David McLintock, Hugh Hauton. 2003. *The Uncanny*. New York, NY: Penguin Books.

Frith, Simon. 1981. *Sound Effects: Youth, Leisure, and the Politics of Rock'n'Roll*. New York, NY: Pantheon Books.

Foucault, Michel. 2003. *Society Must be Defended*. London: Penguin.

Foucault, Michel and Robert Hurley. 1998. *The Will to Knowledge*. London: Penguin Books.

Fukuyama, Francis. 1989. "The End of History?" http://ps321.community.uaf.edu/files/2012/10/Fukuyama-End-of-history-article.pdf (31/03/14).

Gibson, William. 2017. *Neuromancer*. London: Gollancz.

Gilbert, Jeremy. 2004. "Signifying Nothing: 'Culture', 'Discourse' and the Sociality of Affect," *Culture Machine*, 6.

Gilbert, Jeremy. 2014. *Common Ground: Democracy and Collectivity in an Age of Individualism*. London: Pluto Press.

Gilbert, Jeremy and Ewan Pearson. 1999. *Discographies: Dance Music, Culture and the Politics of Sound*. London: Routledge.

Gilroy, Paul. 2007. *The Black Atlantic: Modernity and Double Consciousness*. London: Verso.

Goodman, Steve. 2009. *Sonic Warfare: Sound, Affect, and the Ecology of Fear*, London: MIT Press.

Grey, Kevin. 2012. "Does AA Really Work? A Round-Up of Recent Studies"—*The Fix*, www.thefix.com/content/the-real-statistics-of-aa7301 (24/09/216).

Hameed, Ayesha, Kodow Eshun and Louis Moreno 2017. "Sonic Utopias The last Angel of History" in *Futures and Fictions*, edited By Henriette Gunkel, Ayesha Hameed, and Simon O'Sullivan, 249–265. London: Repeater.

Harper, Adam. 2011. *Infinite Music: Imagining the Next Millennium of Human Music-making*. Ropley: Zer0.

Hesmondhalgh, David. 2013. *Why Music Matters*. West Sussex, UK: John Wiley & Sons Ltd.

Hester, Helen. 2018. *Xenofeminism*. Cambridge, UK: Polity Press.

Holt, Macon. 2012. *Clips and Clicks: The Consequences of Technology Perfecting Music*. University of Hull: MRes. Thesis.

Holt, Macon. 2018. "Manipulation som markedsførings-katalysator," *Atlas Magasin*. http://atlasmag.dk/kultur/manipulation-som-markedsf%C3%B8rings-katalysator. (11/12/2018).

hooks, bell. 2016. "Moving Beyond Pain," bell hooks Institute, blog—www.bellhooksinstitute.com/blog/2016/5/9/moving-beyond-pain. (21/05/16)

Huxley, Aldous. 2014. *Brave New World*. London: Vintage Books.

James, Robin. 2015. *Resilience & Melancholy*. Hants, UK: Zer0 Books.

James, Robin. 2017. "Is the Post- in Post-Identity the Post- in Post-Genre?" *Popular Music* 36, no. 1, 21–32. doi:10.1017/S0261143016000647.

Kassabian, Anahid. 2013. *Ubiquitous Listening: Affect, Attention, and Distributed Subjectivity*. Berkeley, CA: University of California Press.

Kiberd, Roisin. 2015. *The Rise and Fall of "Boring Dystopia," the Anti-Facebook Facebook Group*, http://motherboard.vice.com/read/the-rise-and-fall-of-boring-dystopia-the-anti-facebook-facebook-group (21/09/16).

Laing, R. D. 1990. *The Politics of Experience; and, the Bird of Paradise*. Harmondsworth: Penguin.

Laing, R. D. and A. David. 2010. *The Divided Self: An Existential Study in Sanity and Madness*. London: Penguin Classics.

Land, Nick 2013. *The Dark Enlightenment*. www.thedarkenlightenment.com/the-dark-enlightenment-by-nick-land/ (17/12/2018).

Land, Nick, Robin Mackay, and Ray Brassier. 2018. *Fanged Noumena: Collected Writings 1987–2007*. Falmouth: Urbanomic Media Ltd.

Lash, Scott and Celia Lury. 2011. *Global Culture Industry: The Mediation of Things*. Cambridge, UK: Polity Press.

Launer, John. 2005. "Anna O and the 'talking cure'," *QJM*, 98, No. 6, 465–466.

Lewis, Sophie. 2019. *Full Surrogacy Now: Feminism Against Family*. New York: Verso.

Lyotard, Jean-François. 2006. *The Postmodern Condition: A Report on Knowledge*. Minneapolis, MN: University of Minnesota Press.

Lyotard, Jean-François and Iain Hamilton Grant. 2015. *Libidinal Economy*. Bloomsbury Academic.

Marx, Karl. 1990. *Capital: A Critique of Political Economy. Vol. 1*, London: Penguin Books.

Marx, Karl. 2014. "Fragment on Machines" in *#Accelerate #: [the accelerationist reader]*, edited by Robin Mackay and Armen Avanessian, 51–99. Falmouth: Urbanomic Media Ltd.

Mason, Paul. 2015. *Postcapitalism: A Guide to Our Future*. London: Lane.

Michaels, S. 2008. "My Stumps: Barack Obama speech turned into music video by will.i.am"—*The Guardian* www.theguardian.com/music/2008/feb/04/news, (12/08/14).

Mirowoski, Philip. 2013. *Never Let a Serious Crisis go to Waste How Neoliberalism Survived the Financial Meltdown*. London: Verso.

Moulier Boutang, Yann. 2011. *Cognitive Capitalism*, Cambridge, UK: Polity.

Myers, W. (2013). "A London tube busker dishes the dirt"—*The Guardian* www.theguardian.com/music/2013/jan/09/london-tube-busker-wayne-myers (1/11/2013).

Oppenhiem, Maya. (2016). "Beyonce's Ivy Park sportswear line denies claims its clothes were produced by 'sweatshop workers paid £4.30 a day'"—*The Independent*. www.independent.co.uk/news/people/beyonces-ivy-park-sportswear-line-denies-claims-its-clothes-were-produced-by-sweatshop-workers-a7035926.html. (24/09/2016).

Orwell, George. 2013. *Nineteen Eighty-Four*. London: Penguin Books.

Oswald, J. 1985. "Plunderphonics, or Audio Piracy as a Compositional Prerogative" Plunderphonics—www.plunderphonics.com/ (19/04/2012).

Parisi, Luciana. 2017. "Automate Sex: Xenofeminism, Hyperstition and Alienation" in *Futures and Fictions*, edited by Henriette Gunkel, Ayesha Hameed, and Simon O'Sullivan, 213–230. London: Repeater.

Parisi, Luciana. and Steve Goodman. 2011. "Mnemonic Control" in *Beyond Biopolitics: Essays on the Governance of Life and Death*, edited by P. T. Clough and C. Willes, 163–176. Durham, NC: Duke University Press.

Poulsen, Frank. 2010. *Blood in the Mobile*. Denmark: Koncern.

Preciado, Paul B. 2017. *Testo Junkie: Sex, Drugs, and Biopolitics in the Pharmacopornographic Era*. New York, NY: Feminist Press at the City University of New York.

Ravn, Olga. 2018. *De Ansatte: roman*. Copenhagen: Gyldendals.

Robinson, Zandria. 2016. "We Slay, Part 1," New Southern Negress, http://newsouthnegress.com/southernslayings.

Russolo Luigi. 2008. "The Art of Noises: Futurist Manifesto" in *Audio Culture: Readings in Modern Music*, edited by Christoph Cox and Daniel Warner, 10-14. New York, NY: Continuum.

Schulze, Holger. 2013. "Adventures in Sonic Fiction: A Heuristic for Sound Studies," in the *Journal Of Sonic Studies*, Vol. 4, No. 1, http://journal.sonicstudies.org/vol04/nr01/a10. (03/03/2015).

Schulze, Holger. 2018. *The Sonic Persona: An Anthropology of Sound*. London: Bloomsbury Academic.

Schulze, Holger. 2020. *Sonic Fiction*. London: Bloomsbury Academic.

Self, Will amd Slavoj Žižek. 2017. *Slavoj Žižek Vs Will Self in Dangerous Ideas*. How To Academy. www.youtube.com/watch?v=CId1iOWQUuo. (17/12/2018)

Serra, J. et al. 2012, "Measuring the Evolution of Contemporary Western Popular Music," *Nature*, No. 2, 521

Sloboda, John A. and Patrick N. Juslin, 2001. "Psychological Perspectives on Music and Emotion" in *Series in Affective Science. Music and Emotion: Theory and Research*, edited by Patrick N. Juslin and John. A. Sloboda, 71-104. New York, NY: Oxford University Press.

Small, Christopher. 2011. *Music of the Common Tongue: Survival and Celebration in African American Music*. Middletown: Wesleyan University Press.

Smith, Zadie. 2009. *Changing My Mind: Occasional Essays*. New York, NY: Penguin Press.

Spivak, Gayatri Chakravorty. 2013. *An Aesthetic Education in the Era of Globalization*. Cambridge, MA: Harvard University Press.

Stewart Kathleen. 2011. "Atmospheric Attunements; Environment and Planning" *Society and Space*, 29, No. 3, 445-453.

Stiegler, Bernard. 1998. *Technics and Time. 1, The Fault of Epimetheus*, Stanford, CA: Stanford University Press.

Stiegler, Bernard. 2013. *What Makes Life Worth Living: On Pharmacology*, Cambridge, UK: Polity.

Stockhausen, Karlheinz et al. 2008. "Stockhausen vs. the 'Technocrats'" in *Audio Culture: Readings in Modern Music*, edited by Christoph Cox and Daniel Warner, 381-385. New York, NY: Continuum.

Strickland, Bonnie B. 2001. *The Gale Encyclopedia of Psychology*. Detroit, MI: Gale.

Swartz, Aaron. 2009. "What Happens at the End of Infinite Jest? (or, the Infinite Jest ending explained)". www.aaronsw.com/weblog/ijend. (05/05/15).

Taylor, Timothy. D. 2012. *The Sounds of Capitalism: Advertising, Music, and the Conquest of Culture*. Chicago, IL: University of Chicago Press.

TFL (2013). *Culture and Heritage*. www.tfl.gov.uk/corporate/about-tfl/culture-and-heritage (29/10/2013).

Thomas, Andy. 2010. "Is Parental Advisory sticker still being affixed to albums these days? If so, how effective is it? Actually, was it ever effective?" www.westword.com/music/is-parental-advisory-sticker-still-being-affixed-to-albums-these-days-if-so-how-effective-is-it-actually-was-it-ever-effective-5708676 (23/09/2016).

Torrey, E Fuller. 2013. "Ronald Reagan's Shameful Legacy: Violence, the Homeless, Mental Illness," in *Salon*, www.salon.com/2013/09/29/ronald_reagans_shameful_legacy_violence_the_homeless_mental_illness/ (17/12/2018).

VanderMeer, Jeff. 2015. *Annihilation*. London: Fourth Estate.

Wallace, David Foster. 2007. *Infinite Jest: A Novel*. London: Abacus.

Wallace, David Foster. 2009. *This Is Water: Some Thoughts, Delivered on a Significant Occasion, about Living a Compassionate Life*. New York, NY: Little, Brown

Wallace, David Foster. 2013. *Consider the Lobster and Other Essays*. London: Abacus.

Walsh, Matt. 2016. "Beyoncé is destroying your daughter, not empowering her," *The Blaze*. www.theblaze.com/contributions/beyonce-is-destroying-your-daughter-not-empowering-her.

Weheliye, A. G. (2005). *Phonographies: Grooves in Sonic Afro-modernity*. Durham, NC: Duke University Press.

Wilderson, Frank. 2017. *Irreconcilable Anti-Blackness: A Conversation With Dr. Frank Wilderson III*. www.youtube.com/watch?v=k1W7WzQyLmI. (17/12/2018)

Williamson, Mark. 2014. "Streaming now included in the Official UK Charts—what does this mean for artists?" www.spotifyartists.com/streaming-now-included-in-the-official-uk-charts-what-does-this-mean-for-artists/ (10/04/2015).

Young, A. (2016). "All Michelle Obama wants to talk about is Beyoncé"—*Consequences of Sound*, http://consequenceofsound.net/2016/09/all-michelle-obama-wants-to-talk-about-is-beyonce/ (24/09/2016).

Žižek, Slavoj. 2004. *Organs Without Bodies: Deleuze and Consequences*. New York, NY: Routledge.

Žižek, Slavoj. 2008. *The Sublime Object of Ideology*. London: Verso.

Žižek, Slavoj. 2010. *Living in the End Times*. London: Verso.

Ørntoft, Theis. 2018. *Solar: roman*. Copenhagen: Gyldendal.

Discography

Andrea True Connection, Andrea True, and Gregg Diamond. 1997. More, more, more: the best of the Andrea True Connection. Hollywood, CA: Right Stuff.

Avalanches. 2001. Frontier psychiatrist. Londres: Virgin records international.

Band Aid, Bob Geldof, and Midge Ure. 1984. Do they know it's Christmas? West Germany: Mercury.

Beyoncé, White, J., Weekend, Blake, J., Lamar, K., Shire, W., Melo-X, Joseph, K., & Anyanwu, O. 2016. *Lemonade*. New York: Parkwood Entertainment: Columbia.
Beyoncé. 2008. *I am– Sasha Fierce*. New York, NY: Music World Music/Columbia.
Bikini Kill. 1996. *Reject all American*. Olympia, WA: Kill Rock Stars.
Cohen, Leonard. 2011. *Various Positions*. San Rafael, CA: 4 Men with Beards.
Cyrus, Miley. 2008. *Breakout*. Burbank, CA, Hollywood Records.
Cyrus, Miley. 2010. *Can't be tamed*. Burbank, CA, Hollywood Records.
Cyrus, Miley. 2013. *Bangerz*. New York, NY: RCA Records.
Cyrus, Miley. 2015. *Miley Cyrus & Her Dead Petz*, Smiley Miley Inc.
Eels. 2011. *Beautiful Freak*. Europe: Universal Music.
FKA Twigs. 2014. *LP1*. London: Young Turks.
FKA Twigs. 2015. *M3LL155X*. London: Young Turks.
FKA Twigs and Arca. 2013. *EP2*. London: Young Turks.
Glover, Donald and Ludwig Göransson. 2018. *This is America*. New York, NY: mcDJ, RCA.
Goulding, Ellie. 2015. "Love Me Like You Do" from *Fifty Shades of Grey: Original Motion Picture Soundtrack*. New York, NY: Republic.
Hutchings, Shabaka, Sons of Kemet. 2016. "In The Castle of My Skin" from *Lest We Forget What We Came Here To Do*. Salisbury: Naim Jazz.
Jackson, Michael, Michael Boddicker, Jerry Hey, Paul Jackson, Louis Johnson, Quincy Jones, Steve Lukather, et al. 2015. *Thriller*. MJJ Productions.
Jessie J, and B.o.B. 2015. *Who You Are*. New York, NY: Lava; Universal Republic.
Led Zeppelin. 1990. *Led Zeppelin II: remasters*. New York, N.: Atlantic.
Misty, Father John, J. Tillman, Jonathan Wilson, Bryce Gonzales, and Greg Calbi. 2015. *I Love You, Honeybear*. Seattle, WA: Sub Pop Records.
Mumford & Sons. 2010. *Sigh no more*. New York, NY: Glassnote.
Mumford & Sons. 2014. *Babel*. United States: Glassnote Records.
Mumford & Sons. 2015. *Wilder mind*. New York, NY: Glassnote Entertainment Group.
Muse. 2005. *Origin of Symmetry*. Burbank, CA: Warner Bros.
Nine Inch Nails. 1997. *The Perfect Drug*. [S.l.]: Interscope Records.
Nine Inch Nails. 2004. *The Downward Spiral*. Santa Monica, CA: Interscope Records.
O'Connor, Sinéad. 1990. *Nothing Compares 2 U; Jump in the River*. England: Ensign/Chrysalis.
Pixies. 1989. *Surfer Rosa & Come on pilgrim*. London: Beggars Banquet Records.
Puce Mary. 2016. *The Spiral*. Copenhagen: Posh Isolation.
Radiohead. 2009. *Hail to the Thief*. London: Parlophone/EMI.
Radiohead. 2016. *Ok Computer*. [Place of publication not identified]: XL Recordings.
REM. 2016. *Monster*. Europe: Universal Music.
Rolling Stones. 2018. *Beggars Banquet*. New York, NY: ABKCO Music & Records.
Simon, C., Kunkel, R., McCurry, J., Jason, N., Goldmark, A., Siegel, I., Lebolt, D., Kilgore, R., & Wolk, T. 1985. *Spoiled girl*. Los Angeles, CA: Epic.

Simon and Garfunkel. 2001. *Bridge Over Troubled Water*. New York, NY: Sony Music Entertainment.
Simone, Nina. 2013. *I Put a Spell on You*. Europe: Universal music.
Sheeran, Ed, Rudimental. 2014. *Bloodstream*. USA: Asylum.
Smiths. 2017. *The Queen is Dead*. Burbank, CA: Warner Chappell Artemis Music Ltd.
St. Vincent. 2012. *Strange Mercy*. London: 4AD.
Swift, Taylor. 2014. *1989*. Nashville: Big Machine Records.
Talking Heads. 2006. *Speaking in Tongues*. Burbank, CA: Rhino Entertainment Co.
Will.i.am. 2008. "Yes We Can (Obama Song)." www.youtube.com/watch?v=2fZHou18Cdk&list=PLWZcbo86CxGIQjnJRIe9av1kLAog_mT-K&index=7 (11/08/14).
Will.i.am, Apl.de.ap, Taboo, Fergie, David Guetta, and Frederic Riesterer. 2009. *I Gotta Feeling*. Milwaukee, WI: Cherry River Music Co.
Wonder, Stevie. 2000. *Talking Book*. New York, NY: Motown.
Xiu Xiu. 2006. *Air force*. Olympia, WA: 5 Rue Christine.
Xiu Xiu. 2016 *Xiu Xiu Plays the Music of Twin Peaks*. Champaign, Il: Polyvinyl Record Co.
Xiu Xiu. 2017. Forget. United States: Polyvinyl Records.

Filmography

Allen, Woody, Diane Keaton, and Michael Murphy. 2012. *Manhattan*. Los Angeles: Metro Goldwyn Mayer.
Ball, Alan, Lori Jo Nemhauser, Robert Del Valle, Kate Robin, Rick Cleveland, Bruce Eric Kaplan, Alan Poul, et al. 2009. *Six Feet Under*. New York, NY: HBO Video.
Caine, Michael, Alfonso Cuarón, Phyllis Dorothy James, Julianne Moore, and Clive Owen. 2007. *Children of Men*. Hamburg: Universal Pictures Germany [u.a.].
Coppola, Francis Ford, Al Pacino, Diane Keaton, Marlon Brando, Robert De Niro, and Mario Puzo. 2001. *The Godfather*. Hollywood, CA: Paramount Home Video.
Curtis, Adam. 2007. *The Trap: What Happened to Our Dream of Freedom?* London: BBC.
Curtis, A. 2010. *Oh Dearism*. London: BBC. www.youtube.com/watch?v=YCBG4bvIueA (24/04/13)
Fincher, David, Edward Norton, Brad Pitt, Helena Bonham Carter, and Meat Loaf. 2004. *Fight Club*. UK: Twentieth Century Fox Home Entertainment.
FKA Twigs, Tom Beard. 2013. *Papi Pacify* (music video). London: Young Turks.
FKA Twigs, Jesse Kanda. 2013. *Water Me* (music video). London: Young Turks.
FKA Twigs, Nabil. 2014. *Two Weeks* (music video). London: Young Turks.
FKA Twigs. 2015. *M3LL155X* (short film). London: Young Turks.

Garland, Alex, Scott Rudin, Andrew Macdonald, Allon Reich, Eli Bush, Natalie Portman, Jennifer Jason Leigh, et al. 2018. *Annihilation*. Hollywood, CA: Paramount.
Haneke, Michael, Naomi Watts, and Tim Roth. 2008. *Funny Games*. UK: Tartan Video.
Lucas, George, Harrison Ford, Carrie Fisher, Mark Hamill, James Earl Jones, Billy Dee Williams, Alec Guinness, Peter Cushing, Irvin Kershner, and Richard Marquand. 2004. *Star Wars Trilogy*. [United States]: 20th Century Fox Entertainment.
Lynch, David, Bill Pullman, Patricia Arquette, Balthazar Getty, Angelo Badalamenti, and Peter Deming. 2011. *Lost Highway*. Grünwald: Concorde Home Entertainment.
Mann, Michael, Art Linson, Al Pacino, Robert De Niro, Val Kilmer, Tom Sizemore, Amy Brenneman, et al. 2017. *Heat*. Australia: Twentieth Century Fox Entertainment.
Matsoukas, Melina, Beyoncé, 2016. *Formatmation* (music video). New York, NY: Parkwood Entertainment.
Murai, Hiro, Glover Donald. 2018. *This is America* (music video). New York, NY: Reservoir Media.
Peele, Jordan, Sean McKittrick, Jason Blum, Edward H. Hamm, Daniel Kaluuya, Allison Williams, Bradley Whitford, Caleb Landry Jones, Stephen Root, and Catherine Keener. 2017. *Get Out*. USA: Universal Pictures Home Entertainment.
Romanek, Mark. 1997. *The Perfect Drug* (music video). US: Nothing Records
Winkler, Irwin, Nicholas Pileggi, Martin Scorsese, Robert De Niro, Ray Liotta, Joe Pesci, Lorraine Bracco, et al. 2010. *Goodfellas*. Burbank, CA: Warner Home Video.

Index

4 Hero 17
"6 Inch Heels" 170
1984 (Orwell) 39
1989 (Swift) 72

#Accelerate: Manifesto for an Accelerationist Politics (Srnicek/Williams) 31
Acid Communism (Fisher) 31–3, 180
acid communism, impact 29–33
Adorno, Theodor 11–12, 56–60, 71, 79
    critique 160
    hobbies essay 88
    sublimation 111
    TCT 92
Afrocentric conceptual engineering 10–11
Afrofuturism
    non-essentialist drive 41
    practice 10–11
Afrofuturist science sonic theory-fiction 7–16
Afro NoFuturism 150
afro-pessimism, position 181
A Guy Called Gerald 17
Alcoholics Anonymous (AA)
    renunciation 179–80
    rituals 176
American Psycho (Ellis) 90
And: Phenomenology of the End (Berardi) 161–2, 178
anhedonia 93–9
Annihilation (VanderMeer) 159
anthropocentric framework 120
anti-blackness, deployment 181
Anti-Oedipal reading 126–7
Anti-Oedipus 96–7 160–1
Arctic Monkeys 135, 139
Arendt, Hannah 87
Aristotle 109–11, 133
art-objects-oriented subjectivity 67–70

art-object-to-subject 74
art, super categorical definition (Adorno) 111
artwork, definition (Adorno) 112–13
Astro Jazz 17
Attali, Jacques 57–8, 139
attention 63–7
    absence 51–5
    economy 57
    enforcement 59
    focus 70–6
    mediatized commodities 55–6
attentional data 55–6
attention economics 55–62

Babel (Mumford and Sons) 91
Badly Drawn Boy 79
Ballard, J. G. 8–9
Bam Bam 17
Bangerz (Cyrus) 150
Barnett, Tahliah 146
Bateman, Patrick 90–5
Beller, Jonathan 65
Benjamin, Walter 128
Berardi, Franco 121, 139, 161–2, 177
Beyoncé 127, 164–82
Beyoncé Is Destroying Your Daughter, Not Empowering Her (Walsh) 169
Bieber, Justin (image) 57
Black Atlantic (music) 13
Black Atlantic Futurism 17
Black Eyed Peas, The 60, 72, 75
black masculinity, investment 165
black music 12, 181
    Sonic Fiction, connection 17
blackness
    appropriation 181
    essentializing 12–13
    liberation 30–1
    white appropriations 17
black subjectivities 11

Blood in the Mobile 86
"Bloodstream" (Sheeran/Rudimental) 72
Boltanski, Luc 28, 89
"Bored in the USA" (YouTube video
    removal) 100–3
"Born in the USA" 100
Boswell, Marshall 97, 124
Bown, Alfie 88–9
"Boy Soprano" 184
Brave New World (Huxley) 39
Breakout (Montana) 147
Buchanan, Ian 137–138
Burton, Tim 117
buskers, usage 78
busking 79
Butler, Octavia 9

Candy Crush, capitalism (relationship)
    88–9
Can't Be Tamed (Montana) 147
capital
    accumulation 162
        logic 140
    deterritorialization/reterritorialization
        82
    deterritorializing power 94
    illiterate logic 142
    logic 153
    mapping 81
    valorization 61, 172
capitalism
    cathartic processes 122
    exterior limit 120
    illiteracy 101, 121
    Marxian recognition 171
    overcoming 71
    persistence 30
    pharmapornographic capitalism
        145
    power 56
    products, usage 73
    protean construct 121–2
    schizophrenia, contrast 122
    systemic structure 120–1
    understanding 154
capitalist desiring-production 159
capitalist patriarchy, impact 142
capitalist power structures, protection 92

capitalist realism 21, 58–9, 161
    affects/materials 24–8
    birth 21–4
    concept 28–9
    conceptualization 33
    conditions, impact 169–70
    disentanglement 23
    formation 107
    inertia 154–5
    mechanism 87
    reproduction 76, 164, 171–2
    symptoms 27
Capitalist Realism (Fisher) 29, 32–3, 41, 180
Capitalist Realism (publication) 23
catatonic bliss 124
catharsis 105–10, 114
    compensation 182
    hermetic sealing 126
    oppressive governance, contrast 114
    purging action 111
    substitute satisfaction 101
    term, psychological usage 114
"Cave, The" 91
Cheers! 125
chemical self-obliteration 122
Chiapello, Eve 28, 89
Childish Gambino 166
    music, analysis 62–3
Children of Men 29, 30, 41
chrono-normative relationship
        imperatives 101
chrononormativity 135
Civilization and Its Discontents (Freud) 73, 93
civilization, laws (transgression) 73
Clinton, George 169
"Closer" (Nine Inch Nails) 182
cloud services, subscription 64–5
Cohen, Leonard 77
Coldplay, interpretations 25
Collins, Phil 90
colonialism, intersection 15
Coltrane, Alice 17
communication, ecstasy 5
complicity 81
    discussion 119
conjunction 159
    experience 179–80
consciousness, affirmative affect 108

consumption
  act 94
  libidinizing spectacle 22
content-based critique, defanging 102
Cool Britannia (reapplication) 45
Copenhagen Jazz Festival, popularity 37
Cortés, arrival/injustices 178–9
countercultural movement, Oedipal subjectivity 123–7
"Cruel" (St. Vincent) 86
cruelty 85–90
  culture, movement 93
  maintenance/normalization 87
  persistence 93
  violence, comparison 94
Cuboniks, Laboria 31
CultStud 3
cultural capital, discussion 119
cultural engagements 38
cultural production
  corporate taxation 39
  normative borders 150–1
cultural referentiality 117
cultural theory 40
culture
  desacralization 154
  movement 93
Curtis, Adam 87
CyberCulture 3
Cybernetic Cultures Research Unit (CCRU) 6–9, 23, 41, 122
  theory-fictionalists 24
"cynicism," term (usage) 177
Cyrus, Miley 146–7, 150, 152–3, 177–8
  blackness, appropriation 181
  VMA performance 149

data packages, cost (reduction) 85–6
David (Michelangelo) 29, 30
Davis, Miles 16
Dead Petz 151
"Deleuze and Pop Music" (Buchanan) 137
Deleuze, Gilles 23, 40, 71, 74
  argument 95
  capitalism analysis 66
  formulation 139

passivity 83
philosophical projects 120
stratification 14
Deleuzians, theory-fictions 5
delibidinization 22–3
democracies, subversions 105
Democratic Republic of Congo (DRC) mining operations 86
Den Nye Borgerlige (New Right/Citizens) 36–7
DeNora, Tia 65, 106
de Paul, Vincent 86
depression 110
  characterization 98
depressive hedonia, acceleration 98–9
desire, pulsional force 83
desiring-production 4, 160
despotic cathartic model 121
Destiny's Child 164
deterritorialization 82, 88, 136–7
Dick, Philip K. 9
difference, production 139
digital age, new economy 105
digital homunculus 145
direct violence 105
disassociation 110
Discographies (Gilbert/Pearson) 12
distributed subjectivity 75–6
"Diva" 173
"Don't Hurt Yourself" 167
Dr Octagon 16
Du Bois, W.E.B. 174
dubstep 149–50
Dunkelman, Shayna 186

Eichmann in Jerusalem (Arendt) 87
Elba, Idris 91
Electro 16
electronic dance music (EDM) 72, 146
Ellis, Bret Easton 90
emancipatory capability 153
emancipatory communism, possibility 59–60
emojis, choice 86
epistemic resistance 174
Eros 144–52
  psyche, combination 161

Eshun, Kodwo 3–8, 181
　Fisher, friendship 40–1
　intention 9
ethico-aesthetic comportment 27–8
external authority, impact 115

feedback loop 141–2
　positive feedback loop 136
Feher, Michel 89
feminism, Beyoncé involvement 175–6
feminist anti-racism, improvement 180
"Fictions of All Kinds" (Ballard) 8
fictive ideality, capacity 14–15
Fight Club (movie) 25
Fink, Robert 72
Fisher, Mark 21, 27–31, 38–9, 58, 114, 180
　capitalism 154
　Eshun, friendship 40–1
FKA Twigs 159–60, 178
　dancing iteration 149
　EP2 144–52
　Miley Cyrus, contrast 141–4
　transgressive refrain 154
Flaming Lips, The 151
Flying Lotus 12
Forget (Xiu Xiu) 24–5
"Formation" (Beyoncé) 165–82
　release 173–4
　response 181
Foucault, Michel 10
Frantzen, Mikkel 38
"Free Time" (Adorno) 88
Freud, Sigmund 73, 114, 122, 143
　cathartic method 115
　influence, danger 136
"fridge hum" 65
Friends (watching) 120–3
frontier psychiatrist 114–16
Fukuyama, Francis 21
Funny Games 103
"Further Considerations of Afrofuturism" (Eshun) 11
Futurhythmachine 4, 7, 16

Gabriel, Peter 90
Gambino. *See* Childish Gambino
Gately, Don 176
Genesis (band) 90
geo-cultural determinism 17
Gibson, William 9
Glover, Donald 63
Godfather, The 28
Goldie 17
Good feelings 105–10
Goodfellas 28
Goodman, Steve (music analysis) 62, 63
Google Docs, usage 164
Google Glass 178
　advertisement 154
Goulding, Ellie 72
Grasshopper Lies Heavy, The (Duke) 10
Green, Karen 47
Guattari, Félix 23, 71, 83
　argument 95
　capitalism analysis 66
　passivity 83
　philosophical projects 120
　stratification 14
Guernica (Picasso) 29

Haashim 16
"Hallelujah" (Cohen) 77
Hancock, Herbie 17
HangOuts 31
harmony, privileging 11–12
Heat 28
Heimlich 143–4
　constitution 154
Heroes (Berardi) 121
hip ennui 93–9
　coinage (Wallace) 42
HipHop 16
home state 142
Houston, Whitney 90
"How's That?" 145
Huey Lewis and the News 90
human capital 89
　validation 95
human-security system 17
Huxley, Aldous 39
Hyde Park, Rolling Stones concert 128–31
hyper-competitive capitalism (US) 22
hyperrhythm 13

I Am … Sasha Fierce 173
"I Believe" 91–2
"I Gotta Feeling" (Black Eyed Peas) 60, 72
I Love You, Honebear (Misty) 100
"image of thought" 11
"I'm Your Doll" 151
indirect violence 105
industrial capitalism, technological advances 56
Infinite Jest (Wallace) 40–1, 47, 95, 123–7, 176
　characters, anhedonia 97
Infinite Jest (movie) 124
innovation, sale 139
Intelligent Dance Music (IDM) 149–50
"In the Castle of My Skin" 37
"irony" term (usage) 177
Ivy Park 171, 182

James, Robin 150, 164–5
Jay Z 164
jazz, denouncements (Adorno) 113
Jazz Fission 16
Jessie J 48
jouissance 72–3
　chastisement 74
Jungle 7, 122
Jungle Brothers, The 16

Kafka, Franz 60
Kassabian, Anahid 52, 75, 81
King, Jr., Martin Luther 166
Kirk, Roland 16
K-Punk 23

Lacan, Jacques 72
　mirror stage 160–1
LAD Bible 89
Lady Gaga 164
Laing, R. D. 117
La Malinche 178
Late Show, The 102–3
Lemonade (Beyoncé) 127, 164–9
　conjunctive critique 170–1
　critique (Walsh) 169
Letterman, David 102
Lewis, Huey 90–3
Libertines, The 79

Libidinal Economy (Lyotard) 170
libidinal ecstasy, context 47
listening skills, usage 157
"Little Lion Man" 91
Lloyd-Webber, Julian 79
London Olympics (2012) closing ceremony, music (impact) 45–9
London Underground, busking 77–9
London Underground Busking Scheme 78
Lost Highway (Lynch) 116
"Love Me Like You Do" (Goulding) 72
"Lover of the Light" (video) 91
Lucas, George 134
Lynch, David 116
Lyotard, Jean-François 98, 170, 188 n.2

M3LL155X (Twigs) 151
Macero, Teo 16
Mærsk Group 35
"Mairzy Doats" 186
Malcolm X 171
Manhattan 113
Man in the High Castle, The (Dick) 9–10
Marcuse, Herbert 84, 92–3
　argument 95
market forces, destabilization 26–7
marketing, impact 92
market reterritorialization 137
Marx, Karl 61, 107
M*A*S*H (TV Series) 125
material survival, economic activity 170
maternal plenitude, return 124
M-C-M 140
　mechanism 142
melancholia 110
mental health, theory 115
midrange frequencies, fetishization 63
Miley Cyrus, FKA Twigs (contrast) 141–4
Miley Cyrus & Her Dead Petz 151
Mirowski, Philip 26
mirror stage (Lacan) 160–1
Misty, John 100, 172
Møller, A.P. 35
mommy-daddy-me triangle 126–7
Montana, Hannah 147
More Brilliant than the Sun (Eshun) 3–4, 6, 8–9, 41

multi-racial white supremacist patriarchy
    (MRWaSP) 165, 181
  hegemony 167
Mumford and Sons 90–3
music
  designation 159–60
  meaning, impact 51
  relational phenomenon 172
  vernacular form 138
music criticism, frames 8–9
Myers, Wayne 77
"My New Boyfriend" (Simon) 157
MythScience (Sun Ra) 14

negativity, discharge 117–18
neoliberal capitalism 123
  competitive conditions 119
  connective semiotics 162
  suffering 111
neoliberal foreclosure 177
neoliberalism 26–7
  conservatism, alliance 175
  mismatch 28–9
neoliberal revolution, Reaganomics
    (impact) 47
Neuromancer (Gibson) 9
New Spirit of Capitalism, The (Boltanski/
    Chiapello) 28
"Night Josh Tillman Came to Our Apt.,
    The" 172
Nine Inch Nails 116–17, 182
normative music making, atmospheric
    pressure 53
norm-reproducing media 125
nostalgia
  programming 157
  trap 158

Obama, Michelle 178
Oedipal desire, internal limit 144
Oedipalization 122–3
Oedipal subjectivity 123–7
Oedipal subject, notion 96–7
Oedipus 159
  manifestation 155
  templates 136
"Oh Dearism" (Curtis) 87

oppressive governance, catharsis
    (contrast) 114
oppressive catharsis 113
Orwell, George 39
Oswald, John 52–3, 58, 75

Pale King, The (Wallace) 47
Palmer, Laura 186
"Papi Pacify" 145
"Parental Advisory: Explicit Content"
    (warning logo) 82
peer-hunger 96
penis envy, templates 136
"Perfect Drug, The" (Nine Inch Nails)
    116–20
Perry, Lee 16
pharmapornographic capitalism 145, 146
phenomenological listening subject 74–5
Phuture 17
pitched-down vocals 149
Playford, Rob 17
pleasure, indictment 98
pleasure-seeking, human capital 98
Poetics (Aristotle) 109, 111
Politics of Experience, The (Laing) 118
pop cultural history, existence (freedom)
    134–5
popular music (pop music) 133–40
  atmosphere, entry 51–2
  commodity 81–2
  critique 127
  cultures, emergence 123
  difference 59
  intensity, tendency 88
positive feedback loop 136
possessive individualism 141
post-African repetitions 12
post-punk, production ideology 135
Postsoul 16–19
post-structuralist philosophy, interest 40
Poulsen, Frank 86
power/desire, interconnection 140
power relations, deterritorialization
    169–70
power structure, defusing 27
"Pray You Catch Me" 173
presence, simulation 56

"Price Tag" (Jessie J) 48
primary attention 75
production
　capitalist mode 82
　injection 94
　surplus resources 133–4
productive misreading 142
products/events, synchronizations 82
psyche/Eros, combination 161
psychoanalytic therapy (talking cure) 109
psychological repression 156
Puce, Mary 89

quantitative easing 24–5

racial justice (fight), Beyoncé involvement 175–6
radio signal, feedback 144
Reagan, Ronald (state mental hospital closures) 115–16
reductionism, avoidance 13–14
refrain 133–40
　repetition 140
repressive desublimation 92–3
reproductive futurism 135
responsibilisation 114
Reznor, Trent 116
Rhetorics (Aristotle) 109, 111
rhizomatic network management 90
rhizome, ontological conceptual framework 161
Richards, Keith 129
Robinson, Zandria 173–4
rock music, vigor/exhilaration 108
Rolling Stones, examination 128–31
Ronson, Mark 139
Roof, Dylan 63
Rudimental 72
Russell, George 16
Russolo, Luigi 15

Sakamoto, Ryuichi 16
Sanders, Pharoah 17
satire, catharsis 101
schizophrenia
　capitalism, contrast 122
　examination 120–3
　exterior limit, recognition 121

schizophrenics, treatment 117
Schulze, Holger 4, 5, 15, 54
science fiction 6–7
　depiction 41
　fascination 38–9
　hyperstitional capacity 9
　response 8
　usage 7–8
self-obliteration
　chemical self-obliteration 122
　impulse 107–8
Self, Will 86
semantic language, requirement (absence) 59
semiotic anxiety 163–4
semiotic chains, asignification 46
sensation-stimulus matrix 59
senses, input 75
sensorium 18
"Shake It Off" (Swift) 70–6
Sheeran, Ed 72
shimmer 51–2, 54, 64, 66, 72–3, 76, 83, 98–9, 106, 128, 159–60, 164, 169
shudder 113
Sigh No More (Mumford) 90
Simon, Carly 156–8
simulacra 131
Six Feet Under 110
smartphones, science fiction technology 85–6
Smiths, The 135
Snapchart filters, choice 86
social democracy, containment 22
social exclusion 105
social fact 118
sociality, manifestation 76
social norms, synecdoche 137
social order, norms/values 133
social reality, forms 113
sonic affects 52
sonic crowd control 111–12
Sonic Fiction (Eshun) 13, 16
　conception, limitations 18–19
　concept, vitality 4–5
　practice 18
　problematic potential 14–15
　theory-fiction, comparison 3–7
Sonic Futurism 17

sonic invention 64
sonic shimmer 64
Sons of Kemet 37–8
sounds systems cultures 63
spectacle theory 56–7
Spectral Dub 16
speculative realists 31
Srnicek, Nick 31
Stewart, Jamie 24, 184
Stiegler, Bernard 67–71
Stockhausen, Karlheinz 12, 15
stratification 14
strings, glissando 145
St. Vincent 86, 94
sublimation 111
substitute satisfaction 54, 101
Sun Ra
    claims 18
    music, qualities 15
    narration 13–14
Super Bowl 50 (halftime show) 165
"Superstition" (Wonder) 182
Swift, Taylor 70–6
symbol systems, destabilization 180
"Sympathy for the Devil" 130, 131
syncopated vocal layering 173
synecdoche 137, 165

Taylor, Timothy 106
TechnoTheory 3
TED Talk, attendance 63–7
Thatcher, Margaret 21
theory-fiction, sonic fiction (comparison) 3–7
"There Is a Light That Never Goes Out" (Smiths) 135
"This Is America" (Childish Gambino) 62
Thousand Plateaus, A 89, 137
tidal streams 71
Tillman, Josh 100, 102–3
time
    deterritorialization 135
    rhythmic intensity/re-temporalization 179
    traditional critical theory (TCT) 54–6, 61, 64–7, 92
    approach, applications 112
    articulations 107

pleasure, indictment 98
practitioners, seminars 72
problems 82–3, 88, 113
usage 81, 110
trad sublime 3, 13
transgression 159
Transport for London (TFL) 77–8
Tricky 16
    technological reappropriations 17
truth content 112–13
Twigs. *See* FKA Twigs
"Two Weeks" (video) 148–9, 151

Ubiquitous Listening (Kassabian) 52
ubiquitous music 75
Ultramagnetic MCs 17
"Ultraviolet" 146
uncanny
    concept (Freud) 141, 142
    refrain 154
Unheimlich 143, 146, 150
    constitution 154
    experience 151
United States housing market, financial crisis 46
universal human emancipation 173

valorization, principle 95
value production 98
vampirism 46
VanderMeerian shimmer 51–2
VanderMeer, Jeff 159
"Video Phone" 164
violence
    absence 58
    cruelty, comparison 94
    enjoyment, inexorability 94–5
    impulse, control 93

Wallace, David Foster 40–1, 47, 126, 130, 176
    commencement address (Kenyon College) 48
    struggles 177
"Water Me" 145
"We Can't Stop" (Cyrus) 150
Weird and the Eerie, The (Fisher) 146
Weltschmerz (Romantic glorification) 96

"White Jesus" salvation 102
white supremacist cultural narratives 165
"Whole Lotta Love" (Led Zeppelin) 134
Wilder Mind (Mumford and Sons) 91–2
Will.I.Am 84
   music video 84–5
Williams, Alexander 31
"Winter Wind" 91
"Wolf, The" 91–2
Wonder, Stevie 182
world, ending 29–33

Xenofeminism (Cuboniks) 31
X-Factor 97
Xiu Xiu 24, 183–6

"Yes, We Can" 84
YouTube video, removal 100–3

Zer0 Books 23
Žižek, Slavoj 86, 102

www.ingramcontent.com/pod-product-compliance
Lightning Source LLC
Chambersburg PA
CBHW052040300426
44117CB00012B/1912